Warman's Depression Glass

A VALUE & IDENTIFICATION GUIDE

BY ELLEN T. SCHROY

Published by

krause
publications

700 East State Street, Iola, WI 54990-0001

Please, call or write us for our free catalog of antiques and collectibles publications. To place an order or receive our free catalog, call 800-258-0929. For editorial comment and further information, use our regular business telephone at (715) 445-2214.

Library of Congress Catalog Number: 97-073024
ISBN: 0-87069-754-4
Printed in the United States of America

Table of Contents

Introduction

Patterns, Items and Values

Introduction

Welcome

Welcome to *Warman's Depression Glass*, the latest edition to the Warman's price guides series. This edition is designed to assist collectors, appraisers, auctioneers and those trying to identify that special piece of heirloom Depression glassware. A selection of 140 of the most popular patterns of American glass dinnerware that was manufactured between the 1920s and 1970s is included.

Each pattern is represented by a color photograph and line drawing to help with the identification process. A listing of known manufactured items and current prices will assist in helping to establish the value. When known, the original manufacturer's language has been used to identify the name of the piece. A glossary is included in this edition to help explain some of those terms. The pattern name listed is the one given by the manufacturer, except in the case of numbered patterns, which have now developed more easily recognizable names. A "Shape Library" has been included to give you an idea of the myriad shapes plates were manufactured in during this exciting period of American glassware production.

Prices

The prices of *Warman's Depression Glass* have been established by careful research and compiling data for months from various sources. These sources include advertisements of glassware listed for sale in such sources as *The Daze* and other trade publications. Visits to auctions, antiques shops, malls and flea markets yielded still another source of pricing data. Many specialized Depression glassware shows and general antique shows were visited. The newest and probably most up-to-date pricing venue is the Internet. Several sites were visited daily to observe what was being offered for sale. A careful eye was used to determine which patterns were being offered, as well as which colors seemed most popular and which forms were being offered for sale.

A huge database was electronically created to track what was being offered for sale, as well as what was not being offered at this point in time.

Regional differences were noted, and it seemed apparent that advertised prices were fairly constant. Of course, some patterns are more popular in certain areas, but there is no clear definition of what patterns were being collected by any particular geographic area. Collectors remain individual in their tastes and preferences for certain patterns and colors. Some colors in some patterns are just not being offered for sale in large enough quantities to get a true reading for the price structure. In those cases, a note as to availability has been included to guide the collector in establishing a value. The antiques and collectibles business is based on comparables, and great amounts of data must be analyzed to accurately attribute pricing. Regional differences, condition and collector desirability are all factors that have affected the pricing included in *Warman's Depression Glass*.

Research

Depression glassware is one of the best researched collecting areas available to the U.S. marketplace. This is due in large part to the careful research of several people, including Hazel Marie Weatherman, Gene Florence and Carl F. Luckey. Their volumes are held in high regard by researchers and collectors today. Many Depression glass collectors find their libraries grow as fast as their collections, as they search to find what was manufactured in a particular pattern. By carefully researching company records and archives, these authors have allowed us to view what forms were popular, what colors delighted housewives of the era and what sizes and shapes the patterns include. *Warman's Depression Glass* has responded to these authors by incorporating the best information they offer into a new source for collectors.

Reproductions

Reproductions of Depression glassware have greatly impacted the market. Whole patterns have fallen in value because collectors are wary of continuing to invest in patterns beset by reproductions. Some patterns, like Miss America, are now experiencing reproductions of reproductions. The well-known clues to identifying the Miss America butter dish are now being compounded by having to recognize the second generation reproduction and its identification clues. Known reproductions, as of March 1997, are identified in the introduction of each pattern, as well as being marked in the listing as †. Fantasy pieces, items not originally produced or produced in another color, are also listed as reproductions. Collectors are encouraged to subscribe to the *Antique and Collectors Reproduction News*, P.O. Box 71174, Des Moines, IA 50325. This excellent publication covers all areas of the antiques and collectibles marketplace, as well as information about Depression glassware.

What's Included

Depression glassware, as defined by this edition, designates "patterns" produced between 1920 and the late 1970s. Such an expansive time-span allows patterns to be included from many manufacturers. The patterns selected reflect dinnerware patterns as opposed to elegant patterns or stemware only patterns. To be included in this edition, a pattern had to meet several criteria:

- Be readily available on the marketplace
- Include a basic place-setting, such as a cup and saucer and plates
- Been manufactured during the time-frame established
- Been manufactured in America

Several patterns were included which are considered "hand-made," such as Fostoria's American and Tiffin's Flower Garden with Butterflies. These patterns actually cross over into the elegant glassware associated with Depression glass. Because these patterns are currently very popular with collectors, they were chosen to be included along with the machine-made patterns.

Very expensive items have been included in some patterns to give collectors a comparable value. Depression collectors are referred to other volumes that list rare and expensive Depression glass, to firmly establish prices on those very rare items. As in some other areas of the antiques and collectibles marketplace, rare does not always equate to a high dollar amount. And some more readily found items command lofty prices because of high demand or other factors, not because they are necessarily rare. As collectors tastes range from the simple patterns to the more elaborate patterns, so does the ability of their budget to invest in inexpensive patterns to multi-hundreds of dollars per form patterns.

To maintain the fine tradition of extensive descriptions typically found in Warman's price guides, as much information as possible has been included as far as sizes, shapes, color and so on. Whenever possible, the original manufacturer's language was maintained. A glossary is included to help you identify some of those puzzling names. As the patterns evolved, sometimes other usage names were assigned to pieces. Collectors and dealers today face the constant challenge of identifying not only the pattern, but also understanding the original usage. It takes careful attention to detail to discern the differences between berry, dessert, fruit, sauce and cereal bowls. Color names are also given as the manufacturers originally named them. The Depression glassware researchers have many accurate sources, including company records, catalogs, magazine advertisements, oral and written histories from sales staff and factory workers.

The dates included in the introductions are approximate, as are some of the factory locations. When companies had more than one factory, usually only the main office or factory is listed. With the fine reference books available to collectors, *Warman's Depression* chose to concentrate on the pricing aspects of this segment of the antiques and collectibles market, rather than repeat the known company histories. A time-line is included to give some perspective of the companies actually covered in this edition, which contains general dates. An interesting color time-line has been developed and perhaps it will assist the collector or dealer to determine the date of a piece by the color, as well as the pattern.

Warman's Depression Glass also includes a "Color Identification Guide." This has been included to show the differences between the beautiful colors of Depression Glass. Not every color known to the world of Depression Glass is shown; however, it's a good starting place. The patterns included were chosen because they were good representatives of a specific color. Like the "Shape Library," use this section as a clue to determine what color and pattern you're searching for.

Today's Collectors

It became quite evident, through the compilation and analyzing of the databases, that collectors of Depression glassware tend to use their treasures. Whether it's for every day use or for just special occasions, most reported on enjoying their collections and using them. Some noted that they mix and match patterns, although most seem devoted to one color in a particular pattern. Sometimes colors will be mixed and matched as a collection is created for use purposes. Often, the collectors later sell off those pieces that no longer match or go with their patterns. Many Depression glass collectors become dealers to support their habit and to lessen their groaning cupboards!

Warman's Today's Collector lists Depression Glass as being one of the hottest areas of interest on the Internet. This statement is verified by the ever growing number of sites available to the serious collector and first-time buyer. Information about company histories, interesting articles, listings of shows and shops is becoming more easily accessible, as this worldwide web gathers collectors together.

Many Depression collectors consistently look to each other for support, sharing of knowledge and searching. This is one area where the Internet has answered a need in that some collectors correspond or "chat" daily about their collections, sharing experiences and dreams. During Depression glass antique shows, it is not uncommon to see a dealer or collector offering their opinion about the source of a particular piece, what colors are available and so forth. This is certainly one area of the antiques and collectibles marketplace where knowledge is freely shared. Perhaps this helps explain why so many young collectors are drawn to this colorful glassware. Information is readily available, standard price guides are used to establish prices, and knowledge is freely shared. Add to that excellent reference books and you have an ever-increasing pool of collectors. Many exciting treasures await those who actively search for the rainbow of sparkling colors known today as Depression glass.

Thanks to...

Working on *Warman's Depression Glass* has been a wonderful experience. Hopefully, it will continue to be a work-in-progress, as readers share their discoveries, stories of special pieces and other interesting events with me. No book of this nature can ever be 100% complete—there will always be some unknown pieces, unreported colors or unusual pieces. Company records and catalogs are still to be discovered and shared with collectors. Krause Publications and I are proud to bring you this edition and we hope it will meet your expectations.

To facilitate photographing of all these beautiful patterns, several Depression dealers and private collectors generously loaned us pieces. Each piece was hand selected for the book, told to smile, carefully washed and wrapped for transport. Those who deserve our thanks for this task include: Keith and Jeanean Belk, Gayle Brecka, Jim and Linda Cartin, Joyce Centola, Tony and Jeanne Jacobsen, Fran Jay, Sandra A. Lassari, Bettianne Ludden, Neil and Mildred McCurdy, Al and Rubie Myers and Troy Vozzella. Photographer Donna Chiarelli carefully positioned each and every piece, adjusting lights and cameras to present each one's best side! Ross Hubbard took the pictures of Swankyswigs, Forest Green and Fire King Turquoise Blue.

Another type of artist was employed to develop the line drawings. Jerry O'Brien's patience and attention to detail have resulted in these superb drawings. Whenever possible, he worked from an actual example, measuring details, analyzing the pattern from an artist's point of view. Sometimes an actual plate, saucer, or other of piece was photocopied and then the lines meticulously traced and enhanced to show the details. After Jerry completed a pencil sketch, the drawings were again evaluated for attention to detail. Finally, the drawings were inked in preparation for use in *Warman's*. Other patterns, those with a design in a more geometric arrangement, were drawn using more technical drawing skills. Where the pattern repeats evenly around the piece, only a portion is shown, allowing more room for pertinent information. In other patterns, such as Parrot (Sylvan) the whole pattern is shown, so that collectors can get a proper prospective as to the location of the parrots, foliage, etc. It's our hope that these detailed drawings will help give you a clearer view of the details associated with these beautiful patterns.

After Jerry completed the task of drawing the pattern, he provided us with a drawing of a typical plate to be included in our "Shape Library." As the book progressed, we were all delighted to see the variations of the Depression glassware.

Support and guidance for *Warman's Depression Glass* has been terrific and freely given by many. To those, including Jerry Gallagher, Larry Baker, Troy Vozzella, Jeffrey and Mark Schroy, Larry and Naomi Tischbein, Linda and Brian Fluck, Carl Babino and Jon Brecka, who proof-read, packed glassware and shared their enthusiasm. Thank you!

Glossary

AOP: All-over pattern, often found in descriptions to indicate a design that covers the entire piece rather than in just one location.

Berry Bowl: Used to describe both individual serving dishes and master bowl used as a set to serve berries (strawberries, etc.). Often accompanied by creamer or milk pitcher and sugar bowl.

Bouillon: Generally, cup-shaped bowl for serving broth or clear soups, usually has handles.

Cheese and Cracker Set: Serving piece often consists of a comport to hold cheese and large plate for crackers; forms differ. Sometimes, a sherbet is used as comport.

Cheese Dish: Serving dish, often with domed top, to cover cheese wedge.

Children's Wares: Dish and tea sets designed to be used by children for play.

Chop Plate: Large round plate used to serve individual portions of meat and foul.

Cider Set: Consists of covered cookie jar (used to hold cider), tray and roly-poly cups and ladle.

Closed Handle: Solid glass handle.

Comport: Container used as serving dish, open with handles, sometimes covered.

Compote: Another name for comport.

Console Set: Decorative large bowl with matching candlesticks.

Cream Soup: Bowl used to serve cream-type or chilled soups, usually has handles.

Cup and Saucer: Used to refer to place-setting cup and saucer; some patterns include larger coffee cup or more diminutive tea cup.

Demitasse Cup and Saucer: Term used to describe smaller cup and saucer used for after-dinner beverage.

Domino Tray: Tray used to hold sugar blocks shaped like dominoes.

Egg Cup: Stemware with short stem used to hold egg, usually used with underplate.

Goblet: Stemware used to hold water.

Grill Plate: Dinner-sized plate with lines that divide plate into compartments.

Ice Lip: Small piece of glass inside of top of pitcher to hold ice in pitcher. May also mean a pinched lip that prevents ice from falling from pitcher.

Icer: Vessel with compartment to hold crushed ice to keep main vessel cold, i.e., mayonnaise, cream soup, shrimp, etc.

Individual Sized Pieces: Smaller sized pieces, often designed for bed tray use. Not to be confused with children's wares.

Liner: Underplate or under bowl used to accompany another piece, i.e., finger bowl or sherbet.

Light (Lite): Branch found on candlestick used to hold additional candles, i.e., 2 light, 3 light. Nappy: Shallow bowl used as serving dish or in place-setting; often has small handle.

Oil/Vinegar: Term used to describe cruet or bottle with stopper to hold oil and/or vinegar for salads.

Platter: Small, medium or large oval plate used to serve roasts and foul.

Ring Handle: Figural round handle, ring-shaped.

Salver: Large round plate used as serving piece.

Sandwich Server: Round plate, often with center handle (made of glass or metal) used to serve tea-type sandwiches.

Sherbet: Part of a place-setting used to hold sherbet, often served with matching underplate about the same size as a saucer.

Snack Set: Plate or small tray with indent to hold punch or coffee-type cup.

Spooner: Small, often squatty, open vase-type vessel used to hold spoons upright. Typically, part of table set.

Spoon Tray: Small bowl-shaped vessel used to hold spoons horizontally, often oval. Often used on buffets, etc., to hold extra place-setting spoons.

Stand: Base or additional piece used to hold punch bowl, etc.

Table Set: Name given to set of matching covered butter dish, creamer, covered (or open) sugar and spooner. An extended table service may include syrup, toothpick holder and salt and pepper shakers.

Tab Handle: Small solid glass handle useful to grab bowl, etc.

Toddy Set: Set consists of covered cookie jar (used to hold toddy), tray and roly-poly cups and ladle.

Tumbler: Any footed or flat vessel used to hold water or other liquids. Specialized tumblers include ginger ale, juice, iced tea, lemonade, old fashioned and whiskey.

Wine: Term used to describe stemware used to hold wine. Depression-era wines have a small capacity, by today's standards.

Company Time-Line

19th C Ohio Flint Glass is founded; it later becomes part of National Glass Company conglomerate.

19th C Bottle plant established at Jeannette, Pa., which becomes Jeannette Glass Company.

1853 McKee and Brothers is founded in Pittsburgh.

1887 Fostoria Glass Company is founded in Fostoria, Ohio, but is moved to Moundsville, W.V., when fuel supply is depleted.

1888 McKee moves to Jeannette, Pa.

1890 Westmoreland Specialty Company is established in Grapeville, Pa. Early manufacture includes bottles and food containers. During World War I, glass candy containers are made. The plant continues on to make colored and opaque glassware in both Depression patterns and, later, a giftware line.

1891 U.S. Glass Company organized by combining 18 different glass houses, located in Pennsylvania, Ohio and West Virginia. The main offices are in Pittsburgh, as well as some manufacturing.

1899 MacBeth merges with Evans, creating MacBeth-Evans. Main factory is located in Charleroi, Pa., with others located in Marion, Bethevan and Elwood, Ind., as well as Toledo, Ohio.

1900 Federal Glass Company opens Columbus, Ohio, plant. First wares were crystal with needle etching, various decorations and crackle finish. After switching to automation, it soon begins production of tumblers and many Depression-era patterns, as well as restaurant wares—all at an economical price.

1901 Imperial Glass Company is organized. Produces first glass at Bellaire, Ohio, plant in 1904. Morgantown Glass Works begins production in Morgantown, W.V. New Martinsville Glass Manufacturing Company is established at New Martinsville, W.V.

1902 Hazel Atlas Glass Company established in Washington, Pa. It was a result of the merger of the Hazel Glass Company and its neighboring factory, Atlas Glass and Metal Company; corporate offices are later established at Wheeling, W.V.

1903 Morgantown Glass Works reorganizes as Economy Tumbler Company and operates using that name. Liberty Cut Glass Works established in Egg Harbor, N.J. Primarily a cutting house for years, pressed glass is also made. McKee Brothers reorganize into McKee Glass Company and continue until 1951.

1905 Anchor Hocking Glass Company established in Lancaster, Ohio. Well known by the mid 1920s for its tumbler and tableware production.

1906 Fenton Art Glass Company builds a new factory in Williamstown, W.V. While its giftware lines are well known, some Depression-era glassware is produced.

1907 Indiana Glass Company established at Dunkirk, Ind. Early production is hand-pressed. Assembly-line patterns evolve during the 1920s, although some still required hand work. Later, enters into automobile glassware items and becomes a subsidiary of Lancaster Colony.

1908 Lancaster Glass Company, Lancaster, Ohio, is built by first president of Fostoria.

1911 L.E. Smith begins in the glass trade. Much of the production of this company remains utilitarian in nature, as well as making lenses for automobiles.

1916 Paden City Glass Manufacturing Company is established at Paden City, W.V. Production includes some Depression-era patterns, but is more well known for its elegant lines, vases, lamps and restaurant wares.

1923 Economy Tumbler Company changes name to Economy Glass Company.

1924 Fostoria introduces color and starts national magazine advertising campaign.

Jeannette toted by trade as "one of the most complete automatic factories in the country." Lancaster becomes subsidiary of Hocking Glass Company. It continues to make kitchenware, cut and decorated tableware under the Lancaster name until 1937. Also makes colored blanks for Standard Glass Company (another Hocking subsidiary) in which the glass is etched and cut. Known as Plant #2 to Anchor Hocking.

1927 Jeannette management ceases all hand operations.

1928 Jeannette makes green and pink glass automatically in a continuous tank. A first!
Trade journals proclaim Clarksburg, W.V., Hazel-Atlas factory as "World's Largest Tumbler Factory," which accurately describes the fully automated factory.

1929 Economy Glass Company changes name back to Morgantown Glass Works, Inc.

1932 Liberty Cut Glass Works is destroyed by fire, never to rebuilt.

1937 Corning Glass Works purchases MacBeth-Evans.
Hocking Glass Company merges with Anchor Cap and Closure Corporation, Long Island City, N.Y., creating the huge Anchor-Hocking Glass Company, which has continued to have a major impact on the glassware industry.
Morgantown Glass Works, Inc., closes.

1938 U.S. Glass moves main offices to Tiffin, Ohio, and production decreases.

1939 Morgantown Glassware Guild is organized and reopens factory.

1944 New Martinsville is sold and reorganized as Viking Glass Company.

1949 Westmoreland Glass Company begins to use impressed intertwined "W" and "G" mark.

1951 The only operating company of the former U.S. Glass is Tiffin. The rest have all closed.
McKee is sold to Thatcher Manufacturing Co.

1952 Fire destroys Belmont plant, Bellaire, Ohio. With the fire go the records.

1955 Duncan and Miller molds are acquired by Tiffin, which begins to produce colors and crystal wares with these molds.

1956 Continental Can purchases Hazel-Atlas and continues to sell tableware under name "Hazelware."

1958 Federal Glass becomes a division of Federal Paper Board Company. It continues glassware production.

1961 Jeannette buys old McKee factory in Jeannette, Pa., and moves there to continue production.

1964 Brockway Glass Company buys out Continental Can's interest in Hazel-Atlas and begins operation.

1965 Fostoria Glass Company purchases Morgantown Glassware Guild.

1966 Continental Can takes over operation of Tiffin until 1969, with glass production continuing.

1971 Glass production is terminated at Fostoria's Morgantown facility, ending the Morgantown Glassware Guild.

1973 Imperial Glass Company sold to Lenox, Inc.

1980 Tiffin Glass discontinues operation.

1982 Westmoreland Glass Company closes factory in May. Reorganized in July.

1983 Lancaster Glass purchases Fostoria.
Westmoreland begins to use full name as imprinted mark.

1984 Westmoreland Glass Company again closes Grapeville plant.

Color Time-Line

Apple Green
1925: Jeannette

Amber
1923: McKee
1923: New Martinsville
1924: Paden City
1924: Westmoreland's Transparent Amber
1924-1941: Fostoria
1925: Indiana
Mid 1920s: Hocking, Imperial and L.E. Smith
1926: Jeannette
Late 1920s: Liberty
1931-1942: Federal's Golden Glow
1960: Westmoreland's Golden Sunset

Amethyst
1923: McKee
1924: New Martinsville
Mid 1920s: L.E. Smith
1926: Morgantown's Old Amethyst
1933: Paden City
1939: Morgantown's Light Amethyst

Black
1920s-1930s: L.E. Smith
1922: Morgantown's India Black
1923 and 1930s: Paden City
1923: New Martinsville
1924: Fostoria
1930: McKee
1931: Hazel-Atlas, Imperial, Lancaster

Blue
1920s: Lancaster
1923: McKee's Jap Blue and Transparent Blue
1923: New Martinsville
1924: Paden City
1924-1928: Fostoria
1925: McKee's Sky Blue and Westmoreland's
Mid 1920s: Hocking
1926: Imperial, Morgantown's Azure and transparent blue
1927: Imperial's Blue-Green, Morgantown's Ritz
1928: New Martinsville's Alice Blue (medium shade)
1928-1943: Fostoria's Azure Blue (lighter shade)
Late 1920s: Liberty's pale shade
1930: Hocking's Mayfair Blue (medium shade), McKee's Ritz Blue and Chalaine Blue
1931: Imperial's Ritz Blue, Lancaster's pale blue, Westmoreland's Belgian Blue
1933: Fostoria's Regal Blue
1933-1934: Federal's Madonna Blue (medium shade)
1933-1942: New Martinsville's Ritz Blue
Mid 1930s: MacBeth-Evans' Ritz Blue
1936: Hazel-Atlas's Ritz Blue, McKee's opaque Poudre Blue, Paden City's Ceylon Blue

1939: Morgantown's Copen Blue and Gloria Blue
1940: Anchor-Hocking's Fire King
1950s: Indiana's Blue-Green

Burgundy
1933: Fostoria
1936: Hazel-Atlas (deep shade)

Canary Yellow
1923: McKee
Mid 1920s: Hocking, L.E. Smith
1924: New Martinsville
1924-1927: Fostoria
1925: Lancaster

Cobalt Blue
1930: Liberty
1936: Paden City
1939: Morgantown

Cremax
1939: MacBeth-Evans

Crystal
1923: Paden City
1930s: Imperial
1935: New Martinsville and Westmoreland—most companies produced crystal throughout their years of production

Delphite, Delfite
1936: Jeannette

Fired-On Colors
1920s: Federal and Lancaster
1923: Westmoreland
1926: New Martinsville
Mid 1930s: MacBeth-Evans

French Ivory (opaque)
1933: McKee

Green
1920s: Lancaster
1921: Morgantown's Venetian Green
1922: Morgantown's Meadow Green
1923: McKee
1924: Paden City
1924-1941: Fostoria
Mid 1920s: Hocking, Imperial and L.E. Smith
1925: Indiana, McKee's Grass Green and New Martinsville
1926: New Martinsville's Emerald Green
1926-1936: Federal's Springtime Green
1928: MacBeth-Evans' Emerald
Late 1920s: Liberty
1929: Hazel-Atlas, Imperial
1931: Morgantown's Stiegel Green

1931-1933: New Martinsville's Stiegel Green
1933: Fostoria's Empire Green, Hazel-Atlas's Killarney Green, New Martinsville's Evergreen (dark shade)
1936: Paden City's Forest Green
1939: Morgantown's Shamrock Green
1950s: Anchor-Hocking's Forest Green

Iridescent
1920s: Federal
1920s to present: Jeannette
1934-1935: Federal's Iridescent Amber

Ivory
1929: Imperial
1933: Indiana (opaque)
1940: Anchor-Hocking

Ivrene
1930s: MacBeth-Evans

Jade
1930: McKee
1931: New Martinsville

Jadite
1932: Jeannette

Jade Yellow
1923: McKee

Monax
1920s: MacBeth-Evans

Mulberry
1924: Paden City

Opalescent
1923: Morgantown's Alabaster
1931: Westmoreland's Moonstone (blue)
1942: Anchor-Hocking's Moonstone

Orchid
1927: McKee
1927-1929: Fostoria
1929: Imperial

Pink
Mid 1920s: Imperial's Rose Marie, Rose
1925: Paden City's Cheriglo
1926: McKee's Rose Pink, Morgantown's Anna

Red-Amber
1930: Liberty

Rose
1926: Indiana and Westmoreland
1926-1942: Hocking's Rose (later called Flamingo or Cerise), New Martinsville's Peach Melba (later known as Rose)
1927: Jeannette's Wild Rose, L.E. Smith
1928: MacBeth-Evans
1928-1941: Fostoria's Rose or Dawn
Late 1920s: Liberty

1930: Hazel-Atlas, Lancaster's deep pink
1931-1942: Federal's Rose Glow
1933: Hazel-Atlas's Sunset Pink
1939: Morgantown's Pink Champagne
1947-1949: Jeannette

Royal Blue
1932: Paden City

Ruby
1925: Morgantown
1927: McKee
1931: Imperial
1932: Paden City
1933-1942: New Martinsville
Mid 1930s: MacBeth-Evans
1935: Fostoria's Ruby
1939: Anchor-Hocking's Royal Ruby

Sea Foam
1931: Imperial, Harding Blue, Moss Green or Burnt Almond with opal edge

Seville Yellow
1931: McKee

Shell Pink
1958: Jeannette

Skokie Green
1931: McKee

Tan
1931: McKee's Old Rose

Topaz
1921: Morgantown's 14K Topaz
1925: Jeannette
1928: Hocking
1929: Fostoria
1930: Lancaster, Westmoreland (sometimes combined with crystal or black)
1930-mid 1930s: Indiana
1931: Imperial, Liberty, MacBeth-Evans, McKee, Paden City's Golden Glow
1933: Hazel-Atlas
1938-1940s: Fostoria's Golden Tint
1939: Morgantown's Topaz Mist

Ultramarine
1937-1938: Jeannette

Vaseline
Mid 1920s: Imperial

White
1930s: Hazel-Atlas's Platonite (opaque)
1932: Hocking (Vitrock)
1937-1942: McKee (opal) and after World War II

Wine
1923: New Martinsville

Wisteria
1931-1938: Fostoria

Resources

Collectors' Clubs

Canadian Depression Glass Club
P.O. Box 104
Mississaugua, Ontario L53 2K1 Canada

Fenton Art Glass Collectors of America, Inc.
P.O. Box 384
Williamstown, WV 26187

Fire-King Collectors Club
1167 Teal Rd., SW
Dellroy, OH 44620

Fostoria Glass Collectors
10211 Slater Ave., #103-396
Fountain Valley, CA 92708

Fostoria Glass Society of America, Inc.
P.O. Box 826
Moundsville, WV 26041
Internet: http://home1.gte.net/bartholf.fostoria.htm

Morgantown Glass Collectors of America
420 1st Ave., NW
Plainview, MN 55964

National Depression Glass Association
P.O. Box 8264
Wichita, KS 67208-0264
Internet: http://www.interlabs.bradley.edu/ndga

National Fenton Glass Society
P.O. Box 4008
Marietta, OH 45750

National Imperial Glass Collectors Society
P.O. Box 534
Bellaire, OH 43906

National Westmoreland Glass Collectors Club
P.O. Box 372
Westmoreland City, PA 15692

Tiffin Glass Collectors' Club
P.O. Box 554
Tiffin, OH 44883
20-30-40 Society, Inc.
P.O. Box 856
LaGrange, IL 60525

Westmoreland Glass Society, Inc.
2712 Glenwood
Independence, MO 64052

Internet Sites

The following are three sites that list quality depression-era glassware. Many other dealers offer depression-era glassware on the Internet. These three sites all offer dealer information, as well as show listings, information about reproductions, books for sale and links to other related web sites. Both "DG Shopper Online" and "Mega" offer collectors a place to chat about Depression Glass. As the Internet expands, so will buying and selling opportunities for Depression Glass collectors.

DG Shopper Online, The WWW Depression Era Glassware Magazine
http://www.dgshopper.com/~dgshoppr

Mega Show, Depression Era Glass and China
http://www.glassshow.com

Facets Antiques & Collectibles Mall
http://www.Facets.net

Publications

Antique & Collector's Reproduction News
P.O. Box 12130
Des Moines, IA 50312

Glass Collector's Digest
P.O. Box 553
Marietta, OH 45750

The DAZE, Inc.
P.O. Box 57
Otisville MI 48463
Internet: http://www.thedaze.com

The Fire-King News
K&W Collectibles, Inc.
P.O. Box 473
Addison, AL 35540

Video Tapes

"Fenton: Glass Artistry in the Making, Fenton Art Glass," Michael Dickensen, 1992.

"Popular Patterns of the Depression Era," from the Living Glass Videotape Series, RoCliff Communications, 8422 N. Park Court, Kansas City, MO 64155.

References

General Depression Glass References

Gene Florence: *Collectible Glassware from the 40's, 50's & 60's*, 3rd edition, Collector Books, 1996; *Collector's Encyclopedia of Depression Glass*, 13th edition, Collector Books, 1997; *Elegant Glassware of the Depression Era*, 7th edition, Collector Books, 1996; *Kitchen Glassware of the Depression Era*, 5th edition, Collector Books, 1995; *Pocket Guide to Depression Glass & More*, 10th edition, Collector Books, 1996; *Stemware Identification*, Collector Books, 1996; *Very Rare Glassware of the Depression Years*, 1st Series (1988, 1990 value update), 2nd Series (1990), 3rd Series (1993, 1995 value update), 4th Series (1995), 5th Series (1996), Collector Books.

Jay L. Glickman: *Yellow-Green Vaseline! A Guide to the Magic Glass*, Antique Publications, 1991.

Ralph and Terry Kovel: *Kovel's Depression Glass & Americana Dinnerware Price List*, 5th edition, Crown, 1995.

Carl F. Luckey and Mary Burris: *Identification and Value Guide to Depression Era Glassware*, 3rd edition, Books Americana, 1994.

Naomi L. Over: *Ruby Glass of the 20th Century*, Antique Publications, 1990 (1993-94 value update).

The Daze: *The Daze Past: Volumes 1, 2 and 3*, The Daze.

Marlene Toohey: *A Collector's Guide to Black Glass*, Antique Publications, 1988.

Kent G. Washburn: *Price Survey*, 4th edition, published by author, 1994.

Hazel Marie Weatherman: *Colored Glassware of the Depression Era, Book 2*, published by author, 1974 (available in reprint); *1984 Supplement & Price Trends for Colored Glassware of the Depression Era, Book 1*, published by author, 1984.

Specific Company References

Fenton: Robert E. Eaton, Jr., *Fenton Glass: The First 25 Years Comprehensive Price Guide*, The Glass Press, 1995, distributed by Antique Publications; *Fenton Glass: The 1980's Decade Comprehensive Price Guide*, The Glass Press, 1996, distributed by Antique Publications; William Heacock, *Fenton Glass: The First Twenty-Five Years* (1978), *The Second Twenty-Five Years* (1980), *The Third Twenty-Five Years* (1989), available from Antique Publications; Alan Linn, *Fenton Story of Glass Making*, Antique Publications, 1996; James Measell, *Fenton Glass: The 80's Decade*, Antique Publications, 1996; Members of the Fenton Art Glass Collectors of America, *Fenton Glass: The Third 25 Years Comprehensive Price Guide to Fenton Glass*, Antique Publications, 1995, distributed by Antique Publications; Ferill J. Rice (ed.), *Caught in the Butterfly Net, Fenton Art Glass Collectors of America*, The Glass Press, 1995; Margaret and Kenn Whitmyer, *Fenton Art Glass: 1907-1939*, Collector Books, 1996.

Fostoria: Ann Kerr, *Fostoria: An Identification and Value Guide, Volume I, Pressed, Blown & Hand Molded Shapes*, Collector Books, 1994; *Fostoria: An Identification and Value Guide, Volume II, Etched and Carved & Cut Designs*, Collector Books, 1996; Milbra Long and Emily Seate, *Fostoria Stemware*, Collector Books, 1995; Leslie Pina, *Fostoria Designer George Sakier*, Schiffer Publishing, 1996; Fostoria, Schiffer Publishing, 1995; Joann Schleismann, *Price Guide to Fostoria*, 3rd edition, Park Avenue Publications; Sidney P. Seligson, *Fostoria American, A Complete Guide*, 2nd edition, published by author.

Imperial: Margaret and Douglas Archer, *Imperial Glass*, Collector Books, 1978 (1993 value update); National Imperial Glass Collectors Society, *Imperial Glass Encyclopedia, Volume I: A-Cane*, Antique Publications, 1995; *National Imperial Glass Collectors Society, Imperial Glass 1966 Catalog*, reprint, 1991 price guide, Antique Publications.

Morgantown: Jerry Gallagher, *A Handbook of Old Morgantown Glass, Volume I: A Guide to Identification and Shape*, published by author, 1995.

New Martinsville: James Measell, *New Martinsville Glass*, Antique Publications, 1994.

Tiffin: Fred Bickenhauser, *Tiffin Glassmasters, Book I* (1979), *Book II* (1981), *Book III* (1985), Glassmasters Publications; Bob Page and Dale Fredericksen, *Tiffin Is Forever*, Page-Fredericksen, 1994; Leslie Pina and Jerry Gallagher, *Tiffin Glass*, Schiffer Publishing, 1996.

Westmoreland: Lorraine Kovar, *Westmoreland Glass, Volumes. I and II*, Antique Publications, 1991; Chas West Wilson, *Westmoreland Glass*, Collector Books, 1996.

Color Identification Guide

Blue: (back row, from left) Lace Edge, Radiance, Bubble; (front row from left) Mayfair, Ships.

Green #1: (from left) Floral and Diamond, Colonial, U.S. Swirl, Thistle, Pyramid, Daisy, Fire-King Restaurantware.

Green #2: (from left) Laurel, Rosemary, Westmoreland vaseline basket, Parrot, Thumbprint.

Pink #1: (back row, from left) Nora Bird, Fire-King Swirl, Petalware, Diana; (front row from left) Fortune, Hobnail.

Pink #2: (back row, from left) Lincoln Inn, Open Lace, Ovide; (front row from left) Moondrops (cup and saucer), Sharon, Diana (coaster), Peacock & Wild Rose.

Yellow #1: (from left) Madrid, Patrick, Jubilee, Mayfair, Orchid, Madrid, Roxana.

Yellow #2: (from left) Crow's Foot, Princess (apricot grill plate), Daisy, Rock Crystal (front).

Shape Guide

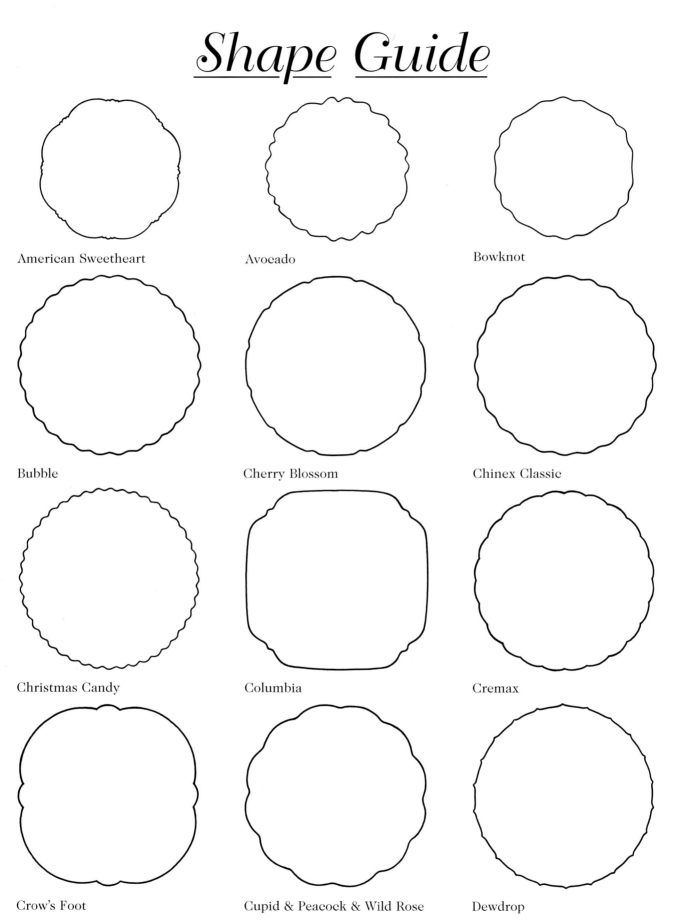

American Sweetheart

Avocado

Bowknot

Bubble

Cherry Blossom

Chinex Classic

Christmas Candy

Columbia

Cremax

Crow's Foot

Cupid & Peacock & Wild Rose

Dewdrop

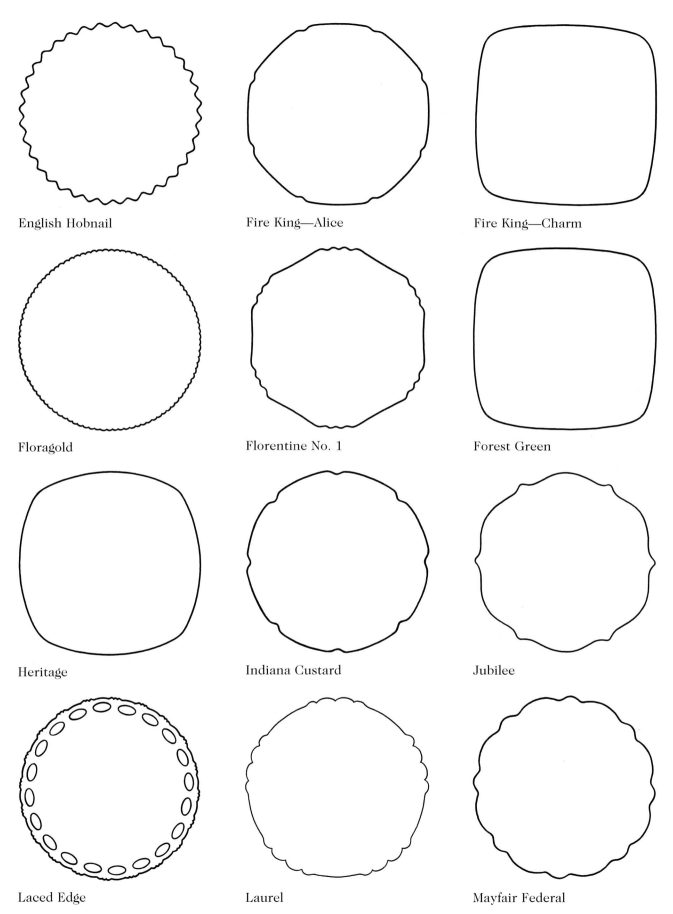

English Hobnail

Fire King—Alice

Fire King—Charm

Floragold

Florentine No. 1

Forest Green

Heritage

Indiana Custard

Jubilee

Laced Edge

Laurel

Mayfair Federal

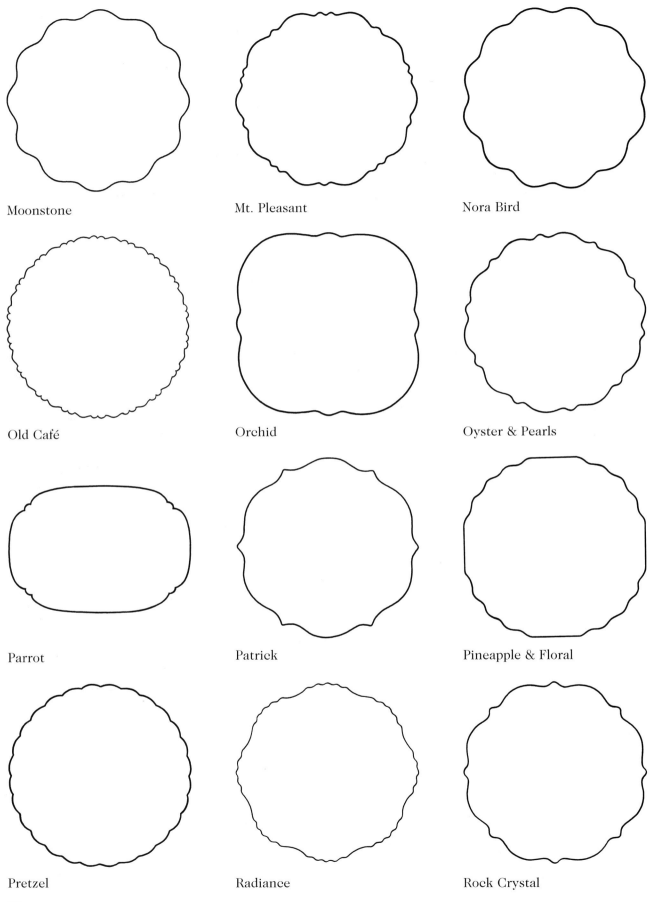

Moonstone

Mt. Pleasant

Nora Bird

Old Café

Orchid

Oyster & Pearls

Parrot

Patrick

Pineapple & Floral

Pretzel

Radiance

Rock Crystal

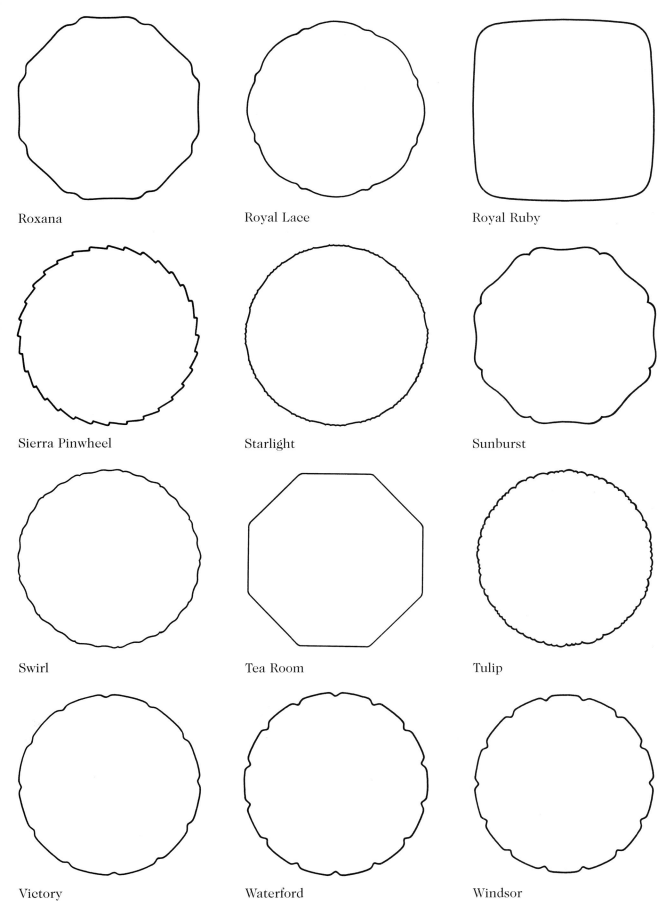

Roxana

Royal Lace

Royal Ruby

Sierra Pinwheel

Starlight

Sunburst

Swirl

Tea Room

Tulip

Victory

Waterford

Windsor

Adam

Manufactured by Jeannette Glass Company, Jeannette, Pa., from 1932 to 1934.

Made in crystal, Delphite blue, green, pink, some topaz and yellow. Delphite 4" h candlesticks are valued at $240 a pair. A yellow cup and saucer are valued at $190, and a 7-3/4" d yellow plate is valued at $100. Production in topaz and yellow was very limited. Crystal prices would be approximately 50% of the prices listed for green.

Reproductions: † Butter Dish in pink and green.

Item	Green	Pink
Ashtray, 4-1/2" d	25.00	32.00
Berry Bowl, small	18.50	16.50
Bowl, 9" d, cov	85.00	75.00
Bowl, 9" d, open	45.00	30.00
Bowl, 10" l, oval	40.00	40.00
Butter Dish, cov †	325.00	95.00
Cake Plate, 10" d, ftd	32.00	30.00
Candlesticks, pr, 4" h	125.00	100.00
Candy Jar, cov, 2-1/2" h	100.00	95.00
Casserole, cov	90.00	75.00
Cereal Bowl, 5-3/4" d	46.00	46.00
Coaster, 3-1/4" d	22.00	32.00
Creamer	22.00	20.00
Cup	22.00	24.00
Dessert Bowl, 4-3/4" d	18.50	16.50
Iced Tea Tumbler, 5-1/2" h	60.00	65.00
Lamp	285.00	265.00
Pitcher, 32 oz, round base	-	125.00
Pitcher, 32 oz, 8" h	48.00	45.00
Plate, 6" d, sherbet	9.50	9.00
Plate, 7-3/4" d, salad, sq	17.00	17.00
Plate, 9" d, dinner, sq	30.00	32.00
Plate, 9" d, grill	20.00	20.00
Platter, 11-3/4" l, rect	32.00	30.00
Relish Dish, 8" l, divided	27.00	20.00
Salt and Pepper Shakers, pr, 4" h	100.00	80.00
Saucer, 6" sq	7.00	7.00
Sherbet, 3"	40.00	35.00
Sugar, cov	48.00	42.00
Tumbler, 4-1/2" h	28.00	30.00
Vase, 7-1/2" h	60.00	250.00
Vegetable Bowl, 7-3/4" d	30.00	30.00

Adam pink pitcher and green ashtray.

American

Line #2056

Manufactured by Fostoria Glass Company, Moundsville, Va., from 1915 to 1986.

Made in crystal, some amber, blue, green, yellow, pink, pink tinting to purple in the late 1920s, white, red in 1980s, currently in red and crystal for Lancaster Colony by Dalzell Viking. Prices for colors fluctuate greatly.

Item	Crystal
Almond Bowl, 3-3/4" l, oval	9.00
Appetizer Insert, 3-1/4"	28.00
Appetizer Tray, 10-1/2" l, 6 inserts	250.00
Ashtray, 2-7/8" w, sq	8.00
Ashtray, 3-7/8" l, oval	10.00
Ashtray, 5" w, sq	35.00
Ashtray, 5-1/2" l, oval	20.00
Banana Split, 9" x 3-1/2"	310.00
Basket, 10", c1988	30.00
Basket, 7" x 9", reeded handle	75.00
Beer Mug, 4-1/2" h, 12 oz	65.00
Bell	345.00
Bitter Bottles, 5-3/4" h, 4-1/2 oz	70.00
Boat, 8-1/2" d	15.00
Boat, 9" d, 2 part	12.00
Boat, 12" l	17.50
Bonbon, 6" d, 3 ftd	15.00
Bonbon, 7" h, 3 ftd	15.00
Bonbon, 8" d, 3 ftd	17.50
Bowl, 4-1/2" d, 1 handle, round	10.00
Bowl, 4-1/2" d, 1 handle, sq	12.00
Bowl, 4-1/2" d, oval	15.00
Bowl, 5" d, handle, tricorner	12.50
Bowl, 7" d, 4-1/2" h, cupped	50.00
Bowl, 8" d, deep	50.00
Bowl, 8" d, ftd	55.00
Bowl, 8-1/2" d, 2 handles	48.00
Bowl, 9-1/2" d, 6" w, 3 part	40.00
Bowl, 10" d, deep	35.00
Bowl, 10" d, 14" d liner	50.00
Bowl, 11-1/2" d rolled edge	42.00
Bowl, 11-3/4" l, oval, deep	40.00
Box, cov, 4-1/2" x 4-1/2"	200.00
Brush Tray	50.00
Bud Vase, 6" h, flared	18.00
Bud Vase, 6" h, ftd	18.00
Bud Vase, 8-1/2" h, cupped	24.00

Item	Crystal
Bud Vase, 8-1/2" h, flared	24.00
Butter Dish, cov, 1/4 lb	28.00
Butter Dish, cov, 7-1/4" d, round plate	90.00
Cake Plate, 10" d, 2 handles	24.00
Cake Plate, 12" d, 3 ftd	20.00
Cake Stand, 10" round, pedestal foot	65.00
Cake Stand, 10" sq, pedestal foot	90.00
Cake Stand, 11" d, round, pedestal foot	65.00
Cake Tray, 10-1/2" d, crook-shaped handle	35.00
Candelabrum, 6-1/2", 2 light, bell base, bobeche, pr	125.00
Candle Lamp, 8-1/2" h, chimney, candle part, 3-1/2"	170.00
Candlestick, 2", chamber, fingerhold	40.00
Candlesticks, pr, 3", round, ftd	24.00
Candlesticks, pr, 4-3/8", 2-light, round foot	95.00
Candlesticks, pr, 6", octagon foot	60.00
Candlesticks, pr, 6-1/2", 2-light, bell base	95.00
Candlesticks, pr, 6-1/4", round foot	45.00
Candlesticks, pr, 7", sq, column	95.00
Candlesticks, pr, 7-1/4", Eiffel Tower	130.00
Candy Box, cov, 3 part, triangular	75.00
Candy Box, cov, pedestal foot	40.00
Catsup Bottle	115.00
Celery Tray, 10" l, oblong	18.00
Centerpiece Bowl, 9-1/2" d	45.00
Centerpiece Bowl, 11" d	45.00
Centerpiece Bowl, 11" d, tricorner	45.00
Centerpiece Bowl, 15" d, hat-shape	165.00
Cheese and Cracker, 5-3/4" comport, 11-1/2" d plate	65.00
Chocolate Tray, 7" x 5" x 1-7/8" deep	675.00
Cigarette Box, cov, 4-3/4"	40.00
Claret, 4-5/8" h, 3-1/2 oz, plain bowl, #5056	14.00
Claret, 4-7/8" h, 7 oz, #2056	40.00
Coaster, 3-3/4" d	8.00
Cocktail, 2-7/8" h, cone, ftd, 3 oz, #2506	12.00

Item	Crystal
Cocktail, 4" h, 3-1/2 oz, plain bowl, #5056	10.00
Cologne Bottle, orig stopper, 5-3/4" h, 6 oz	75.00
Cologne Bottle, orig stopper, 7-1/4" h, 8 oz	85.00
Cologne Bottle, orig stopper, 7-1/4" h, 9 oz	90.00
Comport, 5" d, covered	25.00
Comport, 8-1/2" d, 4" h	42.00
Comport, 9-1/2" d, 5-1/2" h	50.00
Condiment Bottle	115.00
Condiment Set, 2 oils, 2 shakers, mustard, tray	325.00
Condiment Tray, clover leaf	165.00
Cookie Jar, cov, 8-3/4" h	285.00
Cordial Bottle, 7-1/4" h, 9 oz	85.00
Cordial Set, scotch, rye, and gin decanters, rack	395.00
Cordial, 3-1/8" h, 1 oz, plain bowl, #5056	25.00
Cream Soup Bowl, 5" d, two handles	48.00
Cream Soup Liner	12.00
Creamer and Sugar Tray, 6-3/4" l, handle	15.00
Creamer, 3 oz, 2-3/8" h, tea size	9.00
Creamer, 4-3/4 oz, individual size	10.00
Creamer, 9-1/2 oz	14.00
Cruet, orig stopper, 5 oz	32.00
Cruet, orig stopper, 7 oz	35.00
Crushed Fruit, cov, spoon, 10" h	1,350.00
Cup, flat	8.00
Cup, ftd, 7 oz	7.00

Item	Crystal
Decanter, stopper, 24 oz, 9-1/4" h	85.00
Finger Bowl, 4-1/2" d, smooth edge	18.00
Float Bowl, 10" d	45.00
Float Bowl, 10" l, oval	35.00
Float Bowl, 11-1/2" d	55.00
Float Bowl, 11-1/2" l, oval	45.00
Fruit Bowl, 10-1/2" d, 3 ftd	38.00
Fruit Bowl, 11-1/2" d, 2-3/4" h, rolled edge	45.00
Fruit Bowl, 13" d, shallow	65.00
Fruit Bowl, 4-3/4" d, flared	18.00
Fruit Bowl, 16" d, pedestal foot	150.00
Fruit Cocktail, 4-3/4" h, 4-1/2 oz, hex foot, #2506	37.50
Glove Box, cov, 9-1/2" x 3-1/2"	295.00
Goblet, 9 oz, 4-3/8" h, low foot, #2056	10.00
Goblet, 10 oz, 6-1/8" h, plain bowl, #5056	12.50
Goblet, 10 oz, 6-7/8" h, hex foot, #2056	14.00
Hair Receiver, 3" x 3"	295.00
Hairpin Box, cov, 3-1/2" x 1-3/4"	315.00
Handkerchief Box, cov, 5-5/8" x 4-5/8"	295.00
Hat, 2-1/8"	25.00
Hat, 3" h	20.00
Hat, 4" h	40.00
Hat, western style	200.00
Hurricane Lamp, 12" h, complete	175.00
Ice Bucket, tongs	60.00
Ice Cream Saucer, 2 styles	55.00

American relish, plate and tumbler.

Item	Crystal
Ice Cream Tray, 13-1/2" l, oval	170.00
Ice Dish for 4 oz crab or 5 oz tomato liner	50.00
Ice Dish Insert	80.00
Ice Tub, with liner, 5-3/8"	95.00
Ice Tub, with liner, 6-1/2"	100.00
Iced Tea Tumbler, handle	215.00
Iced Tea Tumbler, 12 oz, 5-3/4" h, 12 oz, low foot, #2056	17.50
Jam Pot, cov	55.00
Jelly Bowl, 4-1/4" d, 4-1/4" h	15.00
Jelly Bowl, cov, 4-1/2" d, 6-3/4" h	24.00
Jelly Comport, 4-1/2" d	15.00
Jelly Comport, 5" d, flared	36.00
Jelly Comport, cov, 6-3/4" d	28.00
Jewel Box, cov, 2 drawer, 4-1/4" x 3-1/4"	1,800.00
Jewel Box, cov, 5-1/4" x 2-1/4"	325.00
Juice Tumbler, 5 oz, straight sides, #2056-1/2, flat	12.00
Juice Tumbler, 4-1/8" h, 5 oz, ftd, plain bowl	12.00
Juice Tumbler, 4-3/4" h, 5 oz, ftd, #2056	12.00
Lemon Bowl, cov, 5-1/2" d	45.00
Lily Pond Bowl, 12" d	65.00
Marmalade, cov, chrome spoon	55.00
Mayonnaise, div	18.00
Mayonnaise, ladle, pedestal foot	42.00
Mayonnaise, liner, ladle	35.00
Molasses Can, 11 oz, 6-3/4" h, 1 handle	350.00

Item	Crystal
Muffin Tray, 10" l, 2 upturned sides	35.00
Mustard, cov	45.00
Napkin Ring	12.00
Nappy, 4-1/2"	8.00
Nappy, 5" d	10.00
Nappy, 5" d, cov	28.00
Nappy, 6" d	15.00
Nappy, 7" d	17.50
Nappy, 8" d	20.00
Old Fashioned Tumbler, 3-3/8" h, 6 oz, flat	10.00
Olive, 6" l, oblong	11.00
Oyster Cocktail, 3-1/2" h, 4-1/2 oz, #2056	17.50
Oyster Cocktail, 3-1/2" h, 4 oz, plain bowl, #5056	15.00
Pickle Jar, pointed cov, 6" h	300.00
Pickle, 8" l, oblong	10.00
Picture Frame	18.00
Pin Tray, oval, 5-1/2" x 4-1/2"	120.00
Pitcher, 1 pt, 5-3/8" h, flat	28.00
Pitcher, 1 qt, flat	32.00
Pitcher, 1/2 gal, 8", ftd	72.00
Pitcher, 1/2 gal, ice lip, 8-1/4", flat bottom	60.00
Pitcher, 1/2 gal, without ice lip	250.00
Pitcher, 2 pt, 7-1/4" h, ftd	60.00
Pitcher, 3 pt, 8", ftd	72.00
Pitcher, 3 pt, ice lip, 6-1/2", ftd, fat	55.00
Plate, 6" d, bread and butter	10.00

American bowl.

Item	Crystal
Plate, 7" d, salad	10.00
Plate, 7-1/2" x 4-3/8", crescent salad	10.00
Plate, 8" d, sauce liner, oval	20.00
Plate, 8-1/2" d, lunch	15.00
Plate, 9-1/2" d, dinner	22.50
Platter, 10-1/2" l, oval	40.00
Platter, 12" l, oval	52.00
Pomade Box, 2" sq	365.00
Preserve Bowl, cov, 5-1/2" d, two handles	85.00
Puff Box, cov, 3-1/8" x 2-3/4"	220.00
Punch Bowl, 14" d, high foot, base, 2 gallon	250.00
Punch Bowl, 14" d, low foot, base	275.00
Punch Bowl, 18" d, low, 3-3/4 gallon	325.00
Punch Cup, flared rim	12.00
Punch Cup, straight edge	10.00
Relish Boat, 12" l, 2 part	16.50
Relish Tray, 6-1/2" x 9", 4 part	42.00
Relish/Celery, 11" l, 3 part	26.00
Ring Holder	215.00
Rose Bowl, 3-1/2" d	18.00
Rose Bowl, 5" d	10.00
Salt and Pepper Shakers, pr, individual, tray, 2" h	24.00
Salt Shaker, 3" h	20.00
Salt Shaker, 3-1/2" h	7.50
Salt Shaker, 3-1/4" h	9.50
Salt, individual	10.00
Sandwich Plate, 9" d, small center	14.00
Sandwich Plate, 10-1/2" d, small center	22.00
Sandwich Plate, 11-1/2" d, small center	22.00
Sandwich Tray, 12" d, center handle	35.00
Sauce Boat and Liner	45.00
Saucer	3.25
Service Tray, 9-1/2", 2 handle	32.00
Sherbet, 4-1/2 oz, 3-1/2" h, handle	75.00
Sherbet, 4-1/2 oz, 4-3/8" h, flared, #2056	8.50
Sherbet, 4-1/2 oz, 4-1/2" h, #2056-1/2	8.50
Sherbet, 5 oz, 3-1/2" h, low, #2056-1/2	6.00
Sherbet, 5-1/2 oz, 4-1/8" h, plain bowl, #5056	7.50
Shrimp Bowl, 12-1/4" d	345.00
Spooner, 3-3/4" h	37.50
Strawholder, 10" h, cov	265.00
Sugar Shaker	50.00
Sugar, cov, 2 handles	22.00
Sugar, cov, 6-1/4" h	65.00
Sugar, handle, 3-1/4" h	15.00
Sugar, tea, 2-1/4" h	9.00
Sundae, 3-1/8" h, 6 oz, low foot, #2056	8.50
Sweet Pea Vase, 4-1/2" h	72.00
Syrup, drip-proof top	55.00
Syrup, 6 oz, non-pour screw top, 5-1/2" h	200.00
Syrup, 6-1/2 oz, Sani-cut server, #2056-1/2	75.00
Syrup, 10 oz, glass cov, 6" liner plate	145.00
Tea Tumbler, 5" h, 12 oz, straight sides, #2056-1/2	17.50

Item	Crystal
Tea Tumbler, 5-1/2" h, plain bowl, #5056	15.00
Tea Tumbler, 5-1/4" h, 12 oz, flat, flared	17.50
Tidbit Tray, metal crook-shaped handle	30.00
Toddler set, baby tumbler, bowl	85.00
Tom and Jerry Mug, 3-1/4" h, 5-1/2 oz	42.00
Tom and Jerry, 12" d, small punch bowl, pedestal foot	240.00
Toothpick Holder	25.00
Torte Plate, 13-1/2" d, oval	40.00
Torte Plate, 14" d	38.00
Torte Plate, 18" d	90.00
Torte Plate, 20" d	95.00
Torte Plate, 24" d	175.00
Tray, 10" w, sq	115.00
Tray, 10" w, sq, 4 part	85.00
Tray, 10-1/2" x 5", oval, handle	48.00
Tray, 10-1/2" x 7-1/2", rect	75.00
Tray, 10-3/4" sq, 4 part	135.00
Tray, 12" d, round	145.00
Tray, 5" x 2-1/2", rect	80.00
Tray, 6", oval, handle	40.00
Tray, 14-1/8", 5 part	125.00
Trophy Cup, 8" d, ftd, 2 handles	115.00
Tumbler, 3-7/8" h, straight sides, #2056-1/2	17.50
Tumbler, 4-1/8" h, 8 oz, flat, flared	9.00
Tumbler, 4-7/8" h, 9 oz, ftd	10.00
Urn, 6" h, sq, pedestal foot	13.00
Urn, 7-1/2" sq, pedestal foot	60.00
Vase, 6" h, straight side	38.00
Vase, 6-1/2" h, flared rim	18.00
Vase, 7" h, flared	75.00
Vase, 8" h, flared	85.00
Vase, 8" h, porch, 5" d	315.00
Vase, 8" h, straight side	45.00
Vase, 9" h, sq pedestal foot	48.00
Vase, 9-1/2" h, flared	115.00
Vase, 10" h, cupped in top	155.00
Vase, 10" h, flared	95.00
Vase, 10" h, porch, 8" d	295.00
Vase, 10" h, straight side	95.00
Vase, 10" h, swung	295.00
Vase, 12" h, straight side	125.00
Vase, 12" h, swung	295.00
Vase, 14" h, swung	310.00
Vase, 20" h, swung	325.00
Vegetable Bowl, 9" l, oval	30.00
Vegetable Bowl, 10" l, oval, 2 part	32.00
Wash Bowl and Pitcher	2,650.00
Water Bottle, 9-1/4" h, 44 oz	565.00
Wedding Bowl, cov, 6-1/2" w, 5-1/4" h, sq, edestal	65.00
Whiskey, 2 oz	12.00
Whiskey Tumbler, 2-1/4" h, 6 oz, #2056	12.00
Wine, 4-3/8" h, 2-1/2 oz, hex foot, #2056	13.00

American Pioneer

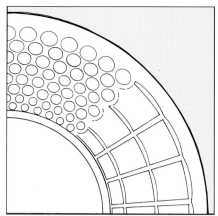

Manufactured by Liberty Works, Egg Harbor, N.J., from 1931 to 1934.

Made in amber, crystal, green and pink.

Item	Amber	Crystal
Bowl, 5" d, handle	44.00	22.00
Bowl, 8-3/4" d, cov	-	85.00
Bowl, 9" d, handle	-	24.00
Bowl, 9-1/4" d, cov	-	95.00
Bowl, 10" d	-	50.00
Candlesticks, pr, 6-1/2" h	-	75.00
Candy Jar, cov, 1 pound	-	100.00
Candy Jar, cov, 1-1/2 pound	-	70.00
Cheese and Cracker Set, indented plate and compote	-	50.00
Coaster, 3-1/2" d	-	18.00
Cocktail, 3 oz, 3-13/16" h	45.00	-
Cocktail, 3-1/2 oz, 3 -15/16" h	45.00	-
Console Bowl, 10-3/4" d	-	50.00
Creamer, 2-3/4" h	-	18.00
Creamer, 3-1/2" h	60.00	30.00
Cup	24.00	10.00
Dresser Set, 2 cologne bottles, powder jar, 7-1/2" tray	-	300.00
Goblet, 8 oz, 6" h, water	-	40.00
Ice Bucket, 6" h	-	50.00
Juice Tumbler, 5 oz	-	32.00
Lamp, 1-3/4", metal pole, 9-1/2"	-	-
Lamp, 5-1/2" round, ball shape	-	-
Lamp, 8-1/2" h	-	90.00
Mayonnaise, 4-1/4"	-	60.00
Pilsner, 5-3/4" h, 11 oz	-	100.00
Pitcher, cov, 5" h	265.00	150.00
Pitcher, cov, 7" h	300.00	175.00
Plate, 6" d	-	12.50
Plate, 6" d, handle	25.00	12.50
Plate, 8" d	28.00	10.00
Plate, 11-1/2" d, handle	40.00	20.00
Rose Bowl, 4-1/4" d, ftd	-	40.00
Saucer, 6" sq	11.00	4.00
Sherbet, 3-1/2" h	-	18.00
Sherbet, 4-3/4" h	-	32.50
Sugar, 2-3/4" h	-	20.00
Sugar, 3-1/2" h	50.00	20.00
Tumbler, 8 oz, 4" h	-	32.00
Tumbler, 12 oz, 5" h	-	40.00
Vase, 7" h, 4 styles	-	85.00
Vase, 9" h, round	-	-
Whiskey, 2 oz., 2-1/4" h	-	48.00

Item	Green	Pink
Bowl, 5" d, handle	24.00	22.00
Bowl, 8-3/4" d, cov	125.00	85.00
Bowl, 9" d, handle	30.00	24.00
Bowl, 9-1/4" d, cov	130.00	95.00
Bowl, 10" d	70.00	50.00
Candlesticks, pr, 6-1/2" h	95.00	75.00
Candy Jar, cov, 1 pound	115.00	110.00
Candy Jar, cov, 1-1/2 pound	125.00	95.00
Cheese and Cracker Set, indented plate and compote	65.00	55.00
Coaster, 3-1/2" d	32.00	30.00
Console Bowl, 10-3/4" d	75.00	60.00
Creamer, 2-3/4" h	20.00	25.00
Creamer, 3-1/2" h	32.00	30.00
Cup	12.00	12.00
Dresser Set, 2 cologne bottles, powder jar, 7-1/2" tray	345.00	365.00
Goblet, 8 oz, 6" h, water	45.00	40.00
Ice Bucket, 6" h	80.00	65.00
Juice Tumbler, 5 oz	37.50	35.00
Lamp, 1-3/4", metal pole, 9-1/2"	65.00	-
Lamp, 5-1/2" round, ball shape	-	70.00
Lamp, 8-1/2" h	115.00	110.00
Mayonnaise, 4-1/4"	90.00	60.00
Pilsner, 5-3/4" h, 11 oz	110.00	100.00
Pitcher, cov, 5" h	225.00	165.00
Pitcher, cov, 7" h	250.00	195.00
Plate, 6" d	17.50	12.50
Plate, 6" d, handle	17.50	12.50
Plate, 8" d	13.00	14.00
Plate, 11-1/2" d, handle	24.00	20.00
Rose Bowl, 4-1/4" d, ftd	50.00	45.00
Saucer, 6" sq	5.00	5.50
Sherbet, 3-1/2" h	22.00	20.00
Sherbet, 4-3/4" h	40.00	30.00
Sugar, 2-3/4" h	27.50	25.00
Sugar, 3-1/2" h	27.50	25.00
Tumbler, 8 oz, 4" h	55.00	35.00
Tumbler, 12 oz, 5" h	55.00	40.00
Vase, 7" h, 4 styles	110.00	90.00
Vase, 9" h, round	235.00	-
Whiskey, 2 oz, 2-1/4" h	48.00	-

American Pioneer green plate, cup & saucer.

American Sweetheart

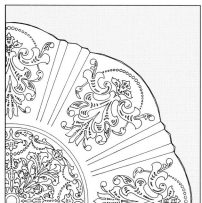

Manufactured by MacBeth-Evans Glass Company, Charleroi, Pa., from 1930 to 1936.

Made in blue, Monax, pink and red. Limited production in Cremax and color-trimmed Monax.

Item	Blue	Cremax	Monax
Berry Bowl, 3-1/4"d, flat	-	-	-
Berry Bowl, 9" d	-	36.00	60.00
Cereal Bowl, 6" d	-	11.00	14.00
Chop Plate, 11" d	-	-	15.00
Console Bowl, 18" d	1,000.00	-	375.00
Cream Soup, 4-1/2" d	-	-	120.00
Creamer, ftd	115.00	-	9.00
Cup	100.00	75.00	8.00
Lamp Shade	-	450.00	400.00
Pitcher, 60 oz, 7-1/2" h	-	-	-
Pitcher, 80 oz, 8" h	-	-	-
Plate, 6" d, bread and butter	-	-	4.50
Plate, 8" d, salad	75.00	25.00	7.50
Plate, 9" d, luncheon	-	-	10.00
Plate, 9-3/4" d, dinner	-	-	14.00
Plate, 10-1/4" d, dinner	-	-	24.00
Platter, 13" l, oval	-	-	75.00
Salt and Pepper Shakers, pr, ftd	-	-	325.00
Salver Plate, 12" d	180.00	-	18.00
Saucer	25.00	-	3.00
Serving Plate, 15-1/2" d	375.00	-	200.00
Sherbet, 3-3/4" h, ftd	-	-	10.50
Sherbet, 4-1/4" h, ftd	-	-	20.00
Soup Bowl, flat, 9-1/2" d	-	-	65.00
Sugar Lid	-	-	300.00
Sugar, open, ftd	115.00	-	7.50
Tidbit, 2 tier	250.00	-	95.00
Tidbit, 3 tier	650.00	-	275.00
Tumbler, 5 oz, 3-1/2" h	-	-	-
Tumbler, 9 oz, 4-1/4" h	-	-	-
Tumbler, 10 oz, 4-3/4" h	-	-	-
Vegetable Bowl, 11"	-	-	90.00

Item	Monax with color-trim	Pink	Red
Berry Bowl, 3-1/4"d, flat	-	50.00	-
Berry Bowl, 9" d	150.00	50.00	-
Cereal Bowl, 6" d	37.50	16.00	-
Console Bowl, 18" d	-	-	850.00
Cream Soup, 4-1/2" d	-	75.00	-
Creamer, ftd	85.00	12.00	110.00
Cup	70.00	15.00	75.00
Pitcher, 60 oz, 7-1/2" h	-	675.00	-
Pitcher, 80 oz, 8" h	-	575.00	-
Plate, 6" d, bread and butter	13.00	5.50	-
Plate, 8" d, salad	-	11.00	75.00
Plate, 9" d, luncheon	35.00	-	-
Plate, 9-3/4" d, dinner	70.00	38.00	-
Plate, 10-1/4" d, dinner	-	38.00	-
Platter, 13" l, oval	-	55.00	-
Salt and Pepper Shakers, pr, ftd	-	425.00	-
Salver Plate, 12" d	-	22.00	125.00
Saucer	25.00	5.75	20.00
Serving Plate, 15-1/2" d	-	-	300.00
Sherbet, 3-3/4" h, ftd	-	22.00	-
Sherbet, 4-1/4" h, ftd	70.00	17.00	-
Soup Bowl, flat, 9-1/2" d	90.00	75.00	-
Sugar, open, ftd	11.00	100.00	
Tidbit, 2 tier	-	200.00	
Tidbit, 3 tier	-	-	575.00
Tumbler, 5 oz, 3-1/2" h	-	100.00	-
Tumbler, 9 oz, 4-1/4" h	-	85.00	-
Vegetable Bowl, 11"	-	65.00	-

*American Sweetheart
Monax large plate.*

Anniversary

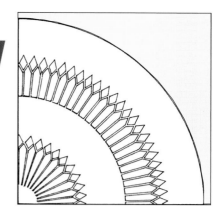

Manufactured by Jeannette Glass Company, Jeannette, Pa., from 1947 to 1949, late 1960s to mid 1970s. Made in crystal, iridescent and pink.

Item	Crystal	Iridescent	Pink
Berry Bowl, 4-7/8" d	3.50	4.50	11.00
Butter Dish, cov.	30.00	-	57.00
Cake Plate, 12-3/8" w, square	7.00	-	16.50
Cake Plate, 12-1/2" d, round	7.50	-	17.50
Cake Plate, metal cover	15.00	-	-
Candlesticks, pr, 4-7/8" h	16.00	24.00	-
Candy Jar, cov	24.00	-	45.00
Comport, open, 3 legs	5.00	5.00	16.00
Comport, ruffled, 3 legs	6.50	-	-
Creamer, ftd	5.00	6.50	14.00
Cup	5.00	4.00	9.00
Fruit Bowl, 9" d	10.00	14.00	24.00
Pickle Dish 9" d	5.50	7.50	12.00
Plate, 6-1/4" d, sherbet	2.00	3.50	4.00
Plate, 9" d, dinner	5.00	8.00	17.00
Relish Dish, 8" d	5.60	7.50	14.00
Sandwich Server, 12-1/2" d	6.50	10.00	20.00
Saucer	1.00	1.50	6.00
Sherbet, ftd	4.00	-	10.00
Soup Bowl, 7-3/8" d	7.00	7.50	17.00
Sugar, cov	10.00	8.00	18.50
Tidbit, metal handle	14.00	-	-
Vase, 6-1/2" h	14.00	-	28.00
Wall Pocket	15.00	-	30.00
Wine, 2-1/2 oz	8.00	-	18.00

Anniversary iridescent plate.

Aunt Polly

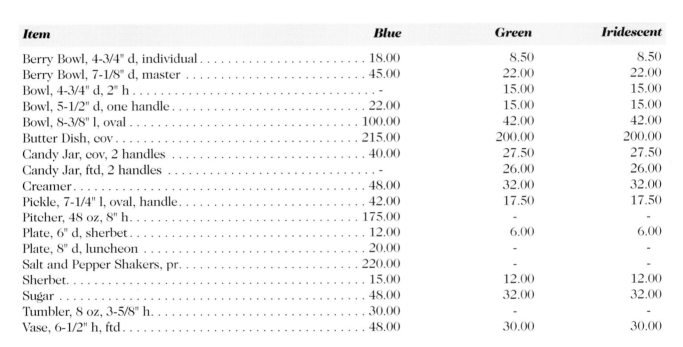

Manufactured by U.S. Glass Company, Pittsburgh, in the late 1920s.

Made in blue, green and iridescent.

Item	Blue	Green	Iridescent
Berry Bowl, 4-3/4" d, individual	18.00	8.50	8.50
Berry Bowl, 7-1/8" d, master	45.00	22.00	22.00
Bowl, 4-3/4" d, 2" h	-	15.00	15.00
Bowl, 5-1/2" d, one handle	22.00	15.00	15.00
Bowl, 8-3/8" l, oval	100.00	42.00	42.00
Butter Dish, cov	215.00	200.00	200.00
Candy Jar, cov, 2 handles	40.00	27.50	27.50
Candy Jar, ftd, 2 handles	-	26.00	26.00
Creamer	48.00	32.00	32.00
Pickle, 7-1/4" l, oval, handle	42.00	17.50	17.50
Pitcher, 48 oz, 8" h	175.00	-	-
Plate, 6" d, sherbet	12.00	6.00	6.00
Plate, 8" d, luncheon	20.00	-	-
Salt and Pepper Shakers, pr.	220.00	-	-
Sherbet	15.00	12.00	12.00
Sugar	48.00	32.00	32.00
Tumbler, 8 oz, 3-5/8" h	30.00	-	-
Vase, 6-1/2" h, ftd	48.00	30.00	30.00

Aunt Polly blue sherbet.

Aurora

Manufactured by Hazel Atlas Glass Company, Clarksburg, W.V., and Zanesville, Ohio, in the late 1930s.

Made in cobalt (Ritz) blue, crystal, green and pink.

Item	Cobalt Blue	Crystal	Green	Pink
Bowl, 4-1/2" d	50.00	-	-	50.00
Breakfast Set, 24 pcs, service for 4	485.00	-	-	-
Cereal Bowl, 5-3/8" d	17.50	10.00	7.50	14.00
Cup	18.00	5.00	9.00	13.50
Milk Pitcher	24.00	-	-	22.00
Plate, 6-1/2" d	12.00	-	-	12.00
Saucer	6.00	2.00	3.00	6.00
Tumbler, 10 oz, 4-3/4" h	22.00	-	-	22.00

Aurora blue cereal bowl, berry bowl and milk pitcher.

Avocado

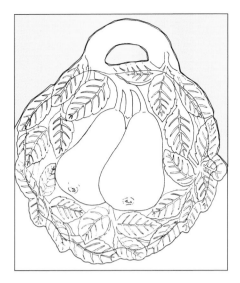

Manufactured by Indiana Glass Company, Dunkirk, Ind., from 1923 to 1933.

Made in crystal, green, pink and white.

Reproductions: † Creamer, 8" pickle, pitcher, plates, sherbet, sugar and tumblers. Reproductions can be found in amethyst, blue, dark green, frosted green, frosted pink, pink, red and yellow, representing several colors not made originally.

Item	Crystal	Green	Pink	White
Bowl, 5-1/4" d, 2 handles	12.00	37.00	27.50	-
Bowl, 8" d, 2 handles, oval	17.50	30.00	25.00	-
Bowl, 8-1/2" d	20.00	60.00	50.00	-
Bowl, 9-1/2" d, 3-1/4" deep	35.00	155.00	125.00	-
Cake Plate, 10-1/4" d, 2 handles	17.50	60.00	40.00	-
Creamer, ftd †	17.50	40.00	35.00	-
Cup, ftd	-	36.00	30.00	-
Pickle Bowl, 8" d, 2 handles, oval †	17.50	30.00	25.00	-
Pitcher, 64 oz †	365.00	1,100.00	800.00	425.00
Plate, 6-3/8" d, sherbet †	6.00	22.00	15.00	-
Plate, 8-1/4" d, luncheon †	7.50	25.00	20.00	-
Preserve Bowl, 7" l, handle	10.00	32.00	28.00	-
Relish, 6" d, ftd	10.00	32.00	28.00	-
Salad Bowl, 7-1/2" d	9.00	55.00	37.50	-
Saucer	6.00	24.00	15.00	-
Sherbet, ftd †	-	55.00	50.00	-
Sugar, ftd †	17.50	40.00	35.00	-
Tumbler †	25.00	250.00	150.00	35.00

Avocado green sugar and creamer.

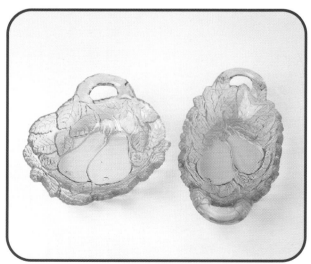

Avocado green bowl and relish dish.

Beaded Block

Manufactured by Imperial Glass Company, Bellaire, Ohio, from 1927 to the 1930s.

Made in amber, crystal, green, ice blue, iridescent, milk white (1950s), opalescent, pink, red and vaseline. Some pieces are still being made in pink and are embossed with the "IG" trademark. The only form known in red is the 4-1/2" lily bowl, valued at $135. The secondary market for milk white is still being established. The pitcher is currently valued at $185, and the 4-1/2" d bowl with a handle is $18.

Item	Amber	Crystal	Green	Ice Blue
Bowl, 4-1/2" d, lily 8.00		6.00	10.00	18.00
Bowl, 4-1/2" d, 2 handles 10.00		8.00	10.00	18.00
Bowl, 5-1/2" sq 8.50		6.00	8.50	9.00
Bowl, 5 -/2 d, 1 handle 8.50		6.00	8.50	9.00
Bowl, 6" deep 12.00		10.00	12.00	12.50
Bowl, 6-1/4" d 9.00		7.00	9.00	9.50
Bowl, 6-1/2" d, 2 handles 9.00		7.00	9.00	9.50
Bowl, 6-3/4" d 12.00		10.00	12.00	11.00
Bowl, 7-1/4" d, flared 12.00		10.00	12.00	11.00
Bowl, 7-1/2" d, fluted 22.00		20.00	22.00	21.00
Bowl, 7-1/2" plain 20.00		18.00	20.00	18.50
Candy Dish, cov, pear shaped . . . . -		-	275.00	-
Celery, 8-1/4" d 15.00		12.00	15.00	16.00
Creamer, ftd 20.00		16.00	20.00	18.50
Jelly, 4-1/2" h, stemmed 10.00		8.00	10.00	10.00
Jelly, 4-1/2" h, stemmed, flared lid 12.00		10.00	12.00	11.00
Pitcher, 1 pt, 5-1/4" h 85.00		95.00	100.00	95.00
Plate, 7-3/4" sq 7.50		5.00	7.50	7.50
Plate, 8-3/4" 20.00		16.00	20.00	20.00
Sugar, ftd 20.00		16.00	20.00	20.00
Syrup . . . . -		-	-	-
Vase, 6" h, ftd 15.00		12.00	18.00	20.00

Beaded Block cobalt blue bud vase and clear compote.

Beaded Block vaseline square plate and iridescent round plate.

Item	Iridescent	Opal	Pink	Vaseline
Bowl, 4-1/2" d, lily	15.00	18.00	15.00	18.00
Bowl, 4-1/2" d, 2 handles	16.00	18.00	10.00	20.00
Bowl, 5-1/2" sq	7.50	9.00	8.50	9.00
Bowl, 5 -/2 d, 1 handle	7.50	9.00	18.00	9.00
Bowl, 6" deep	10.00	12.50	15.00	12.00
Bowl, 6-1/4" d	9.00	9.50	8.00	9.00
Bowl, 6-1/2" d, 2 handles	9.00	9.50	8.00	9.00
Bowl, 6-3/4" d	12.00	12.00	11.00	10.00
Bowl, 7-1/4" d, flared	12.00	12.00	11.00	10.00
Bowl, 7-1/2" d, fluted	18.00	22.00	21.00	22.00
Bowl, 7-1/2" plain	18.50	20.00	18.00	20.00
Candy Dish, cov, pear shaped	-	-	-	600.00
Celery, 8-1/4" d	15.00	15.00	14.00	15.00
Creamer, ftd	18.50	20.00	18.00	20.00
Jelly, 4-1/2" h, stemmed	9.00	8.50	9.00	10.00
Jelly, 4-1/2" h, stemmed, flared lid	12.00	12.00	11.00	10.00
Pitcher, 1 pt, 5-1/4" h	90.00	85.00	175.00	85.00
Plate, 7-3/4" sq	7.00	7.00	6.00	7.50
Plate, 8-3/4"	17.50	17.50	16.00	17.50
Sugar, ftd	17.50	17.50	16.00	17.50
Syrup	-	-	-	150.00
Vase, 6" h, ftd	15.00	15.00	14.00	20.00

Block Optic

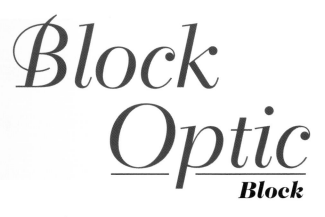 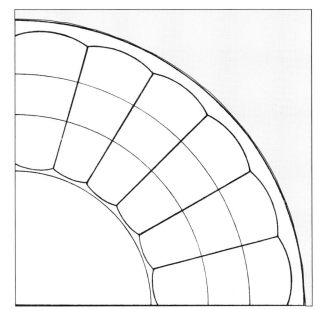

Block

Manufactured by Hocking Glass Company, Lancaster, Ohio, from 1929 to 1933.

Made in amber, crystal, green, pink and yellow. Production in amber was very limited. A 11-3/4" d console bowl is valued at $50, while a pair of matching 1-3/4" h candlesticks is valued at $110.

* There are five styles of creamers and four styles of cups, each have a relative value.

Item	Crystal	Green	Pink	Yellow
Berry Bowl, 8-1/2" d	20.00	35.00	40.00	-
Bowl, 4-1/4" d, 1-3/8" h	4.00	8.00	10.00	-
Bowl, 4-1/2" d, 1-1/2" h	-	28.00	-	-
Butter Dish, cov	-	50.00	-	-
Cake Plate, 10" d, ftd	18.00	-	-	-
Candlesticks, pr, 1-3/4" h	-	100.00	80.00	-
Candy Jar, cov, 2-1/4" h	30.00	60.00	55.00	65.00
Candy Jar, cov, 6-1/4" h	40.00	80.00	60.00	-
Cereal Bowl, 5-1/2" d	-	16.00	27.50	-
Champagne, 4-3/4" h	10.00	27.50	16.50	15.00
Cocktail, 4" h	-	35.00	35.00	-
Comport, 4" wide	-	36.00	70.00	-
Console Bowl, 11-3/4" d, rolled edge	-	70.00	95.00	-
Creamer*	10.00	12.50	18.00	15.00
Cup*	6.00	7.00	6.50	6.50
Goblet, 9 oz, 5-3/4" h	10.00	24.00	30.00	-
Goblet, 9 oz, 7-1/2" h, thin	15.00	-	-	22.00
Ice Bucket	-	40.00	48.00	-
Ice Tub, open	-	48.00	-	-
Mug	-	35.00	-	-
Pitcher, 54 oz, 7-5/8" h, bulbous	-	70.00	70.00	-
Pitcher, 54 oz, 8-1/2" h	-	42.00	40.00	-
Pitcher, 80 oz, 8" h	-	90.00	80.00	-
Plate, 6" d, sherbet	1.50	3.50	3.25	3.50
Plate, 8" d, luncheon	3.50	5.50	7.00	8.50
Plate, 9" d, dinner	11.00	27.50	35.00	42.00
Plate, 9" d, dinner, snowflake center	-	16.50	-	-
Plate, 9" d, grill	15.00	27.50	30.00	42.00
Salad Bowl, 7-1/4" d	-	155.00	-	-

Block Optic green covered candy dish, sherbet, sugar and creamer.

Block Optic green large and small berry bowl and salad bowl.

Item	Crystal	Green	Pink	Yellow
Salt and Pepper Shakers, pr, ftd . . . . -		37.50	80.00	80.00
Salt and Pepper Shakers, pr, squatty . . . . -		90.00	-	-
Sandwich Plate, 10-1/4" d. . . . . -		27.50	30.00	-
Sandwich Server, center handle . . . . -		65.00	50.00	-
Saucer, 5-3/4" d . . . . -		12.00	10.00	-
Saucer, 6-1/8" d	2.00	8.00	10.00	3.50
Sherbet, cone. . . . . -		6.00	5.50	-
Sherbet, 5-1/2 oz, 3-1/4" h . . . . -		6.50	9.50	7.50
Sherbet, 6 oz, 4-3/4" h.	7.00	15.00	15.00	16.00
Sugar, cone . . . . -		12.00	9.50	12.00
Sugar, flat. . . . . -		10.00	10.00	-
Sugar, round, ftd	10.00	12.00	18.00	-
Tumbler, 3 oz, 2-5/8" h. . . . . -		27.50	25.00	-
Tumbler, 3 oz, 3-1/4" h, ftd. . . . . -		27.50	25.00	-
Tumbler, 5 oz, 3-1/2" h, flat . . . . -		20.00	17.50	-
Tumbler, 5-3/8" h, ftd . . . . -		-	19.50	18.00
Tumbler, 9" h, ftd . . . . -		-	17.50	22.00
Tumbler, 9-1/2 oz, 3-13/16" h, flat . . . . -		17.50	14.00	-
Tumbler, 10 oz, 6" h, ftd	10.00	-	-	-
Tumbler, 10 or 11 oz, 5" h, flat. . . . . -		24.00	22.00	-
Tumbler, 12 oz, 4-7/8" h, flat . . . . -		27.50	24.00	-
Tumbler, 15 oz, 5-1/4" h, flat . . . . -		27.50	24.00	-
Tumble-Up, 3" h tumbler and bottle . . . . -		90.00	75.00	-
Vase, 5-3/4" h, blown . . . . -		285.00	-	-
Whiskey, 1 oz, 1-5/8" h	20.00	40.00	45.00	-
Whiskey, 2 oz, 2-1/4" h	15.00	35.00	30.00	-
Wine, 3-1/2" h . . . . -		415.00	415.00	-
Wine, 4-1/2" h	15.00	35.00	32.00	-

Bowknot

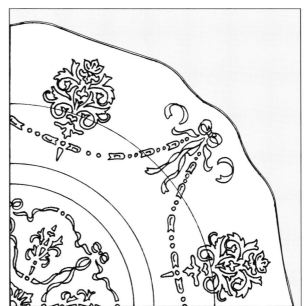

Unknown maker, late 1920s.
Made in green.

Item	Green
Berry Bowl, 4-1/2" d	16.00
Cereal Bowl, 5-1/2" d	20.00
Cup	14.00
Plate, 7" d, salad	12.50
Sherbet, low, ftd	24.00
Tumbler, 10 oz, 5" h, flat	15.00
Tumbler, 10 oz, 5" h, ftd	15.00

Bowknot green tumbler and footed berry bowl.

Bubble

Bullseye Provincial

Manufactured originally by Hocking Glass Company, and followed by Anchor Hocking Glass Corporation, Lancaster, Ohio, from 1937 to 1965.

Made in crystal (1937); forest green (1937); pink, Royal Ruby (1963); and sapphire blue (1937). Production in pink was limited. The master berry bowl is valued at $750.

Item	Crystal	Forest Green	Royal Ruby	Sapphire Blue
Berry Bowl, 4" d	4.25	-	6.00	17.50
Berry Bowl, 8-3/4" d	12.00	15.00	18.00	17.50
Bowl, 9" d, fanged	8.00	-	-	335.00
Candlesticks, pr	24.00	40.00	-	-
Cereal Bowl, 5-1/4" d	7.00	16.50	-	15.00
Cocktail, 3-1/2 oz	4.50	10.00	10.00	-
Cocktail, 4-1/2 oz	4.50	12.50	12.50	-
Creamer	4.00	13.50	17.00	40.00
Cup	4.00	9.00	12.50	14.00
Fruit Bowl, 4-1/2" d	5.00	11.00	9.00	16.00
Goblet, 9 oz, stem, 5-1/2" h	7.50	15.00	15.00	-
Goblet, 9-1/2 oz, stem	7.50	15.00	15.00	-
Iced Tea Goblet, 14 oz	8.00	17.50	-	-
Iced Tea Tumbler, 12 oz, 4-1/2" h	12.50	-	20.00	-
Juice Goblet, 4 oz	3.00	8.00	-	-
Juice Goblet, 5-1/2 oz	5.00	12.50	12.50	-
Juice Tumbler, 6 oz, ftd	4.00	11.50	10.00	-
Lamp, 3 styles	42.00	-	-	-

Item	Crystal	Forest Green	Royal Ruby	Sapphire Blue
Lemonade Tumbler, 16 oz, 5-7/8" h	16.00	-	16.00	-
Old Fashioned Tumbler, 8 oz, 3-1/4" h	6.50	16.00	16.00	-
Pitcher, 64 oz, ice lip	60.00	-	60.00	-
Plate, 6-3/4" d, bread and butter.	3.50	4.50	-	3.75
Plate, 9-3/8" d, dinner	7.50	25.00	22.00	8.00
Plate, 9-3/8" d, grill	-	20.00	-	21.50
Platter, 12" l, oval	10.00	-	-	18.00
Sandwich Plate, 9-1/2" d	7.50	25.00	22.00	8.00
Saucer	1.50	5.00	5.00	1.50
Sherbet, 6 oz	3.50	6.50	12.00	-
Soup Bowl, flat, 7-3/4" d	8.50	-	-	16.00
Sugar	6.00	12.00	-	20.00
Tidbit, 2 tier	-	-	35.00	-
Tumbler, 9 oz, water	5.00	-	10.00	-

Bubble blue grill plate, platter and bowls.

Cameo

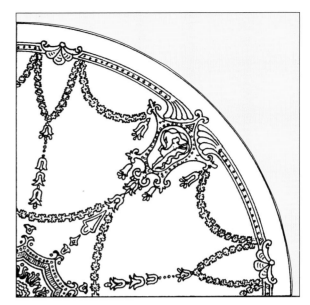

Ballerina, Dancing Girl

Manufactured by Hocking Glass Company, Lancaster, Ohio, from 1930 to 1934.

Made in crystal, green, pink and yellow. Only the crystal has a platinum rim.

Reproductions: † Salt shakers made in blue, green and pink. Recently, children's dishes have been made in green and pink, but were never part of the original pattern.

Item	Crystal	Green	Pink	Yellow
Berry Bowl, 4-1/4" d	13.00	-	-	-
Berry Bowl, 8-1/4" d	-	-	150.00	-
Butter Dish, cov	-	220.00	-	1,400.00
Cake Plate, 10" d, 3 legs	-	22.00	-	-
Cake Plate, 10-1/2" d, flat	-	95.00	150.00	-
Candlesticks, pr, 4" h	-	85.00	-	-
Candy Jar, cov, 4" h	-	75.00	500.00	80.00
Candy Jar, cov, 6-1/2" h	-	150.00	-	-
Cereal Bowl, 5-1/2" d	7.50	30.00	150.00	30.00
Cocktail Shaker	500.00	-	-	-
Comport, 5" w	-	32.00	200.00	-
Console Bowl, 3 legs, 11" d	-	75.00	45.00	95.00
Cookie Jar, cov	-	60.00	-	-
Cream Soup, 4-3/4" d	-	175.00	-	-
Creamer, 3-1/4" h	-	25.00	110.00	23.00
Creamer, 4-1/4" h	-	30.00	85.00	-
Cup	10.00	15.00	-	8.00
Decanter, 10" h	200.00	175.00	-	-
Domino Tray, 7" l	125.00	135.00	250.00	-
Goblet, 6" h, water	-	52.00	165.00	-
Ice Bowl, 3" h, 5-1/2" d	265.00	150.00	600.00	-
Jam Jar, cov, 2" h	175.00	165.00	-	-
Juice Pitcher, 6" h, 36 oz	-	60.00	-	-
Juice Tumbler, 3 oz, ftd	-	55.00	90.00	-
Juice Tumbler, 5 oz, 3-3/4" h	-	25.00	-	-
Pitcher, 8-1/2" h, 56 oz	550.00	50.00	1,200.00	-
Plate, 6" d, sherbet	4.00	6.00	85.00	2.50
Plate, 7" d, salad	12.00	-	-	-
Plate, 8" d, luncheon	14.00	12.00	36.00	10.00
Plate, 8-1/2", luncheon, sq	-	40.00	-	225.00
Plate, 9-1/2" d, dinner	-	18.00	75.00	9.00
Plate, 10-1/2" d, dinner, rimmed	-	90.00	145.00	-
Plate, 10-1/2" d, grill	-	10.00	55.00	6.00
Platter, 12" l	-	20.00	-	40.00
Relish, 7-1/2" l, ftd, 3 part	175.00	30.00	775.00	-

Cameo clear tumbler.

Cameo green vegetable bowl.

Item	Crystal	Green	Pink	Yellow
Salad Bowl, 7-1/4" d . . . . -		60.00	-	-
Salt and Pepper Shakers, pr, ftd † . . . . -		70.00	-	-
Sandwich Plate, 10" d . . . . -		15.00	45.00	37.00
Sandwich Server, center handle . . . . -		3,000.00	-	-
Saucer 4.00		3.00	90.00	4.50
Sherbet, 3-1/8" h, blown . . . . -		15.00	75.00	-
Sherbet, 3-1/8" h, molded . . . . -		16.00	75.00	40.00
Sherbet, 4-7/8" h . . . . -		30.00	95.00	-
Soup Bowl, rimmed, 9" d . . . . -		62.00	100.00	-
Sugar, 3-1/4" h . . . . -		21.00	-	12.00
Sugar, 4-1/4" h . . . . -		29.00	115.00	-
Syrup Pitcher, 20 oz, 5-3/4" h . . . . -		225.00	-	1,850.00
Tumbler, 9 oz, 4" h 16.00		30.00	80.00	-
Tumbler, 9 oz, 5" h, ftd . . . . -		30.00	115.00	14.00
Tumbler, 10 oz, 4-3/4" h, flat . . . . -		30.00	95.00	-
Tumbler, 11" oz, 5" h, flat . . . . -		30.00	90.00	48.00
Tumbler, 11 oz, 5-3/4" h, ftd . . . . -		60.00	125.00	-
Tumbler, 15 oz, 5-1/4" h . . . . -		65.00	125.00	-
Tumbler, 15 oz, 6-3/8" h, ftd . . . . -		425.00	-	-
Vase, 5-3/4" h . . . . -		215.00	-	-
Vase, 8" h . . . . -		40.00	-	-
Vegetable, oval, 10" l . . . . -		30.00	-	45.00
Wine, 3-1/2" h . . . . -		750.00	800.00	-
Wine, 4" h . . . . -		65.00	250.00	-

Cherryberry

Manufactured by U.S. Glass Company, Pittsburgh, early 1930s.

Made in crystal, green, iridescent and pink.

Cherryberry clear bowl.

Item	Crystal	Green	Iridescent	Pink
Berry Bowl, 4" d.	6.50	8.75	6.50	8.75
Berry Bowl, 7-1/2" d, deep	17.50	20.00	17.50	20.00
Bowl, 6-1/4" d, 2" deep	40.00	55.00	40.00	55.00
Butter Dish, cov.	150.00	170.00	150.00	170.00
Comport, 5-3/4"	17.50	25.00	17.50	25.00
Creamer, large, 4-5/8"	40.00	45.00	40.00	45.00
Creamer, small.	15.00	20.00	15.00	20.00
Olive Dish, 5" l, one handle	10.00	15.00	10.00	15.00
Pickle Dish, 8-1/4" l, oval	10.00	15.00	10.00	15.00
Pitcher, 7-3/4" h	165.00	175.00	165.00	175.00
Plate, 6" d, sherbet	6.50	11.00	6.50	11.00
Plate, 7-1/2" d, salad.	8.50	15.00	9.00	15.00
Salad Bowl, 6-1/2" d, deep	17.50	22.00	17.50	22.00
Sherbet	9.00	10.00	9.00	12.00
Sugar, large, cov.	45.00	75.00	45.00	75.00
Sugar, small, open	15.00	20.00	15.00	20.00
Tumbler, 9 oz, 3-5/8" h.	20.00	35.00	20.00	35.00

Cherry Blossom

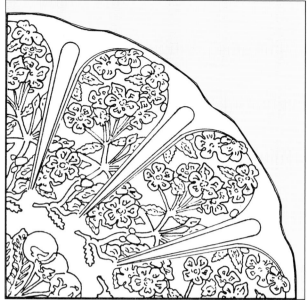

Manufactured by Jeannette Glass Company, Jeannette, Pa., from 1930 to 1939.

Made in Crystal, Delphite, green, jadite, pink and red (production was very limited in crystal, jadite and red).

Reproductions: † Reproductions include: small berry bowl, 8-1/2" d bowl, cov butter dish, cake plate, cereal bowl, cup, pitcher, 6" and 9" plates, divided 13" platter, salt shaker, sandwich tray, saucer, ftd tumbler. Reproductions have been made in cobalt blue, Delphite, green, pink and red. A children's butter dish has also been made, which was never included in the original production.

Item	Delphite	Green	Pink
Berry Bowl, 4-3/4" d †	15.00	19.00	16.00
Berry Bowl, 8-1/2" d †	50.00	48.00	42.00
Bowl, 9" d, 2 handles	25.00	65.00	46.00
Butter Dish, cov †	-	85.00	75.00
Cake Plate, 10-1/4" d, 3 legs †	-	28.00	25.00
Cereal Bowl, 5-3/4" d †	-	35.00	32.00
Coaster	-	15.00	15.00
Creamer	19.00	26.00	24.00
Cup †	20.00	25.00	20.00
Fruit Bowl, 10-1/2" d	32.00	89.00	89.00
Mug, 7 oz	-	185.00	250.00
Pitcher, 36 oz, 6-3/4" h, 36 oz †	89.00	55.00	70.00
Pitcher, 36 oz, 8", PAT, ftd	-	55.00	55.00
Pitcher, 42 oz, 8", PAT, flat	-	52.00	52.00
Plate, 6" d, sherbet †	6.00	6.00	10.00
Plate, 7" d, salad	-	21.00	17.00
Plate, 9" d, dinner †	18.00	26.00	22.00
Plate, 9" d, grill	-	22.00	22.00
Plate, 10" d, grill	-	26.00	-
Platter, 11" l, oval	40.00	48.00	35.00
Platter, 13" d	-	72.00	43.00
Platter, 13" divided †	-	72.00	43.00
Salt and Pepper Shakers, pr, scalloped base †	-	975.00	1,200.00
Sandwich Tray, 10-1/2" d †	20.00	24.00	24.00
Saucer †	5.00	7.50	5.00
Sherbet	15.00	18.00	17.00
Soup, flat, 7-3/4" d	-	55.00	50.00

Item	Delphite	Green	Pink
Sugar	18.00	21.00	19.00
Tumbler, 1 oz, 3-1/2"	-	18.00	15.00
Tumbler, 3-3/4" h, AOP, ftd †	-	20.00	20.00
Tumbler, 5" h	20.00	70.00	72.00
Tumbler, 8 oz, 4-1/2" h, scalloped ftd base, AOP	-	30.00	30.00
Tumbler, 9 oz, 4-1/4" h	-	22.00	20.00
Tumbler, 9 oz, 4-1/2" h †	16.00	27.00	30.00
Vegetable Bowl, 9" l, oval	45.00	38.00	35.00

Children's

Item	Delphite	Pink
Creamer	47.50	45.00
Cup †	35.00	35.00
Plate, 6" d	13.00	12.00
Saucer	7.50	6.50
Sugar	47.50	45.00
14-Piece Set	300.00	400.00

Cherry Blossom delphite small bowls.

Chinex Classic

Manufactured by MacBeth-Evans Division of Corning Glass Works, from the late 1930s to early 1940s.

Made in Chinex (ivory) and Chinex with Classic Bouquet or Classic Castle decal.

Item	Chinex	Chinex, Classic Bouquet decal	Chinex, Classic Castle decal
Bowl, 11" d	18.00	36.00	48.00
Butter Dish, cov.	55.00	80.00	135.00
Cake Plate, 11-1/2" d	8.00	15.00	25.00
Cereal Bowl, 5-3/4" d	6.00	8.50	15.00
Creamer	7.50	12.00	20.00
Cup	5.00	7.50	17.50
Plate, 6-1/4" d, sherbet	2.50	3.50	8.00
Plate, 9-3/4" d, dinner	4.00	8.00	16.00
Sandwich Plate, 11-1/2" d	8.00	15.00	25.00
Saucer	1.50	4.00	7.00
Sherbet, low, ftd.	7.50	12.00	30.00
Soup Bowl, 7-3/4" d	14.00	25.00	40.00
Sugar, open	7.50	12.50	20.00
Vegetable Bowl, 7" d	15.00	25.00	35.00
Vegetable Bowl, 9" d	15.00	25.00	35.00

Chinex Classic plate with castle decal.

Christmas Candy

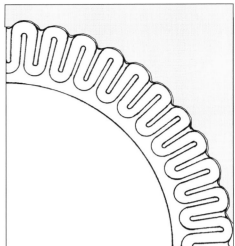

No. 624

Manufactured by Indiana Glass Company,
Dunkirk, Ind., 1950s.
Made in crystal and Terrace Green (teal).

Item	Crystal	Terrace Green
Bowl, 5-3/4" d	5.00	-
Creamer	12.00	27.50
Cup	8.00	35.00
Mayonnaise, ladle, liner	24.00	-
Plate, 6" d, bread and butter	4.00	16.00
Plate, 8-1/4" d, luncheon	8.00	28.00
Plate, 9-5/8"d, dinner	12.00	36.00
Sandwich Plate, 11-1/4" d	24.00	65.00
Saucer	5.00	15.00
Soup Bowl, 7-3/8" d	11.00	75.00
Sugar	12.00	35.00
Tidbit, 2 tier	20.00	-
Vegetable Bowl, 9-1/2" d	-	235.00

Christmas Candy crystal sugar and creamer.

Circle

Manufactured by Hocking Glass Company, Lancaster, Ohio, in the 1930s.

Made in crystal, green and pink. Crystal is listed in the original catalogs, but few pieces have surfaced to date. A 3-1/8" d sherbet is known and valued at $4.

Item	Green	Pink
Bowl, 4-1/2" d	14.00	14.00
Bowl, 5-1/2" d, flared	15.00	15.00
Bowl, 8" d	16.00	16.00
Bowl, 9-3/8" d	18.50	18.50
Creamer, ftd	9.00	16.00
Cup	5.00	6.00
Goblet, 8 oz, 5-3/4" h	16.50	15.00
Iced Tea Tumbler, 10 oz	17.50	17.50
Juice Tumbler, 4 oz	9.50	9.00
Pitcher, 60 oz	35.00	35.00
Pitcher, 80 oz	30.00	32.00
Plate, 6" d, sherbet	2.50	2.50
Plate, 8-1/4"d, luncheon	11.00	11.00
Plate, 9-1/2" d, dinner	12.00	12.00
Sandwich Plate, 10" d	15.00	17.50
Saucer, 6" d	2.50	2.50
Sherbet, 3-1/8"	4.00	5.00
Sherbet, 4-3/4"	11.00	12.00
Sugar, ftd	8.00	16.00
Tumbler, 8 oz	10.00	10.00
Tumbler, 15 oz, flat	17.50	17.50
Wine, 4-1/2" h	15.00	15.00

Circle green cup.

Cloverleaf

Manufactured by Hazel Atlas Glass Company, Clarksburg, W.V., and Zanesville, Ohio, from 1930 to 1936.

Made in black, crystal, green, pink and yellow. Collector interest in crystal is minimal; prices would be about 50% of those listed for green.

Item	Black	Green	Pink	Yellow
Ashtray, match holder in center, 4" d	65.00	-	-	-
Ashtray, match holder in center, 5-3/4" d	75.00	20.00	-	-
Bowl, 8" d	-	50.00	-	-
Candy Dish, cov	-	45.00	-	95.00
Cereal Bowl, 5" d	-	25.00	-	34.00
Creamer, 3-5/8" h, ftd	18.00	9.00	-	18.00
Cup	16.00	8.00	7.00	10.00
Dessert Bowl, 4" d	-	18.00	15.00	25.00
Plate, 6" d, sherbet	38.00	4.50	-	7.00
Plate, 8" d, luncheon	15.00	6.00	7.00	14.00
Plate, 10-1/4" d, grill	-	20.00	-	34.00
Salad Bowl, 7" d	-	40.00	-	48.00
Salt and Pepper Shakers, pr	75.00	14.00	-	100.00
Saucer	7.00	4.00	4.00	5.00
Sherbet, 3" h, ftd	18.00	12.00	6.50	11.00
Sugar, 3-5/8" h, ftd	15.00	12.00	-	20.00
Tumbler, 9 oz, 4" h, flat	-	50.00	-	-
Tumbler, 10 oz, 3-3/4" h, flat	-	35.00	22.50	-
Tumbler, 10 oz, 5-3/4" h, ftd	-	22.00	-	32.00

Cloverleaf green saucer and pink plate and cup.

Colonial

Knife and Fork

Manufactured by Hocking Glass Company,
Lancaster, Ohio, from 1934 to 1938.
Made in crystal, green and pink.

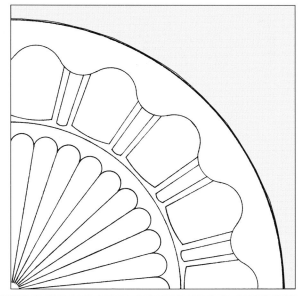

Item	Crystal	Green	Pink
Berry Bowl, 3-3/4" d	-	-	45.00
Berry Bowl, 4-1/2"	10.00	17.00	15.00
Berry Bowl, 9" d	24.00	55.00	35.00
Butter Dish, cov	37.00	60.00	625.00
Cereal Bowl, 5-1/2" d	32.00	85.00	60.00
Claret, 4 oz, 5-1/4" h	20.00	25.00	-
Cocktail, 3 oz, 4" h	15.00	25.00	-
Cordial, 1 oz, 3-3/4" h	20.00	30.00	-
Cream Soup Bowl, 4-1/2" d	70.00	70.00	70.00
Creamer, 8 oz, 5" h	17.00	25.00	60.00
Cup	8.00	12.00	12.00
Goblet, 8-1/2 oz, 5-3/4" h	24.00	35.00	40.00
Ice Tea Tumbler, 12 oz	28.00	55.00	45.00
Juice Tumbler, 5 oz, 3" h	17.50	27.50	20.00
Lemonade Tumbler, 15 oz	47.50	75.00	65.00
Milk Pitcher, 8 oz, 5" h	17.00	25.00	60.00
Mug, 12 oz, 5-1/2" h	-	825.00	500.00
Pitcher, 54 oz, 7" h, ice lip	40.00	45.00	48.00
Pitcher, 54 oz, 7" h, no lip	40.00	45.00	48.00
Pitcher, 68 oz, 7-3/4" h, ice lip	35.00	72.00	65.00
Pitcher, 68 oz, 7-3/4" h, no lip	35.00	72.00	65.00
Plate, 6" d, sherbet	4.50	7.50	6.50
Plate, 8-1/2" d, luncheon	8.00	9.00	11.00
Plate, 10" d, dinner	32.00	45.00	46.00
Plate, 10"d, grill	17.50	27.00	27.00
Plate, 12" d, oval	17.50	25.00	30.00
Platter, 12" l, oval	17.50	25.00	30.00
Salt and Pepper Shakers, pr	65.00	140.00	145.00
Saucer	4.50	7.50	6.50
Sherbet, 3" h	-	-	24.00
Sherbet, 3-3/8" h	10.00	15.00	10.00
Soup Bowl, 7" d	30.00	95.00	85.00
Spoon Holder or Celery Vase	80.00	125.00	135.00
Sugar, cov	35.00	38.00	42.00
Sugar, 5", open	10.00	12.00	15.00

Item	Crystal	Green	Pink
Tumbler, 3 oz, 3-1/4" h, ftd	11.00	15.00	14.00
Tumbler, 5 oz, 4" h, ftd	15.00	35.00	30.00
Tumbler, 9 oz, 4" h	15.00	20.00	25.00
Tumbler, 10 oz, 5-1/4" h, ftd	30.00	46.50	50.00
Tumbler, 11 oz, 5-1/8" h	25.00	37.00	40.00
Vegetable Bowl, 10" l, oval	18.00	25.00	30.00
Whiskey, 2-1/2" h, 1-1/2 oz	9.00	20.00	15.00
Wine, 4-1/2" h, 2-1/2 oz	16.00	28.00	11.00

Colonial crystal wine and cocktail.

Colonial green sugar and creamer.

Colonial green saucer.

Colonial Block

Manufactured by Hazel Atlas Glass Company, Clarksburg, W.V., and Zanesville, Ohio, early 1930s.

Made in black, cobalt blue (rare), crystal, green, pink and white (1950s).

Item	Black	Crystal	Green	Pink	White
Bowl, 4" d.	-	6.00	7.50	7.50	-
Bowl, 7" d.	-	16.00	20.00	20.00	-
Butter Dish, cov	-	40.00	45.00	45.00	-
Butter Tub, cov.	-	35.00	40.00	40.00	-
Candy Jar, cov	-	30.00	40.00	40.00	-
Compote, 4" h, 4-3/4" w	-	12.00	-	-	-
Creamer	-	15.00	16.00	15.00	7.50
Goblet, 5-3/4" h	-	9.00	14.50	15.00	-
Pitcher, 20 oz, 5-3/4" h	-	40.00	50.00	50.00	-
Powder Jar, cov	30.00	20.00	24.00	24.00	-
Sherbet	-	6.00	9.50	9.50	-
Sugar, cov.	-	20.00	25.00	25.00	8.00
Sugar, open	-	15.00	8.00	8.00	18.00

Colonial Block green covered butter dish.

Colonial Fluted

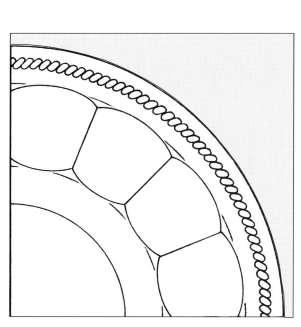

Rope

Manufactured by Federal Glass Company, Columbus, Ohio, from 1928 to 1933.
Made in crystal and green.

Item	Crystal	Green
Berry Bowl, 4" d.	10.00	11.00
Berry Bowl, 7-1/2" d.	16.00	18.00
Cereal Bowl, 6" d	12.00	14.00
Creamer, ftd.	12.00	14.00
Cup	5.00	7.50
Plate, 6" d, sherbet.	2.50	4.00
Plate, 8" d, luncheon	5.00	10.00
Salad Bowl, 6-1/2" d, 2-1/2" deep	18.00	20.00
Saucer.	2.50	4.00
Sherbet	6.00	8.50
Sugar, cov	21.00	25.00
Sugar, open	4.00	5.00

Colonial Fluted green sugar and creamer.

Columbia

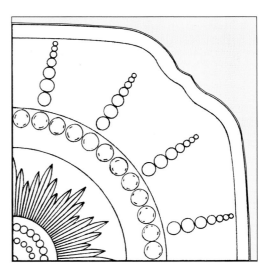

Manufactured by Federal Glass Company, Columbus, Ohio, from 1938 to 1942.

Made in crystal and pink. Several flashed (stained) colors are found, and some decaled pieces are known.

Item	Crystal	Flashed	Pink
Bowl, 10-1/2" d, ruffled edge	24.00	20.00	-
Butter Dish, cov	20.00	18.00	-
Cereal Bowl, 5" d	17.00	-	-
Chop Plate, 11" d	17.00	12.00	-
Crescent Shaped Salad	27.00	-	-
Cup	8.00	9.00	24.00
Cup and Saucer	11.00	11.50	34.00
Plate, 6" d, bread & butter	5.00	-	14.00
Plate, 9-1/2" d, luncheon	15.00	-	32.00
Salad Bowl, 8-1/2" d	20.00	-	-
Saucer	3.00	2.50	10.00
Snack Plate	24.00	-	-
Snack Set, plate and cup	35.00	-	-
Soup Bowl, 8" d, low	22.00	-	-
Tumbler, 4 oz	30.00	-	-
Tumbler, 9 oz	42.50	-	-

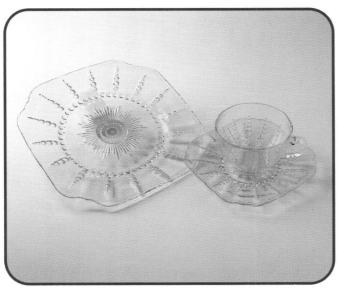

Columbia crystal plate, cup and saucer.

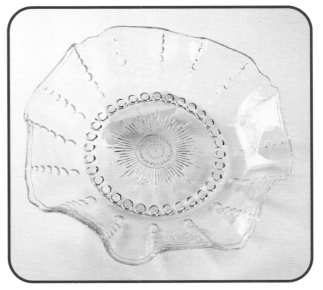

Columbia crystal ruffled bowl.

Coronation

Banded Fine Rib, Saxon

Manufactured by Hocking Glass Company, Lancaster, Ohio, from 1936 to 1940.

Made in crystal, green, pink and Royal Ruby.

Item	Crystal	Green	Pink	Royal Ruby
Berry Bowl, 4-1/4" d	-	32.00	8.00	6.50
Berry Bowl, 8" d, handle	-	-	15.00	18.00
Berry Bowl, 8" d	-	150.00	-	-
Cup	5.00	-	6.00	7.50
Nappy Bowl, 6-1/2" d	15.00	-	7.50	15.00
Pitcher, 68 oz, 7-3/4" h	-	-	500.00	-
Plate, 6" d, sherbet	2.00	-	4.50	-
Plate, 8-1/2" d, luncheon	5.00	42.00	12.00	8.50
Saucer	2.00	-	4.00	-
Sherbet	-	70.00	7.00	-
Tumbler, 10 oz, 5" h, ftd	-	165.00	33.00	-

Coronation ruby handled bowl.

Cremax

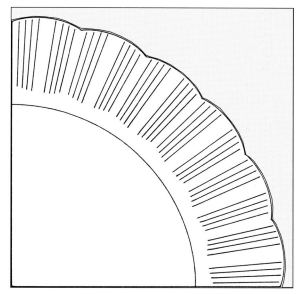

Manufactured by MacBeth-Evans Division of Corning Glass Works, late 1930s to early 1940s.

Made in Cremax, Cremax with fired-on colors, Delphite and Robin's Egg Blue. One set is known as Bordette.

Item	Bordette	Cremax Fired-On	Cremax	Delphite	Robin's Egg Blue
Cereal Bowl, 5-3/4" d	3.00	4.00	3.00	8.00	8.00
Creamer.	4.00	4.50	4.00	9.00	9.00
Cup	3.00	4.00	3.50	5.00	5.00
Demitasse Cup.	8.00	14.00	16.00	24.00	24.00
Demitasse Saucer.	4.00	5.00	6.00	10.00	10.00
Egg Cup, 2-1/4" h	10.00	-	-	-	-
Plate, 6-1/4" d, bread and butter.	2.00	2.50	3.50	5.00	5.00
Plate, 9-3/4" d, dinner.	12.00	5.00	13.00	10.00	10.00
Sandwich Plate, 11-1/2" d.	5.00	6.00	12.50	15.00	15.00
Saucer	1.50	2.00	2.00	4.00	4.00
Sugar, open	4.00	4.50	4.00	9.00	9.00
Vegetable Bowl, 9" d	8.50	9.00	8.00	17.50	17.50

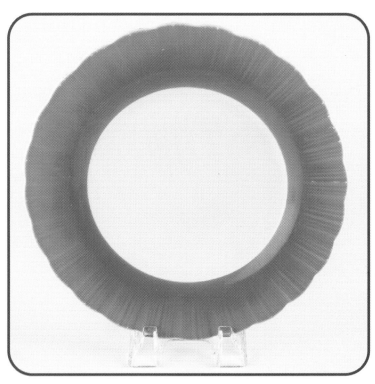

Cremax plate with blue edge.

Crow's Foot

Line #412 and Line #890

Manufactured by Paden City Glass Company, Paden City, W.V., 1930s. The square-shaped pieces are Line #412, the round line is Line #890.

Made in amber, amethyst, black, crystal, pink, Ritz blue, ruby red, white and yellow.

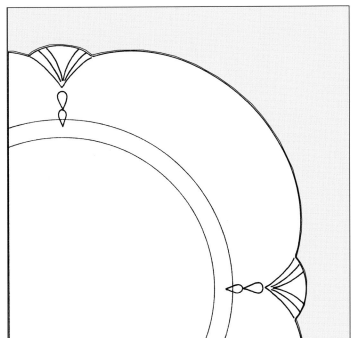

Item	Black Ritz Blue	Colors	RubyRed
Bowl, 4-7/8" w, sq	32.00	13.00	25.00
Bowl, 6" d	35.00	15.00	32.00
Bowl, 6-1/2" d, round, 2-1/2" h, 3-1/2" d base	50.00	24.00	45.00
Bowl, 8-1/2" d, sq, 2 handles	60.00	30.00	50.00
Bowl, 8-3/4" w, sq	55.00	25.00	45.00
Bowl, 10" d, ftd	75.00	35.00	70.00
Bowl, 10" w, sq, 2 handles	75.00	35.00	89.00
Bowl, 11" l, oval	45.00	20.00	40.00
Bowl, 11" w, sq	72.00	32.00	60.00
Bowl, 11" w, sq, rolled edge	75.00	35.00	70.00
Cake Plate, sq, low pedestal foot	95.00	45.00	90.00
Candlesticks, pr, 5-3/4" h	60.00	25.00	50.00
Candlesticks, pr, round base, tall	170.00	75.00	145.00
Candlesticks, pr, sq, mushroom	90.00	45.00	75.00
Candy, 6-1/8" w, 3-1/4" h, 3 legs, round	195.00	85.00	165.00
Candy, cov, 6-1/2" d, 3 part	65.00	25.00	55.00
Cheese Stand, 5" h	35.00	15.00	30.00
Comport, 3-1/4" h, 6-1/4" w	35.00	15.00	30.00
Comport, 4-3/4" h, 7-3/8" w	55.00	30.00	45.00
Comport, 6-5/8" h, 7" w	70.00	35.00	55.00
Console Bowl, 11-1/2" d, 3 legs, round	100.00	45.00	85.00
Console Bowl, 11-1/2" w, sq	95.00	40.00	80.00
Cracker Plate, 11" d	50.00	25.00	45.00
Cream Soup Bowl, flat	25.00	12.00	22.00
Cream Soup Bowl, ftd	25.00	12.00	22.00
Creamer, flat	17.50	10.00	15.00
Creamer, footed	17.50	10.00	15.00
Cup, flat	14.00	6.00	11.00
Cup, ftd	14.00	6.00	11.00
Gravy Boat, flat	100.00	45.00	85.00

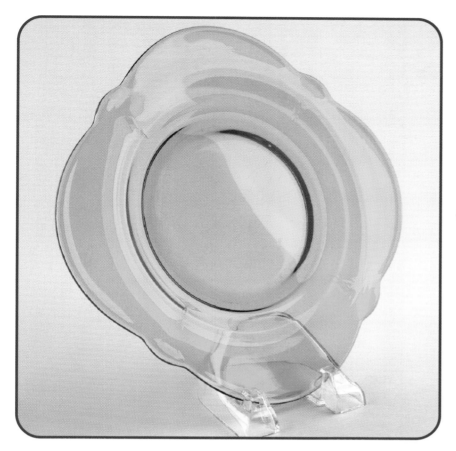

Crow's Foot amber plate.

Item	Black Ritz Blue	Colors	RubyRed
Gravy Boat, ftd 145.00		70.00	130.00
Mayonnaise, 3 legs. 60.00		25.00	50.00
Nasturium bowl, 3 legs 200.00		100.00	175.00
Plate, 5-3/4" d 4.00		2.00	3.00
Plate, 8" d, round. 12.00		5.00	10.00
Plate, 8-1/2" w, sq 10.00		7.00	8.00
Plate, 9-1/4" d, round, dinner. 40.00		20.00	35.00
Plate, 9-1/2" d, 2 handles 75.00		35.00	65.00
Plate, 10-3/8" d, round, 2 handles 65.00		30.00	55.00
Plate, 10-3/8" w, sq, 2 handles 65.00		30.00	55.00
Plate, 10-1/2" d, dinner 100.00		45.00	90.00
Platter, 12" l 35.00		17.50	30.00
Relish, 11" l, 3 part 100.00		48.00	85.00
Sandwich Server, center handle, round 75.00		35.00	70.00
Sandwich Server, center handle, sq 45.00		25.00	50.00
Saucer, 6" d, round 4.00		2.00	5.00
Saucer, 6" w, sq 4.00		2.00	5.00
Sugar, flat 17.50		10.00	15.00
Sugar, ftd. 17.50		10.00	15.00
Tumbler, 4-1/4" h. 80.00		35.00	75.00
Vase, 4-5/8" h 75.00		45.00	65.00
Vases, 10-1/4" h, cupped 110.00		50.00	90.00
Vases, 10-1/4" h, flared 85.00		35.00	70.00
Vases, 11-3/4" h, flared 185.00		125.00	165.00
Whipped Cream Bowl, 3 legs 70.00		30.00	60.00

Cube *Cubist*

Manufactured by Jeannette Glass Company, Jeannette, Pa., from 1929 to 1933.

Made in amber, crystal, green, pink, ultramarine and white. Production in amber and white is limited to the 2-3/8" h sugar bowl, and is valued at $3.

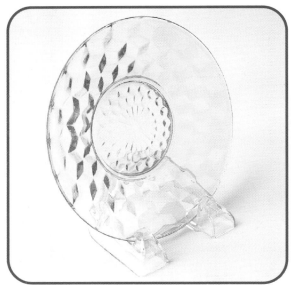

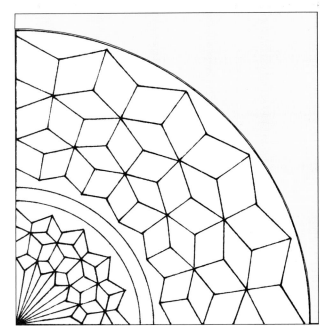

Cube pink plate.

Item	Crystal	Green	Pink	Ultramarine
Bowl, 4-1/2" d, deep	-	7.00	8.00	35.00
Butter Dish, cov	-	60.00	65.00	-
Candy Jar, cov, 6-1/2" h	-	30.00	28.00	-
Coaster, 3-1/4" d	-	8.50	7.00	-
Creamer, 2-5/8" h	5.00	10.00	9.00	70.00
Creamer, 3-9/16" h	-	8.50	9.00	-
Cup	-	7.00	8.00	-
Dessert Bowl, 4-1/2" d	3.50	8.50	7.50	-
Pitcher, 8-3/4" h, 45 oz	-	235.00	215.00	-
Plate, 6" d, sherbet	-	11.00	3.75	-
Plate, 8" d, luncheon	-	8.50	7.50	-
Powder Jar, cov, 3 legs	-	30.00	25.00	-
Salad Bowl, 6-1/2" d	6.00	15.00	15.00	-
Salt and Pepper Shakers, pr	-	36.00	36.00	-
Saucer	1.50	3.00	3.50	-
Sherbet, ftd	-	8.00	11.00	-
Sugar, cov, 2-3/8" h	4.00	22.00	6.00	-
Sugar, cov, 3" h	-	25.00	25.00	-
Sugar, open, 3"	5.00	8.00	7.00	-
Tray, 7-1/2" l	9.00	-	5.00	-
Tumbler, 9 oz, 4" h	-	70.00	65.00	-

Cupid

Manufactured by Paden City Glass Company, Paden City, W.V., 1930s.

Made in amber, black, canary yellow, crystal, green, light blue, peacock blue and pink. Prices for colors, such as amber, black, canary yellow and light blue, are still being established as more pieces of this pattern arrive on the secondary market. This expensive pattern is one to keep your eyes open for while searching at flea markets and garage sales.

Item	Crystal	Green	Peacock Blue	Pink
Bowl, 8-1/2" l, oval, ftd	-	185.00	-	175.00
Bowl, 9-1/4" d, center handle	-	175.00	-	185.00
Bowl, 10-1/2" d, rolled edge	-	140.00	-	140.00
Cake Plate, 11-3/4" h	-	155.00	-	155.00
Cake Stand, 2" h, ftd	-	245.00	-	155.00
Candlesticks, pr, 5" h	-	160.00	-	160.00
Candy, cov, 3 part	-	200.00	-	200.00
Candy, cov, 5-1/4" h	-	235.00	-	235.00
Champagne, 5-7/8" h	14.00	-	-	-
Cocktail, 5-1/8" h	12.50	-	-	-
Comport, 4-1/2" h, ftd	-	95.00	-	90.00
Comport, 6-1/4" h, ftd	-	-	165.00	-
Console Bowl, 11" d	-	140.00	-	140.00
Creamer, 4-1/2" h, ftd	25.00	95.00	-	95.00
Creamer, 5" h, ftd	-	95.00	-	95.00
Fruit Bowl, 9-1/4" d, ftd	-	185.00	-	185.00
Fruit Bowl, 10-1/4" d	-	155.00	-	155.00
Ice Bucket, 6" h	-	195.00	-	195.00
Ice Tub, 4-3/4" h	-	180.00	-	180.00
Mayonnaise, 6" d, spoon, 8" d plate	-	275.00	245.00	145.00
Plate, 10-1/2" d	-	100.00	150.00	95.00
Samovar	-	800.00	-	800.00
Sugar, 4-1/4" h, ftd	-	85.00	-	85.00
Sugar, 5" h, ftd	-	95.00	-	95.00
Tray, 10-3/4" d, center handle	-	125.00	-	125.00
Tray, 10-7/8" l, oval, ftd	-	155.00	-	155.00
Vase, 8-1/4" h, elliptical	-	465.00	-	465.00
Wine, 5-1/8" h	12.50	-	-	-

Cupid pink low pedestal-foot comport.

Daisy

No. 620

Manufactured by Indiana Glass Company, Dunkirk, Ind., from late 1930s to 1980s.

Made in amber (1940s), crystal (1933-40), dark green (1960s-80s), fired-on red (late 1930s) and milk glass (1960s-80s).

Item	Amber or Fired-On Red	Crystal	Dark Green or Milk White
Berry Bowl, 4-1/2" d	9.00	5.00	5.00
Berry Bowl, 7-3/8" d deep	15.00	7.50	7.50
Berry Bowl, 9-3/8" d, deep	30.00	12.00	12.00
Cake Plate, 11-1/2" d	14.50	12.00	12.00
Cereal Bowl, 6" d	25.00	10.00	10.00
Cream Soup Bowl, 4-1/2" d	13.50	7.50	7.50
Creamer, ftd	8.50	6.00	6.00
Cup	5.00	4.50	6.00
Plate, 6" d, sherbet	3.00	2.50	2.50
Plate, 7-3/8" d, salad	7.00	3.00	3.00
Plate, 8-3/8" d, luncheon	7.75	5.00	5.00
Plate, 9-3/8" d, dinner	9.00	7.50	7.50
Plate, 10-3/8" d, grill	15.00	8.00	8.00
Plate, 10-3/8" d, grill, indent for soup	15.00	8.00	8.00
Platter, 10-3/4" d	14.00	11.00	11.00
Relish Dish, 8-3/8" d, 3 part	22.00	12.00	12.00
Sandwich Plate, 11-1/2" d	14.50	12.00	12.00
Saucer	2.00	1.50	2.00
Sherbet, ftd	9.00	5.00	5.00
Sugar, ftd	8.50	6.00	6.00
Tumbler, 9 oz, ftd	16.00	10.00	10.00
Tumbler, 12 oz, ftd	40.00	15.00	15.00
Vegetable Bowl, 10" l, oval	15.00	10.00	10.00

Daisy green luncheon plate.

Daisy amber luncheon plate.

Daisy crystal sandwich plate.

Delilah Bird

Manufactured by Paden City Glass Company, Paden City, WV., 1930s.

Made in amber, crystal, green, pink, red and yellow.

Delilah Bird amber candle holders.

Item	Colors
Bowl, 4-17/8" w, sq	37.50
Bowl, 8-3/4" w, sq	85.00
Bowl, 8-3/4" w, sq, handles	95.00
Candlesticks, pr, 5-13/4" h, sq base	135.00
Candy Dish, 6-1/2" w, sq	140.00
Comport, 3-1/4" h, 6-1/4" w	60.00
Comport, 4-1/4" h, 7-3/8" w	70.00
Console Bowl, 11-3/4" d	80.00
Creamer, 2-3/4" h, flat	80.00
Cup	75.00
Plate, 5-3/4" d, sherbert	24.00
Plate, 8-31/2" d, luncheon	45.00
Plate, 10-3/8" d, 2 handles	155.00
Saucer	20.00
Server, center handle	85.00
Sherbert 4-5/8" h, 3-3/8" d	48.00
Sherbert 4-7/8" h, 3-5/8" d	48.00
Tumbler, 10 oz, 4" h, flat	65.00
Vase, 10" h	100.00

Della Robbia

#1058

Manufactured by Westmoreland Glass Company, Grapeville, Pa., from late 1920s to 1940s.

Made in crystal, with applied luster colors and milk glass. Examples of milk white prices are: hand-painted dec candy jar, $45; creamer, $15; goblet, $20; tumbler, $15; wine, $17.50.

Item	Crystal
Basket, 9"	185.00
Basket, 12"	265.00
Bowl, 8" d, bell, handle	48.00
Bowl, 8"d, heart shape, handle	95.00
Bowl, 12" d, ftd	12.00
Bowl, 13" d, rolled edge	115.00
Bowl, 14" d, oval, flange	155.00
Bowl, 15" d, bell	175.00
Cake Salver, 14" d, ftd	120.00
Candlesticks, pr, 4" h	65.00
Candlesticks, pr, 4" h, 2 light	160.00
Candy Jar, cov, scalloped edge	85.00
Champagne, 6 oz.	24.00
Chocolate Candy, round, flat	75.00
Cocktail, 3-1/4 oz.	15.00
Comport, 12" d, ftd, bell	115.00
Comport, 13" d, flanged	125.00
Creamer, ftd	18.00
Cup, coffee	18.00
Finger Bowl, 5" d	30.00
Ginger Ale Tumbler, 5 oz	25.00
Goblet, 8 oz., 6" h	28.00
Iced Tea Tumbler 11 oz., ftd	35.00
Iced Tea Tumbler 12 oz., 5-3/16" h, straight	40.00
Iced Tea Tumbler 12 oz., bell	32.00
Iced Tea Tumbler, 12 oz., bell, ftd	32.00
Mint Comport, 6-1/2" d, 3-5/8" h, ftd	45.00
Nappy, 7-1/2"d	42.00

Item	Crystal
Nappy, 8" d, bell	45.00
Nappy, 4-1/2" d	30.00
Nappy, 6" d, bell	35.00
Nappy, 6-1/2"d , one handle	32.00
Nappy, 9" d	60.00
Pitcher, 32 oz.	200.00
Plate, 6" d, finger bowl liner	10.00
Plate, 6-1/8" d, bread & butter	10.00
Plate, 7-1/4" d, salad	18.00
Plate, 9" d, luncheon	20.00
Plate, 10-1/2" d, dinner	85.00
Plate, 18" d	170.00
Platter, 14" l, oval	165.00
Punch Bowl, 14"d	200.00
Punch Bowl Liner, 18" d plate, upturned edge	155.00
Punch Bowl Set, 15 pcs	625.00
Punch Cup	15.00
Salt and Pepper Shakers, pr	55.00
Saucer	10.00
Sherbet, 5 oz, low foot	22.00
Sherbet, 5 oz, 4-3/4" h, ftd	24.00
Sugar, ftd	27.50
Sweetmeat Comport, 8" d bell	100.00
Torte Plate, 14"d	85.00
Tumbler 8 oz., ftd	27.50
Tumbler, 8 oz, water	30.00
Wine, 3 oz	25.00

Della Robbia clear plate.

Della Robbia stained decorated compote.

Dewdrop

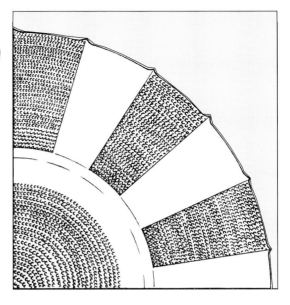

Manufactured by Jeannette Glass Company, Jeannette, Pa., from 1953 to 1956.

Made in crystal. Some pieces known in shell pink and iridescent.

Item	Crystal
Bowl, 4-3/4" d	7.00
Bowl, 8-1/2" d	20.00
Bowl, 10-3/8" d	20.00
Butter, cov	30.00
Candy Dish, cov, 7" d	24.00
Casserole, cov	24.00
Creamer	8.50
Iced Tea Tumbler, 15 oz	17.50
Lazy Susan, 13" d tray	29.00

Item	Crystal
Pitcher, 1/2 gallon, ftd	48.00
Plate, 11-1/2" d	20.00
Punch Cup	4.00
Punch Bowl Set, bowl, 12 cups	65.00
Snack Cup	4.00
Snack Plate, indent for cup	5.00
Relish, leaf-shape, handle	9.00
Sugar, cov	14.00
Tumbler, 9 oz	15.00

Dewdrop crystal sugar and creamer.

Dewdrop clear tumbler and iridescent pitcher.

Diamond Quilted

Flat Diamond

Manufactured by Imperial Glass Company, Bellaire, Ohio, from late 1920 to early 1930s.

Made in amber, black, blue, crystal, green, pink, and red. Amber and red prices would be valued slightly higher than black.

Item	Black	Blue	Crystal
Bowl, 5-1/2" d, one handle	18.50	-	-
Bowl, 7" d, crimped edge	18.50	-	-
Cake Salver, 10" d, tall	-	-	-
Candlesticks, pr.	60.00	-	50.00
Candy Jar, cov, ftd	-	-	25.00
Cereal Bowl, 5" d	15.00	-	6.00
Champagne, 9 oz, 6" h	-	-	-
Compote, 6" h, 7-1/4" w	-	-	-
Compote, cov, 11-1/2" d	-	-	-
Console Bowl, 10-1/2" d, rolled edge	65.00	60.00	15.00
Cordial, 1 oz	-	-	-
Cream Soup Bowl, 4-3/4" d	22.00	20.00	20.00
Creamer	18.50	20.00	15.00
Cup	18.00	18.50	7.00
Ice Bucket	90.00	90.00	-
Iced Tea Tumbler, 12 oz	-	-	-
Mayonnaise Set, comport, plate, ladle	60.00	65.00	25.00
Pitcher, 64 oz	-	-	-
Plate, 6" d, sherbet	10.00	8.50	7.50
Plate, 7" d, salad	10.00	10.00	8.00
Plate, 8" d, luncheon	12.00	12.00	9.00
Punch Bowl and Stand	-	-	-
Sandwich Plate, 14" d	-	-	-
Sandwich Server, center handle	50.00	50.00	20.00
Saucer	5.00	5.00	2.00
Sherbet	16.00	16.00	14.00
Sugar	20.00	25.00	12.00
Tumbler, 6 oz, ftd	-	-	-
Tumbler, 9 oz	-	-	-
Tumbler, 9 oz, ftd	-	-	-
Tumbler, 12 oz, ftd	-	-	-
Vase, fan	80.00	75.00	-
Whiskey, 1-1/2" oz	-	-	-
Wine, 2 oz	-	-	-
Wine, 3 oz	-	-	-

Item	Green	Pink
Bowl, 5-1/2" d, one handle	12.00	15.00
Bowl, 7" d, crimped edge	10.00	10.00
Cake Salver, 10" d, tall	60.00	65.00
Candlesticks, pr	32.00	28.00
Candy Jar, cov, ftd	65.00	65.00
Cereal Bowl, 5" d	8.50	8.00
Champagne, 9 oz, 6" h	12.00	-
Compote, 6" h, 7-1/4" w	45.00	48.00
Compote, cov, 11-1/2" d	80.00	75.00
Console Bowl, 10-1/2" d, rolled edge	20.00	24.00
Cordial, 1 oz.	12.00	15.00
Cream Soup Bowl, 4-3/4" d	12.00	14.00
Creamer	9.00	10.00
Cup	10.00	12.00
Ice Bucket	50.00	50.00
Iced Tea Tumbler, 12 oz	10.00	10.00
Mayonnaise Set, comport, plate, ladle	37.50	40.00
Pitcher, 64 oz	50.00	55.00
Plate, 6" d, sherbet	7.00	7.50
Plate, 7" d, salad	8.50	8.50
Plate, 8" d, luncheon	6.50	8.50
Punch Bowl and Stand	450.00	450.00
Sandwich Plate, 14" d	15.00	15.00
Sandwich Server, center handle	25.00	25.00
Saucer	4.00	4.00
Sherbet	6.00	5.00
Sugar	15.00	13.50
Tumbler, 6 oz, ftd	9.00	10.00
Tumbler, 9 oz	14.00	16.00
Tumbler, 9 oz, ftd	14.00	16.00
Tumbler, 12 oz, ftd	15.00	15.00
Vase, fan	50.00	50.00
Whiskey, 1-1/2" oz	10.00	12.00
Wine, 2 oz	12.50	12.50
Wine, 3 oz	15.00	15.00

Diamond Quilted pink sugar and creamer.

Diana

Manufactured by Federal Glass Company, Columbus, Ohio, from 1937 to 1941.

Made in amber, crystal and pink.

Reproductions: † A 13-1/8" d scalloped pink bowl has been made, which was not original to the pattern.

Item	Amber	Crystal	Pink
Ashtray, 3-1/2" d . . . . -		3.00	4.00
Bowl, 12" d, scalloped edge 18.00		7.00	30.00
Candy Jar, cov, round 36.00		18.50	48.00
Cereal Bowl, 5" d 14.00		4.00	10.00
Coaster, 3-1/2" d 12.00		3.00	7.00
Console/Fruit Bowl, 11"d 6.50		20.00	44.00
Cream Soup Bowl, 5-1/2" d 16.00		12.00	22.00
Creamer, oval 9.00		4.00	12.50
Cup 7.00		4.00	19.00
Demitasse Cup and Saucer, 2 oz, 4-1/2" d saucer . . . -		12.00	50.00
Junior Set, 6 cups and saucers, rack . . . . -		125.00	300.00
Plate, 6" d, bread & butter 3.00		2.00	5.00
Plate, 9-1/2" d, dinner 8.00		6.00	18.00
Platter, 12" l, oval 15.00		6.00	28.00
Salad Bowl, 9"d 17.50		14.00	20.00
Salt and Pepper Shakers, pr 100.00		30.00	75.00
Sandwich Plate, 11-3/4" d 8.00		7.00	28.00
Saucer 2.00		1.50	6.00
Sherbet 10.00		4.00	12.00
Sugar, open, oval 10.00		10.00	16.00
Tumbler, 9 oz, 4-1/8" h 27.50		18.00	40.00

Diana clear tumbler.

Diana pink sherbet.

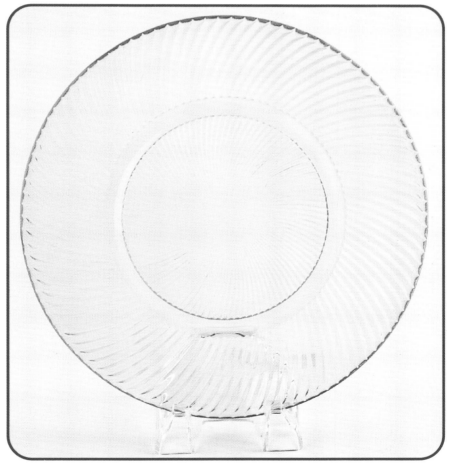

Diana pink plate.

Dogwood

Apple Blossom, Wild Rose

Manufactured by MacBeth-Evans Company, Charleroi, Pa., from 1929 to 1932.

Made in Cremax, crystal, green, Monax, pink and yellow. Yellow is rare; a cereal bowl is known and valued at $85. Crystal items are valued at 50% less than green.

Dogwood pink sugar, creamer and plate.

Item	Cremax or Monax	Green	Pink
Berry Bowl, 8-1/2" d 40.00		100.00	65.00
Cake Plate, 11" d, heavy solid foot. . . . . -		-	650.00
Cake Plate, 13" d, heavy solid foot 185.00		130.00	165.00
Cereal Bowl, 5-1/2" d 6.00		32.00	32.00
Coaster, 3-1/4" d . . . . -		-	500.00
Creamer, 2-1/2" h, thin . . . . -		48.00	18.00
Creamer, 3-1/4" h, thick . . . . -		-	17.50
Cup, thin. . . . . -		32.00	14.00
Cup, thick 36.00		40.00	25.00
Fruit Bowl, 10-1/4" d 100.00		250.00	435.00
Pitcher, 8" h, 80 oz, (American Sweetheart style) . . . -		-	420.00
Pitcher, 8" h, 80 oz, decorated. . . . . -		500.00	265.00
Plate, 6" d, bread & butter 22.00		10.00	9.50
Plate, 8" d, luncheon . . . . -		9.00	9.00
Plate, 9-1/4" d, dinner . . . . -		-	38.00
Plates, 10-1/2" d, grill, AOP or border design only . . -		20.00	20.00
Platter, 12" d, oval . . . . -		-	500.00
Salver, 12"d 20.00		-	35.00
Saucer 20.00		10.00	7.00
Sherbet, low, ftd . . . . -		95.00	40.00
Sugar, 2-1/2" h, thin . . . . -		50.00	18.00
Sugar, 3-1/4" h, thick, ftd. . . . . -		-	18.50
Tidbit, 2 tier . . . . -		-	90.00
Tumbler, 10 oz, 4" h, decorated. . . . . -		85.00	55.00
Tumbler, 11 oz, 4-3/4" h, decorated. . . . . -		95.00	75.00
Tumbler, 12 oz, 5" h, decorated. . . . . -		100.00	65.00
Tumbler, moulded band. . . . . -		-	25.00

Doric

Manufactured by Jeannette Glass Company, Jeannette, Pa., from 1935 to 1938.

Made in Delphite, green, pink and yellow. Yellow is rare.

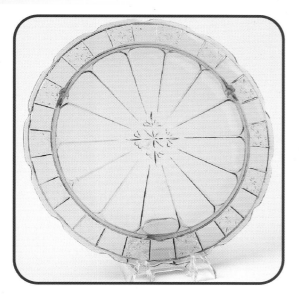

Doric green cake plate.

Item	Delphite	Green	Pink
Berry Bowl, 4-1/2" d	42.00	10.00	10.00
Berry Bowl, 8-1/4" d	135.00	25.00	17.00
Bowl, 9" d, two handles	-	45.00	45.00
Butter Dish, cov	-	90.00	75.00
Cake Plate, 10" d, 3 legs	-	22.00	30.00
Candy Dish, cov, 8" d	-	40.00	45.00
Candy Dish, 3 part	8.00	7.50	12.50
Cereal Bowl, 5-1/2" d	-	65.00	90.00
Coaster, 3" d	-	28.00	20.00
Cream Soup, 5" d, 2 handles	-	385.00	-
Creamer, 4" h	-	17.00	14.00
Cup	-	10.00	10.00
Cup and Saucer	-	17.00	17.00
Pitcher, 36 oz, 6" h, flat	1,000.00	45.00	45.00
Pitcher, 48 oz, 7-1/2" h, ftd.	-	850.00	450.00
Plate 9" d, grill	-	20.00	25.00
Plate, 6" d, sherbet	-	6.50	6.50
Plate, 7" d, salad	-	20.00	18.00
Plate, 9" d, dinner	-	24.00	12.00
Platter, 12" l, oval	-	32.00	35.00
Relish Tray, 4" x 4"	-	12.00	14.00
Relish Tray, 4" x 8"	-	10.00	11.00
Salt and Pepper Shakers, pr	-	24.00	47.00
Saucer	-	7.00	7.00
Sherbet, footed	10.00	17.50	15.00
Sugar, cov	-	35.00	32.00
Tray, 8" x 8", serving	-	28.00	24.00
Tray, 10" l, handle	-	25.00	16.00
Tumbler, 9 oz, 4-1/2" h, flat	-	100.00	66.00
Tumbler, 10 oz, 4" h, ftd.	-	85.00	60.00
Tumbler, 12 oz, 5" h, ftd.	-	125.00	85.00
Vegetable Bowl, 9" l, oval	-	35.00	30.00

Doric and Pansy

Manufactured by Jeannette Glass Company, Jeannette, Pa., from 1937 to 1938.

Made in ultramarine, with limited production in pink and crystal.

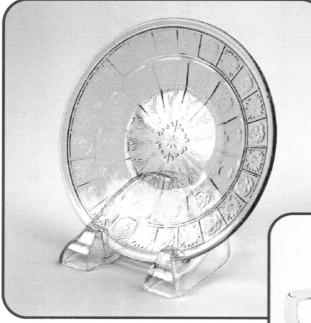

Doric and Pansy pink plate.

Doric and Pansy teal child's creamer and sugar.

Item	Crystal	Pink	Ultramarine
Berry Bowl, 4-1/2" d	7.50	8.00	16.00
Berry Bowl, 8" d	-	20.00	75.00
Bowl, 9" d, handle	14.00	15.00	35.00
Butter Dish, cov.	-	-	500.00
Cup and Saucer	13.00	14.00	24.00
Creamer	70.00	70.00	115.00
Plate, 6" d, sherbet	7.00	7.50	10.00
Plate, 7" d, salad	-	-	35.00
Plate, 9" d, dinner	7.50	8.00	30.00
Salt and Pepper Shakers, pr.	-	-	400.00
Sugar, open	65.00	70.00	115.00
Tray, 10" l, handles	45.00	-	25.00
Tumbler, 9 oz, 4-1/2" h	-	-	78.00

Children's

Item	Pink	Ultramarine
Creamer	35.00	45.00
Cup	32.50	48.00
Plate	8.00	12.00
Saucer	7.00	8.50
Sugar	35.00	45.00
14-pc set	320.00	375.00

English Hobnail

Line #555

Manufactured by Westmoreland Glass Company, Grapeville, Pa., from the 1920s to 1983.

Made in amber, cobalt blue, crystal, crystal with various color treatments, green, ice blue, pink, red and turquoise blue. Values for cobalt blue, red or turquoise blue pieces would be about 25% higher than ice blue values. Crystal pieces with a color accent would be slightly higher than crystal values.

English Hobnail clear tumbler.

Item	Amber	Crystal	Green	Ice Blue	Pink
Ashtray, 3" d	20.00	20.00	22.00	-	22.00
Ashtray, 4-1/2" d	9.00	9.00	15.00	24.00	15.00
Ashtray, 4-1/2" sq	9.50	9.50	15.00	-	15.00
Basket, 5" d, handle	17.50	17.50	-	-	-
Basket, 6" d, handle, tall	36.00	36.00	-	-	43.00
Bonbon, 6-1/2" h, handle	15.00	16.00	27.50	38.00	27.50
Bowl, 7" d, 6 part	17.50	17.50	-	-	-
Bowl, 7" d, oblong spoon	17.50	17.50	-	-	-
Bowl, 8" d, ftd.	28.00	28.00	48.00	-	48.00
Bowl, 8" d, hexagonal foot, 2 handles	38.00	38.00	75.00	115.00	75.00
Bowl, 8", 6 pt	24.00	24.00	-	-	-
Bowl, 9-1/2" d, round, crimped	30.00	30.00	-	-	-

Item	Amber	Crystal	Green	Ice Blue	Pink
Bowl, 10" d, flared	30.00	30.00	40.00	-	40.00
Bowl, 10" l, oval, crimped	35.00	35.00	-	-	-
Bowl, 11" d, bell	32.00	32.00	-	-	-
Bowl, 11" d, rolled edge	35.00	35.00	40.00	85.00	40.00
Bowl, 12" d, flared	32.00	32.00	40.00	-	95.00
Bowl,12" l, oval crimped	32.00	32.00	-	-	-
Candelabra, 2 light	18.00	18.00	-	-	-
Candlesticks, pr, 3-1/2" h, round base	18.00	32.00	36.00	-	60.00
Candlesticks, pr, 5-1/2" h, sq base	30.00	32.00	-	-	-
Candlesticks, pr, 9" h, round base	50.00	36.00	72.00	-	125.00
Candy Dish, 3 foot	35.00	38.00	50.00	-	50.00
Candy Dish, cov, 1/2 lb, cone shape	35.00	40.00	55.00	-	90.00
Celery, 12" l, oval	24.00	45.00	36.00	-	36.00
Celery, 9" d	18.00	20.00	32.00	-	32.00
Champagne, two ball, round foot	8.00	7.00	20.00	-	20.00
Chandelier, 17" shade, 200 prisms	425.00	400.00	-	-	-
Cheese, cov, 6" d	40.00	42.00	-	-	-
Cheese, cov, 8-3/4" d	50.00	48.00	-	-	-
Cigarette Box, cov, 4-1/2" x 2-1/2"	24.50	24.50	30.00	-	55.00
Cigarette Jar, cov, round	16.00	18.00	25.00	-	65.00
Claret, 5 oz, round	15.00	17.50	-	-	-
Coaster, 3"	5.00	5.00	-	-	-
Cocktail, 3 oz, round	8.50	12.00	-	-	37.50
Cocktail, 3-1/2 oz, round, ball	15.00	17.50	-	-	-
Compote, 5" d, round, round foot	22.00	20.00	25.00	-	25.00
Compote, 5" d, round, sq foot	24.00	24.00	-	-	-
Compote, 5-1/2" d, bell	12.00	15.00	-	-	-
Compote, 5-1/2" d, bell, sq foot	20.00	20.00	-	-	-
Console Bowl, 12" d, flange	30.00	30.00	40.00	-	40.00
Cordial, 1 oz, round, ball	15.00	15.00	-	-	-
Cordial, 1 oz, round, foot	15.00	15.00	-	-	-
Cream Soup Bowl	12.00	12.00	-	-	-
Cream Soup Liner, round	5.00	5.00	-	-	-
Creamer, hexagonal foot	20.00	20.00	25.00	-	48.00
Creamer, low, flat	10.00	10.00	-	-	-
Creamer, sq foot	24.00	24.00	45.00	-	45.00
Cruet, 12 oz	-	25.00	-	-	-
Cup	6.50	6.50	18.00	-	25.00
Decanter, 20 oz	55.00	55.00	-	-	-
Demitasse Cup	17.50	17.50	55.00	-	55.00
Dish, 6" d, crimped	15.00	15.00	-	-	-
Egg Cup	10.00	10.00	-	-	-
Finger Bowl, 4-1/2" d	7.00	7.00	15.00	35.00	15.00
Finger Bowl, 4-1/2" sq, foot	8.50	8.50	18.00	40.00	18.00
Finger Bowl Liner, 6" sq	6.00	6.00	20.00	-	20.00
Finger Bowl Liner, 6-1/2" d, round	12.00	12.00	10.00	-	10.00
Ginger Ale Tumbler, 5 oz, flat	10.00	10.00	18.00	-	20.00
Ginger Ale Tumbler, 5 oz, round foot	10.00	10.00	-	-	-
Ginger Ale Tumbler, 5 oz, sq foot	8.00	8.00	32.00	-	35.00
Goblet, 8 oz, 6-1/4" h, round, water	11.00	11.00	-	50.00	35.00
Goblet, 8 oz, sq foot, water	9.00	9.00	-	-	50.00
Grapefruit Bowl, 6-1/2" d	12.00	12.00	22.00	-	24.00
Hat, high	15.00	15.00	-	-	-

Item	Amber	Crystal	Green	Ice Blue	Pink
Hat, low	12.00	12.00	-	-	-
Honey Compote, 6" d, round foot	18.00	18.00	35.00	-	35.00
Honey Compote, 6" d, sq foot	18.00	18.00	-	-	-
Ice Tub, 4" h	18.00	18.00	50.00	-	85.00
Ice Tub, 5-1/2" h	36.00	36.00	65.00	-	100.00
Iced Tea Tumbler, 10 oz	14.00	14.00	30.00	-	30.00
Iced Tea Tumbler, 11 oz, round, ball	12.00	12.00	-	-	-
Iced Tea Tumbler, 11 oz, sq foot	13.50	13.50	-	-	-
Iced Tea Tumbler, 12-1/2 oz, round foot	14.00	14.00	-	-	-
Iced Tea Tumbler, 12 oz, flat	14.00	14.00	32.00	-	32.00
Icer, sq base, patterned insert	45.00	45.00	-	-	-
Ivy Bowl, 6-1/2" d, sq foot, crimp top	35.00	35.00	-	-	-
Juice Tumbler, 7 oz, round foot	7.50	7.50	-	-	-
Juice Tumbler, 7 oz, sq foot	6.50	6.50	-	-	-
Lamp Shade, 17" d	175.00	165.00	-	-	-
Lamp, 6-1/2" h, electric	45.00	45.00	50.00	-	50.00
Lamp, 9-1/2" d, electric	45.00	45.00	115.00	-	115.00
Lamp, candlestick	32.00	32.00	-	-	-
Marmalade, cov	40.00	40.00	45.00	-	70.00
Mayonnaise, 6"	12.00	12.00	22.00	-	22.00
Mustard, cov, sq, foot	18.00	18.00	-	-	-
Nappy, 4-1/2" d, round	8.00	8.00	15.00	30.00	15.00
Nappy, 4-1/2" w, sq	8.50	8.50	-	-	-
Nappy, 5" d, round	10.00	10.00	15.00	35.00	15.00
Nappy, 5-1/2" d, bell	12.00	12.00	-	-	-
Nappy, 6" d, round	10.00	10.00	17.50	-	17.50
Nappy, 6" d, sq	10.00	10.00	17.50	-	17.50
Nappy, 6-1/2" d, round	12.50	12.50	20.00	-	20.00
Nappy, 6-1/2" d, sq	14.00	14.00	-	-	-
Nappy, 7" d, round	14.00	14.00	24.00	-	24.00
Nappy, 7-1/2" d, bell	15.00	15.00	-	-	-
Nappy, 8" d, cupped	22.00	22.00	30.00	-	30.00
Nappy, 8" d, round	22.00	22.00	35.00	-	35.00
Nappy, 9" d, bell	25.00	25.00	-	-	-
Nut, individual, ftd	6.00	6.00	14.50	-	14.50
Oil Bottle, 2 oz, handle	24.00	24.00	-	-	-
Oil Bottle, 6 oz, handle	26.00	26.00	-	-	-
Oil/Vinegar Combination, 6 oz	40.00	40.00	-	-	-
Old Fashioned Tumbler, 5 oz	12.00	12.00	-	-	-
Oyster Cocktail, 5 oz, sq foot	10.00	10.00	17.50	-	17.50
Parfait, round foot	15.00	15.00	-	-	-
Pickle, 8" d	15.00	15.00	-	-	-
Pitcher, 23 oz, rounded	48.00	48.00	150.00	-	165.00
Pitcher, 32 oz, straight side	50.00	50.00	175.00	-	175.00
Pitcher, 38 oz, rounded	62.00	62.00	215.00	-	215.00
Pitcher, 60 oz, rounded	65.00	65.00	295.00	-	295.00
Pitcher, 64 oz, straight side	75.00	72.00	310.00	-	310.00
Plate, 5-1/2" d, round	7.00	7.00	10.00	-	10.00
Plate, 6" w, sq	5.00	5.00	-	-	-
Plate, 6-1/2" d, round	6.00	6.00	10.00	-	10.00
Plate, 6-1/2" d, round, depressed center	6.00	6.00	-	-	-
Plate, 8" d, round	9.00	9.00	14.00	-	14.00
Plate, 8" d, round, ftd	13.00	13.00	-	-	-

Item	Amber	Crystal	Green	Ice Blue	Pink
Plate, 8-1/2" d, plain edge	9.00	9.00	-	-	-
Plate, 8-1/2" d, round	7.00	9.00	17.50	-	28.00
Plate, 8-3/4" w, sq	9.00	9.00	-	-	-
Plate, 10" d, round	14.00	14.00	45.00	-	65.00
Plate, 10" w, sq	14.00	14.00	-	-	-
Plate, 10-1/2" d, round, grill	15.00	15.00	-	-	-
Plate, 12" w, sq	20.00	20.00	-	-	-
Plate, 15" w, sq	28.00	28.00	-	-	-
Preserve, 8" d	15.00	15.00	-	-	-
Puff Box, cov, 6" d, round	20.00	20.00	47.50	-	80.00
Punch Bowl and Stand	215.00	215.00	-	-	-
Punch Cup	7.00	7.00	-	-	-
Relish, 8" d, 3 part	18.00	18.00	-	-	-
Rose Bowl, 4" d	17.50	17.50	48.00	-	50.00
Rose Bowl, 6" d	20.00	20.00	-	-	-
Salt and Pepper Shakers, pr, round foot	24.00	24.00	150.00	-	165.00
Salt and Pepper Shakers, pr, sq, foot	10.00	10.00	-	-	-
Saucer, demitasse, round	10.00	10.00	15.00	-	17.50
Saucer, demitasse, sq	10.00	10.00	-	-	-
Saucer, round	2.00	2.00	6.00	-	6.00
Saucer, sq	2.00	2.00	-	-	-
Sherbet, high, round foot	7.00	7.00	18.00	-	37.50
Sherbet, high, sq foot	8.00	8.00	18.00	-	-
Sherbet, high, two ball, round foot	10.00	10.00	-	-	-
Sherbet, low, one ball, round foot	9.00	8.00	-	-	15.00
Sherbet, low, round foot	12.50	7.00	-	-	-
Sherbet, low, sq foot	6.50	6.00	15.00	-	17.50
Straw Jar, 10" h	60.00	58.00	-	-	-
Sundae	9.00	9.00	-	-	-
Sugar, hexagonal, ftd	9.00	9.00	25.00	-	48.00
Sugar, low, flat	8.00	8.00	-	-	-
Sugar, sq foot	9.00	9.00	48.00	-	55.00
Sweetmeat, 5-1/2" d, ball stem	28.00	28.00	-	-	-
Sweetmeat, 8" d, ball stem	40.00	40.00	60.00	-	65.00
Tidbit, 2 tier	26.00	26.00	65.00	85.00	80.00
Toilet Bottle, 5 oz	24.00	24.00	40.00	65.00	40.00
Torte Plate, 14" d, round	35.00	30.00	48.00	-	48.00
Torte Plate, 20-1/2" round	55.00	50.00	-	-	-
Tumbler, 8 oz, water	10.00	10.00	24.00	-	24.00
Tumbler, 9 oz, round, ball, water	10.00	10.00	-	-	-
Tumbler, 9 oz, round, ftd water	10.00	10.00	-	-	-
Tumbler, 9 oz, sq foot, water	10.00	10.00	-	-	-
Urn, cov, 11" h	35.00	35.00	350.00	-	350.00
Vase, 6-1/2" h, sq foot	24.00	24.00	-	-	-
Vase, 7-1/2" h, flip	27.50	27.50	70.00	-	70.00
Vase, 7-1/2" h, flip jar with cov	55.00	55.00	85.00	-	85.00
Vase, 8" h, sq foot	35.00	35.00	-	-	-
Vase, 8-1/2" h, flared top	40.00	40.00	120.00	-	235.00
Whiskey, 1-1/2 oz	10.00	10.00	-	-	-
Whiskey, 3 oz	12.00	12.00	-	-	-
Wine, 2 oz, round foot	13.00	13.00	-	-	-
Wine, 2 oz, sq ft	15.00	15.00	35.00	-	65.00
Wine, 2-1/2 oz, ball, foot	10.00	10.00	-	-	-

Fire King: Alice

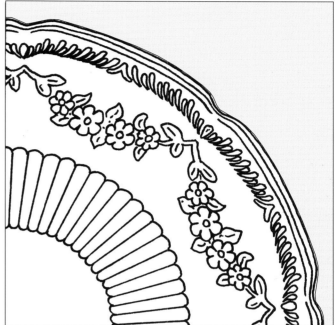

Made in Jade-ite, white with blue trim and white with red rim, early 1940s.

Item	Jade-ite	White, blue trim	White, red trim
Cup 5.00		12.00	15.00
Cup and Saucer 8.00		15.00	20.00
Plate, 9-1/2" d. 22.00		24.00	27.50
Saucer 3.00		3.00	5.00

Fire King Alice Jade-ite cup and saucer.

Fire King: Charm

Made in Azur-ite and Jade-ite, from 1954.

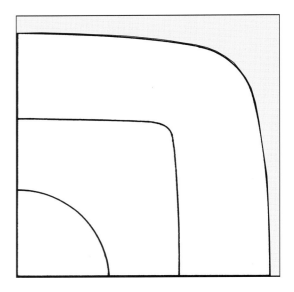

Fire King Charm blue plate, cup and saucer.

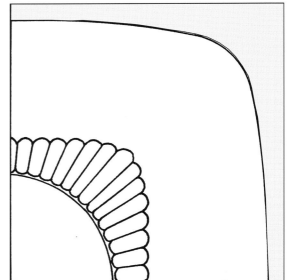

Fire King Charm cup and saucer.

Item	Azur-ite	Jade-ite
Creamer 6.50		17.00
Cup 4.50		10.00
Cup and Saucer 5.00		15.00
Dessert Bowl, 4-3/4" d 5.00		10.00
Plate, 6-5/8" d, salad. 4.00		5.00
Plate, 8-3/4" d, luncheon 7.00		9.00
Plate, 9-1/2" d, dinner 20.00		25.00
Platter, 11" x 8" 15.00		30.00
Salad Bowl, 7-3/8" d 15.00		30.00
Saucer, 5-3/8" d 1.50		2.50
Soup Bowl, 6" d 18.00		24.00
Sugar 6.00		17.00

Fire-King: Dinnerware

Jade-ite Restauraunt Ware

Made from 1950 to 1956.

Fire-King Dinnerware Jade-ite cup & saucer.

Item	Jade-ite
Batter Bowl 30.00	
Bowl, 4-7/8" d. 8.00	
Bowl, 10 oz deep 10.00	
Bowl, 15 oz, deep 12.00	
Butter Dish, cov 95.00	
Cereal Bowl, 8 oz, flanged rim 15.00	
Coffee Mug, 7 oz 6.00	
Cup, 6 oz, straight 7.00	
Cup, 7 oz, extra heavy 6.00	
Cup, 7 oz, narrow rim 6.00	
Egg Cup, double 18.00	
Fruit Bowl, 4-3/4" d 5.00	

Item	Jade-ite
Plate, 5-1/2" d, bread and butter 4.00	
Plate, 6-3/4" d, pie or salad 6.00	
Plate, 8" d, luncheon 10.00	
Plate, 8-7/8" d, oval, partitioned 20.00	
Plate, 9" d, dinner 8.00	
Plate, 9-3/4" l, oval, sandwich 12.00	
Plate, 9-5/8" d, 3 sections 8.00	
Plate, 9-5/8" d, 5 sections 10.00	
Platter, 9-1/2" d, oval 18.00	
Platter, 11-1/2" l, oval 20.00	
Saucer, 6" d 4.00	

Fire-King: Jane Ray

Made in ivory, Jade-ite, Peach Lustre, white and white with gold trim, from 1945 to 1963.

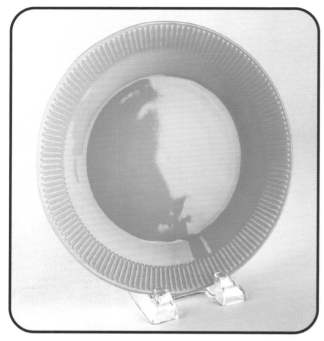

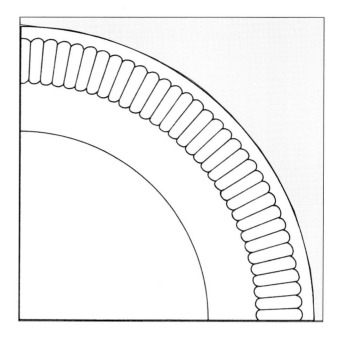

Fire-King Jane Ray Jade-ite plate.

Item	Ivory	Jade-ite	Peach Lustre	White
Cereal Bowl	8.00	11.00	-	8.00
Chili Bowl	8.00	6.00	-	8.00
Creamer	9.00	6.00	10.00	9.00
Cup	5.00	4.00	6.00	5.00
Cup, St. Denis	-	7.50	-	-
Demitasse Cup	18.00	25.00	25.00	18.00
Demitasse Saucer	20.00	25.00	25.00	20.00
Dessert Bowl, 4-7/8" d	4.00	5.50	6.00	4.00
Egg Cup, double	-	12.50	-	-
Mug	-	4.00	-	-
Oatmeal Bowl, 5-7/8" d	8.00	8.00	-	8.00
Plate, 7-3/4" d, salad	9.00	8.00	6.00	9.00
Plate, 9-1/8" d, dinner	12.00	10.00	8.00	12.00
Platter, 9" x 12"	15.00	15.00	-	15.00
Saucer	2.00	3.00	4.00	2.00
Soup Bowl	8.00	16.00	-	8.00
Soup Plate, 7-5/8" d	12.00	15.00	8.00	12.00
Sugar, cov.	10.00	12.00	10.00	10.00
Sugar cover only	5.00	6.00	-	5.00
Sugar, no lid	5.00	5.00	-	5.00
Vegetable Bowl, 8-1/4" d	14.00	18.00	-	14.00

Fire-King: Peach Luster

Laurel Leaf, Gray Laurel

Made from 1952 to 1963.

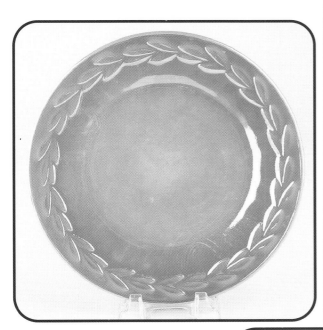

Fire-King Peach Luster
iridescent plate.

Fire-King Peach Luster iridescent
sugar and creamer.

Item	Gray Laurel	Peach Luster
Creamer	5.00	4.00
Cup	4.50	4.00
Dessert Bowl, 4-7/8" d	4.50	3.50
Plate, 7-3/8" d, salad	4.50	4.00
Plate, 9-1/8" d, dinner	8.00	5.00
Saucer, 5-3/4" d	1.00	1.00
Serving Plate, 11" d	15.00	12.50
Soup Plate, 7-5/8" d	6.00	6.50
Sugar, ftd	5.00	4.00
Vegetable Bowl, 8-1/4" d	12.00	10.00

Fire-King: Philbe

Made in blue, crystal, green and pink, from 1937 to 1938.

Fire-King Philbe green creamer.

Item	Blue	Crystal	Green	Pink
Candy Jar, cov, 4" d, low 800.00		220.00	750.00	725.00
Cereal Bowl, 5-1/2" d 65.00		20.00	42.00	42.00
Cookie Jar, cov 1,500.00		625.00	950.00	950.00
Creamer, 3-1/4", ftd 135.00		40.00	115.00	115.00
Cup 150.00		60.00	115.00	115.00
Goblet, 9 oz, 7-1/4" h 225.00		80.00	175.00	175.00
Iced Tea Tumbler, 15 oz, 6-1/2" h, ftd . . . 85.00		45.00	75.00	75.00
Juice Tumbler, 3-1/2" h, ftd 175.00		45.00	150.00	150.00
Pitcher, 36 oz, 6" h 900.00		300.00	625.00	625.00
Pitcher, 56 oz, 8-1/2" h 1,200.00		425.00	950.00	950.00
Plate, 6" d, sherbet. 75.00		35.00	60.00	60.00
Plate, 8" d, luncheon 50.00		22.00	40.00	40.00
Plate, 10-1/2" d, grill 75.00		25.00	65.00	65.00
Platter, 12" l, closed handles 175.00		40.00	125.00	125.00
Salad Bowl, 7-1/4" d. 85.00		30.00	50.00	50.00
Salver, 10-1/2" d. 80.00		25.00	55.00	55.00
Salver, 11-5/8" d. 95.00		25.00	65.00	65.00
Sandwich Plate, 10" d 110.00		30.00	65.00	65.00
Saucer, 6" d 75.00		35.00	60.00	60.00
Sugar, 3-1/4", ftd 135.00		40.00	115.00	115.00
Tumbler, 9 oz, 4" h, flat 125.00		40.00	100.00	100.00
Tumbler, 10 oz, 5-1/4" h. 95.00		35.00	75.00	75.00
Vegetable Bowl, 10" l, oval 150.00		50.00	85.00	85.00

Fire-King: Swirl

Made in Azur-ite, ivory, ivory with gold trim, ivory with red trim, Jade-ite (1960s), pink, white and white with gold trim, 1950s.

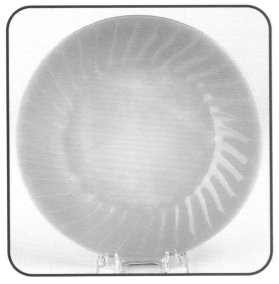

Fire-King Swirl pink plate.

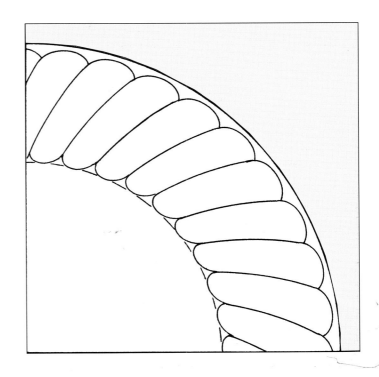

Item	Azur-ite	Ivory	Jade-ite	Pink	White	White/trim
Cereal Bowl, 6-3/8" d . . . . -	-	16.00	-	-	-	
Creamer, flat. 6.00	4.00	-	9.00	4.50	-	
Creamer, ftd . . . . -	5.00	6.00	-	5.00	6.00	
Cup 6.50	3.00	4.00	5.00	3.00	3.50	
Fruit or dessert bowl, 4-7/8" 4.60	3.00	5.00	4.60	4.00	8.00	
Iced Tea Tumbler, 12 oz 7.00	-	-	7.00	-	-	
Juice Tumbler, 1 oz 5.00	-	-	5.00	-	-	
Mixing Bowl, 6" d. . . . . -	-	12.00	-	-	-	
Mixing Bowl, 7" d. . . . . -	-	14.00	-	-	-	
Mixing Bowl, 9" d. . . . . -	-	16.00	-	-	-	
Plate, 7-1/8" d, salad 6.50	4.00	8.50	6.50	4.00	8.00	
Plate, 9-1/8" d, dinner 9.50	5.00	11.00	9.50	5.00	10.00	
Platter, 12" x 9". 18.00	7.00	-	18.00	7.00	20.00	
Saucer, 5-3/4" d 2.00	1.00	1.00	2.00	1.00	7.50	
Serving Plate, 11" d. 18.00	-	-	20.00	-	-	
Soup Plate, 7-5/8" d 9.00	8.00	8.50	12.00	4.00	5.00	
Sugar lid for flat sugar. 6.00	3.00	-	6.00	3.00	-	
Sugar lid for ftd sugar . . . . -	3.00	20.00	-	3.00	-	
Sugar, flat, tab handles 6.50	4.00	-	6.50	4.00	-	
Sugar, ftd, open handles . . . . -	3.50	30.00	-	4.00	6.00	
Tumbler, 9 oz, water 10.00	-	-	10.00	-	-	
Vegetable Bowl, 7-1/4" d 15.00	-	-	15.00	-	-	
Vegetable Bowl, 8-1/4" d 15.00	-	18.00	15.00	7.50	10.00	

Fire-King
Turquoise Blue

Made from 1957 to 1958.

Fire-King Turquoise Blue snack set in original box.

Item	Turquoise Blue
Ashtray, 3-1/2" d	6.00
Ashtray, 4-5/8" d	8.00
Ashtray, 5-3/4" d	12.00
Batter Bowl, spout	200.00
Berry Bowl, 4-1/2" d	6.00
Cereal Bowl, 5" d	14.00
Creamer	6.50
Cup	4.00
Egg Plate, 9-3/4" d	15.00
Mixing Bowl, 1 pt, tear	11.00
Mixing Bowl, 1 qt, round	13.00
Mixing Bowl, 1 qt, tear	15.00
Mixing Bowl, 2 qt, round	12.00
Mixing Bowl, 2 qt, tear	18.00
Mixing Bowl, 3 qt, round	16.00
Mixing Bowl, 3 qt, tear	20.00
Mixing Bowl, 4 qt, round	18.00
Mug, 8 oz	10.00
Plate, 6-1/8" d	12.50
Plate, 7" d	12.00
Plate, 9" d	8.00
Plate, 9" d, cup indent	7.00
Plate, 10" d, dinner	27.50
Relish, 11-1/8" l, 3 part	12.00
Saucer	1.50
Soup/Salad Bowl, 6-5/8"	18.00
Sugar	7.00
Vegetable Bowl, 8" d	15.00

Floragold

Louisa

Manufactured by Jeannette Glass Company, Jeannette, Pa., 1950s.

Made in iridescent. Some large comports were later made in ice blue, crystal, red-yellow and shell pink.

Floragold iridescent plate and ruffled berry bowl.

Item	Iridescent
Ashtray, 4" d	10.00
Bowl, 4-1/2" sq	6.50
Bowl, 5-1/4" d, ruffled	16.00
Bowl, 8-1/2" d, sq	8.00
Bowl, 8-1/2" d, ruffled	12.00
Butter Dish, cov, 1/4 pound, oblong	24.00
Butter Dish, cov, round, 5-1/2" sq base . . .	675.00
Candlesticks, pr, double branch	50.00
Candy Dish, 1 handle	15.00
Candy or Cheese Dish, cov, 6-3/4" d	110.00
Candy, 5-3/4" l, 4 feet	7.50
Celery Vase	395.00
Cereal Bowl, 5-1/2" d, round	35.00
Coaster, 4" d	10.00
Comport, 5-1/4", plain top	595.00
Comport, 5-1/4", ruffled top	695.00
Creamer	10.00
Cup	5.00
Fruit Bowl, 5-1/2" d, ruffled	8.50
Fruit Bowl, 12" d, ruffled, large	8.00
Nappy, 5" d, one handle	11.00
Pitcher, 64 oz	40.00
Plate, 5-1/4" d, sherbet	15.00
Plate, 8-1/2" d, dinner	35.00
Platter, 11-1/4" d	22.00
Salad Bowl, 9-1/2" d, deep	42.50
Salt and Pepper Shakers, pr, plastic tops . .	35.00
Saucer, 5-1/4" d	12.00
Sherbet, low, ftd	16.00
Sugar	15.00
Sugar Lid	15.00
Tidbit, wooden post	35.00
Tray, 13-1/2" d	22.50
Tray, 13-1/2" d, with indent	45.00
Tumbler, 11 oz, ftd	18.00
Tumbler, 10 oz, ftd	18.00
Tumbler, 15 oz, ftd	110.00
Vase	395.00

Floral

Poinsettia

Manufactured by Jeannette Glass Company, Jeannette, Pa., from 1931 to 1935.

Made in amber, crystal, Delphite, green, Jadite, pink, red and yellow. Production in amber, crystal, red and yellow was very limited.

Reproductions: † Reproduction salt and pepper shakers have been made in cobalt blue, dark green, green, pink and red.

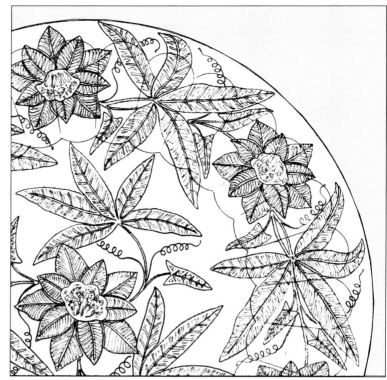

Item	Delphite	Green	Jadite	Pink
Berry Bowl, 4" d	38.00	24.50	-	22.00
Butter Dish, cov	-	90.00	-	85.00
Candlesticks, pr, 4" h	-	90.00	-	95.00
Candy Jar, cov	80.00	43.00	-	45.00
Canister Set	-	-	60.00	-
Casserole, cov	-	45.00	-	28.00
Coaster, 3-1/4" d	-	15.00	-	-
Comport, 9"	-	875.00	-	800.00
Cream Soup, 5-1/2" d	-	735.00	-	735.00
Creamer, flat	-	24.00	-	24.00
Cup	-	13.00	-	12.50
Dresser Set	-	1,250.00	-	-
Dresser Tray, 9-1/4" l, oval	-	200.00	-	-
Flower Frog	-	700.00	-	-
Ice Tub, 3-1/2" h, oval	-	850.00	-	825.00
Juice Tumbler, ftd	-	24.00	-	24.00
Juice Tumbler, 5 oz, 4" h, flat	-	35.00	-	35.00
Lamp	-	275.00	-	260.00
Lemonade Pitcher, 48 oz, 10-1/4" h	-	265.00	-	350.00
Lemonade Tumbler, 9 oz, 5-1/4" h, ftd	-	60.00	-	55.00
Pitcher, 23 or 24 oz, 5-1/2" h	-	50.00	-	-
Pitcher, 32 oz, ftd, cone, 8" h	-	36.00	-	42.00
Plate, 6" d, sherbet	-	7.50	-	6.00
Plate, 8" d, salad	-	15.00	-	14.50
Plate, 9" d, dinner	145.00	30.00	-	20.00
Plate, 9" d, grill	-	185.00	-	-
Plate, 10-3/4" l, oval	-	20.00	-	17.50
Platter, 11" l	150.00	24.00	-	23.00
Refrigerator Dish, cov, 5" sq	-	-	15.00	-
Relish, 2 part oval	165.00	24.00	-	18.50

Item	Delphite	Green	Jadite	Pink
Rose Bowl, 3 legs . . . . -		500.00	-	-
Salad Bowl, 7-1/2" d . . . . -		32.50	-	20.00
Salad Bowl, 7-1/2" d, ruffled. 65.00		125.00	-	120.00
Salt and Pepper Shakers, pr, 4" h, ftd † . . . . . -		45.00	-	45.00
Salt and Pepper Shakers, pr, 6" flat . . . . -		-	-	60.00
Saucer . . . . -		12.50	-	10.00
Sherbet 90.00		18.00	-	20.00
Sugar, cov . . . . -		25.00	-	30.00
Sugar, open 75.00		-	-	-
Tray, 6" sq, closed handles . . . . -		195.00	-	-
Tumbler, 3 oz, 3-1/2" h, ftd. . . . . -		18.00	-	24.00
Tumbler, 7 oz, 4-1/2", ftd 175.00		22.00	-	22.50
Tumbler, 5-1/4" h, ftd . . . . -		60.00	-	55.00
Vase, flared, 3 legs . . . . -		485.00	-	-
Vase, 6-7/8" h . . . . -		475.00	-	-
Vegetable Bowl, 8" d, cov . . . . -		50.00	-	40.00
Vegetable Bowl, 8" d, open. 80.00		-	-	30.00
Vegetable Bowl, 9" l, oval . . . . -		32.00	-	35.00

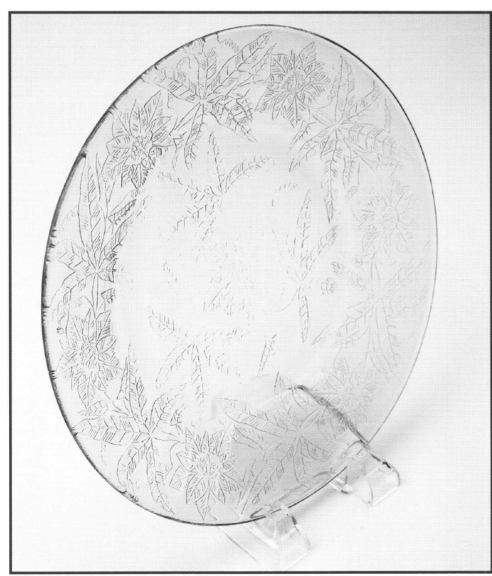

Floral pink plate.

Floral and Diamond Band

Manufactured by U.S. Glass Company, Pittsburgh, late 1920s.

Made in pink and green with limited production in black, crystal and iridescent.

Floral and Diamond Band green plate.

Item	Green	Pink
Berry Bowl, 4-1/2" d	8.00	7.00
Berry Bowl, 8" d	12.00	13.00
Butter Dish, cov	120.00	125.00
Compote, 5-1/2" h	16.50	15.00
Creamer, 4-3/4"	20.00	17.50
Iced Tea Tumbler, 5" h	38.00	32.50

Item	Green	Pink
Nappy, 5-3/4" d, handle	12.00	11.00
Pitcher, 42 oz, 8" h	95.00	90.00
Plate, 8" d, luncheon	40.00	40.00
Sherbet	7.00	6.50
Sugar, 5-1/4"	15.00	14.00
Tumbler, 4" h, water	24.00	22.00

Florentine No. 1

Old Florentine, Poppy No. 1

Manufactured by Hazel Atlas Glass Company, Clarksburg, W.V., and Zanesville, Ohio, from 1932 to 1935.

Made in crystal, green, pink, yellow and limited production in cobalt blue.

Reproductions: † Salt and pepper shakers have been reproduced in cobalt blue, pink and red.

Florentine No. 1 green creamer and covered sugar.

Item	Cobalt Blue	Crystal	Green	Pink	Yellow
Ashtray, 5-1/2" d	-	22.00	24.00	27.50	28.00
Berry Bowl, 5" d	18.00	11.00	12.00	14.00	15.00
Berry Bowl, 8-1/2" d	-	24.00	25.00	28.00	28.00
Butter Dish, cov	-	110.00	115.00	165.00	160.00
Cereal Bowl, 6" d	-	20.00	20.00	22.00	24.00
Coaster/Ashtray, 3-3/4" d	-	18.00	20.00	25.00	25.00
Comport, 3-1/2" h, ruffled	60.00	25.00	25.00	15.00	-
Cream Soup, 5" d, ruffled	50.00	12.00	14.00	18.00	-
Creamer	-	8.00	8.00	25.00	18.00
Creamer, ruffled	65.00	33.00	35.00	37.00	-
Cup	85.00	8.00	8.00	9.00	10.00
Iced Tea Tumbler, 12 oz, 5-1/4" h, ftd	-	28.00	28.00	30.00	24.00
Juice Tumbler, 5 oz, 3-3/4" h, ftd	-	16.00	16.00	20.00	22.00
Lemonade Tumbler, 9 oz, 5-1/4" h	-	-	-	100.00	-
Pitcher, 36 oz, 6-1/2", ftd	850.00	40.00	40.00	50.00	45.00
Pitcher, 48 oz, 7-1/2", flat, with or without ice lip	-	70.00	72.00	115.00	175.00
Plate, 6" d, sherbet	-	6.50	7.00	6.50	7.00
Plate, 8-1/2" d, salad	-	7.50	8.00	12.00	12.00
Plate, 10" d, dinner	-	16.00	16.00	22.00	24.00
Plate, 10" d, grill	-	12.00	12.50	20.00	22.00
Platter, 11-1/2" l, oval	-	19.00	10.00	22.00	28.00
Salt and Pepper Shakers, pr, ftd †	-	22.00	32.00	55.00	58.00
Saucer	18.00	3.50	3.50	4.00	3.00
Sherbet, 3 oz, ftd	-	7.50	7.50	10.00	16.00
Sugar, cov	-	8.00	8.50	25.00	12.00
Sugar, ruffled	55.00	30.00	30.00	35.00	-
Tumbler, 4 oz, 3-1/4" h, ftd	-	15.00	16.00	-	-
Tumbler, 9 oz, 4" h, ribbed	-	14.00	14.00	22.00	-
Tumbler, 10 oz, 4-3/4" h, ftd	-	22.00	20.00	22.00	23.00
Vegetable Bowl, cov, 9-1/2" l, oval	-	40.00	40.00	60.00	60.00

Florentine No. 2

Poppy No. 2

Manufactured by Hazel Atlas Glass Company, Clarksburg, W.V., and Zanesville, Ohio, from 1932 to 1935.

Made in amber, cobalt blue, crystal, green, ice blue, pink and yellow. Ice blue production is limited to 7-1/2" h pitcher, valued at $525. Amber production is limited to 9 oz and 12 oz tumblers, both currently valued at $80; cup and saucer, valued at $75; and sherbet, valued at $45. Cobalt blue production is limited to 3-1/2" comport, valued at $60 and 9 oz tumbler, valued at $80.

Reproductions: † 7-1/2" h cone-shaped pitcher and 4" h ftd tumbler. Reproductions found in cobalt blue, crystal, deep green and pink.

Item	Crystal	Green	Pink	Yellow
Ashtray, 3-1/2" d	18.00	18.00	-	25.00
Ashtray, 5-1/2" d	20.00	25.00	-	35.00
Berry Bowl, 4-1/2" d	12.00	15.00	17.50	22.50
Berry Bowl, 8" d	24.00	26.00	30.00	35.00
Bowl, 5-1/2" d	32.00	35.00	-	42.00
Bowl, 7-1/2" d, shallow	-	-	-	85.00
Bowl, 9" d, flat	27.50	27.50	-	-
Butter Dish, cov	100.00	115.00	-	155.00
Candlesticks, pr, 2-3/4" h	45.00	48.00	-	60.00
Candy Dish, cov	100.00	95.00	95.00	150.00
Cereal Bowl, 6" d	26.00	26.00	-	38.00
Coaster, 3-1/4" d	-	-	-	22.50
Coaster, 3-3/4" d	18.00	18.00	-	25.00
Coaster, 5-1/2" d	20.00	25.00	-	35.00
Cocktail, 3-1/4" h, ftd	-	-	-	12.00
Comport, 3-1/2" d, ruffled	25.00	25.00	25.00	-
Condiment Tray, round	-	-	-	65.00
Cream Soup, 4-3/4" d, 2 handles	14.00	16.00	18.00	20.00
Creamer	8.00	11.00	-	12.00
Cup	7.50	7.50	-	10.00
Custard Cup	60.00	60.00	-	85.00
Gravy Boat	-	-	-	50.00
Gravy Boat Underplate, 11-1/2" l	-	-	-	115.00
Iced Tea Tumbler, 12 oz, 5" h	35.00	35.00	-	45.00
Juice Tumbler, 5 oz, 3-1/8" h, flat	12.00	12.00	12.00	22.00

Item	Crystal	Green	Pink	Yellow
Juice Tumbler, 5 oz, 3-1/8" h, ftd	13.00	15.00	-	21.00
Parfait, 6" h	30.00	32.00	-	60.00
Pitcher, 24 oz, cone, ftd, 6-1/4" h	-	-	-	35.00
Pitcher, 28 oz, cone ftd, 7-1/2" h †	32.00	35.00	-	42.00
Pitcher, 48 oz, 7-1/2" h	60.00	70.00	120.00	32.00
Pitcher, 76 oz, 8-1/4" h	90.00	95.00	225.00	400.00
Plate, 6" d, sherbet	4.00	4.00	-	6.50
Plate, 6-1/2" d, indent	16.00	17.50	-	30.00
Plate, 8-1/2" d, salad	8.50	9.00	9.00	10.00
Plate, 10" d, dinner	14.00	16.00	-	19.00
Plate, 10-1/4" d, grill	15.00	15.00	-	12.00
Plate, 10-1/4" d, grill, cream soup ring	35.00	35.00	-	-
Platter, 11" oval	15.00	16.00	18.00	24.00
Relish, 10" d, divided, 3 part	20.00	22.50	24.00	30.00
Relish, 10" d, plain	20.00	20.00	24.00	30.00
Salt and Pepper Shakers, pr	45.00	45.00	-	55.00
Saucer	5.00	4.00	-	3.50
Sherbet, ftd	10.00	10.00	-	12.00
Sugar, cov	8.50	9.00	-	38.00
Tumbler, 5 oz, 3-1/4" h, ftd	15.00	15.00	15.00	-
Tumbler, 5 oz, 4" h, ftd †	13.00	13.00	17.50	16.50
Tumbler, 5 oz, 3-5/16" h, blown	18.00	18.00	-	-
Tumbler, 6 oz, 3-9/16" h, blown	16.00	18.00	-	-
Tumbler, 9 oz, 4" h	12.00	18.00	16.00	22.50
Tumbler, 9 oz, 4-1/2" h, ftd	25.00	25.00	-	38.00
Tumbler, 10 oz, 4-11/16, blown	19.00	19.00	-	-
Tumbler, 12 oz, 5" h, blown	20.00	20.00	-	20.00
Vase, 6" h	30.00	32.00	-	60.00
Vegetable Bowl, cov, 9" l, oval	55.00	60.00	-	65.00

Florentine No. 2 yellow cup.

REPRODUCTION! Florentine No. 2 green pitcher and tumbler.

Flower Garden with Butterflies

Butterflies and Roses

Manufactured by U.S. Glass Company, Pittsburgh, late 1920s.

Made in amber, black, blue, blue-green, canary yellow, crystal, green and pink.

Item	Amber or Crystal	Black	Blue-Green, Green or Pink	Blue or Canary Yellow
Ashtray	175.00	-	185.00	195.00
Bonbon, cov, 6-5/8" d	-	265.00	-	-
Bowl, 9" d, rolled edge	-	225.00	-	-
Candlesticks, pr, 4" h	50.00	-	60.00	100.00
Candlesticks, pr, 8" h	80.00	285.00	145.00	145.00
Candy, cov, 6" d, flat	135.00	-	165.00	-
Candy, cov, 7-1/2" cone shape	90.00	100.00	165.00	175.00
Candy, cov, heart shape	-	-	1,750.00	3,200.00
Cologne Bottle, 7-1/2" h	-	-	195.00	350.00
Comport, 2-7/8" h	-	250.00	40.00	45.00
Comport, 3" h	25.00	-	30.00	35.00
Comport, 4-1/4" h, 4-3/4" w	-	-	-	65.00
Comport, 4-3/4" h, 10-1/4" w	50.00	250.00	70.00	90.00
Comport, 5-7/8" h, 11" w	60.00	-	-	95.00
Comport, 7-1/4" h, 8-1/4" w	65.00	175.00	85.00	-
Creamer	-	-	75.00	-
Cup	-	-	70.00	-

Flower Garden with Butterflies blue compote.

Item	Amber or Crystal	Black	Blue-Green, Green or Pink	Blue or Canary Yellow
Mayonnaise, ftd, 4-3/4" h, 6-1/4" w, 7" d plate, ladle	70.00	-	85.00	125.00
Orange Bowl, 11" d, ftd	-	250.00	-	-
Plate, 7" d	20.00	-	25.00	30.00
Plate, 8" d	17.50	-	20.00	27.50
Plate, 10" d	-	-	45.00	50.00
Plate, 10" d, indent	35.00	150.00	45.00	50.00
Powder Jar, 3-1/2", flat	-	-	75.00	-
Powder Jar, 6-1/4" h, ftd	80.00	-	130.00	175.00
Powder Jar, 7-1/2" h, ftd	85.00	-	135.00	195.00
Sandwich Server, center handle	55.00	135.00	75.00	100.00
Saucer	-	-	30.00	-
Tray, 5-1/2" x 10", oval	50.00	-	75.00	9.00
Tray, 11-3/4" x 7-3/4", rect	50.00	-	75.00	90.00
Tumbler, 7-1/2 oz	175.00	-	-	-
Vase, 6-1/4" h	75.00	145.00	135.00	145.00
Vase, 8" h, Dahlia, cupped	-	225.00	-	-
Vase, 10" h, 2 handles	-	245.00	-	-
Vase, 10-1/2" h	-	-	140.00	225.00
Wall Pocket, 9" l	-	350.00	-	-

Forest Green

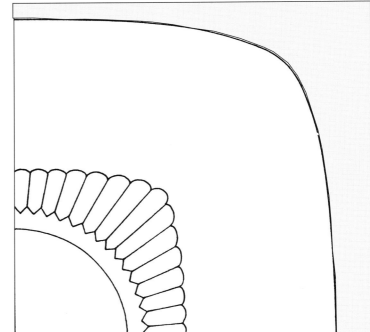

Manufactured by Anchor Hocking Glass Company, Lancaster, Ohio, and Long Island City, N.Y., from 1950 to 1957.

Made only in forest green.

Item	Forest Green
Ashtray, 3-1/2" sq	3.50
Ashtray, 4-5/8" sq	5.50
Ashtray, 5-3/4" hexagon	8.00
Ashtray, 5-3/4" sq	7.50
Batter Bowl, spout	25.00
Berry Bowl, large	15.00
Berry Bowl, small	5.50
Bowl, 4-1/2" w, sq	5.50
Bowl, 5-1/4" deep	8.00
Bowl, 6" w, sq	18.00
Bowl, 6-1/2" d, scalloped	9.00
Bowl, 7-3/8" w, sq	30.00
Bowl, 7-1/2" d, crimped	10.00
Cocktail, 3-1/2 oz	12.00
Cocktail, 4-1/2 oz	14.00
Creamer, flat	7.50
Cup, sq	7.00
Dessert Bowl, 4-3/4" d	5.00
Goblet, 9 oz	10.00
Goblet, 9-1/2 oz	14.00
Iced Tea Tumbler, 13 oz	8.00
Iced Tea Tumbler, 14 oz, Boopie	8.00
Iced Tea Tumbler, 15 oz, tall	10.00
Iced Tea Tumbler, 32 oz, giant	18.00
Ivy Ball, 4" h	5.00
Juice Tumbler, 4 oz	10.00
Juice Tumbler, 5-1/2 oz	12.50
Juice Roly Poly Tumbler, 3-3/8" h	5.00
Ladle, all green glass	80.00
Mixing Bowl, 6" d	8.00
Pitcher, 22 oz	22.50
Pitcher, 36 oz	25.00

Forest Green tumbler.

Item	Forest Green
Pitcher, 86 oz, round	45.00
Plate, 6-3/4" d, salad	7.50
Plate, 7" w, sq	6.75
Plate, 8-3/8" d, luncheon	7.00
Plate, 9-1/4" d, dinner	30.00
Platter, 11" l, rect	22.00
Popcorn Bowl, 5-1/4" d	10.00
Punch Bowl	25.00
Punch Bowl and Stand	45.00
Punch Cup	2.25
Roly Poly Tumbler, 5 1/8" h	6.50
Salad Bowl, 7-3/8" d	12.00
Saucer, 5-3/8" w	3.00
Sherbet, 6 oz	9.00
Sherbet, 6 oz, Boopie	7.00
Sherbet, flat	7.50
Soup Bowl, 6" d	17.00
Sugar, flat	7.00
Tray, 6" x 10", 2 handles	30.00
Tumbler, 5 oz, 3-1/2" h	4.00
Tumbler, 7 oz	4.50
Tumbler, 5-1/4" h	4.00
Tumbler, 9-1/2 oz, tall	8.00
Tumbler, 9 oz, fancy	7.00
Tumbler, 9 oz, table	5.00
Tumbler, 10 oz, 4-1/2" h, ftd	7.50
Tumbler, 11 oz	7.00
Tumbler, 14 oz, 5" h	8.00
Tumbler, 15 oz, long boy	10.00
Vase, 6-3/8" h	4.00
Vase, 9" h	8.00
Vegetable Bowl, 8-1/2" l, oval	24.00

Fortune

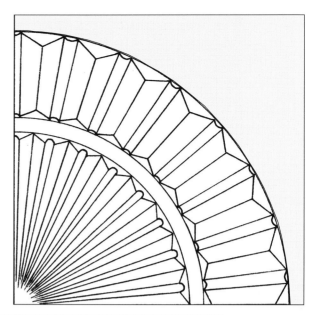

Manufactured by Hocking Glass Company, Lancaster, Ohio, from 1937 to 1938. Made in crystal and pink.

Fortune pink fruit bowl.

Item	Crystal	Pink
Berry Bowl, 4" d	5.00	6.00
Berry Bowl, 7- 3/4" d	15.00	15.00
Bowl, 4-1/2" d, handle	4.50	4.50
Bowl, 5-1/4" d, rolled edge	6.00	6.50
Candy Dish, cov, flat	22.50	25.00
Cup	7.50	10.00
Dessert Bowl, 4-1/2" d	4.50	4.50
Juice Tumbler, 5 oz, 3-1/2" h	8.00	10.00
Plate, 6" d, salad	5.00	12.50
Plate, 8" d, luncheon	17.50	17.50
Salad Bowl, 7-3/4" d	15.00	15.00
Saucer	4.00	6.50
Tumbler, 9 oz, 4" h	10.00	10.00

Fruits

Manufactured by Hazel Atlas Company, and several other small glass companies, from 1931 to 1935.

Made in crystal, green, iridized, and pink. Iridized production includes only a 4" tumbler, valued at $10.

Fruits green cup and saucer.

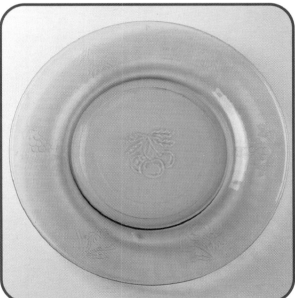

Fruits green plate.

Item	Crystal	Green	Pink
Berry Bowl, 5" d	14.00	28.00	22.00
Berry Bowl, 8" d	30.00	60.00	40.00
Cup	5.00	10.00	7.00
Juice Tumbler, 5 oz, 3-1/2" h	12.00	24.00	22.00
Pitcher, 7" h	45.00	85.00	-
Plate, 8" d, luncheon	3.00	7.00	6.50
Saucer	2.50	5.00	4.50
Sherbet	4.50	9.00	7.50
Tumbler, 4" h, multiple fruits	14.00	28.00	22.00
Tumbler, 4" h, single fruit	10.00	20.00	17.50
Tumbler, 12 oz, 5" h	70.00	140.00	95.00

Georgian *Lovebirds*

Manufactured by Federal Glass Company, Columbus, Ohio, from 1931 to 1936.

Made in green. A crystal hot plate is valued at $25.

Georgian green sherbet.

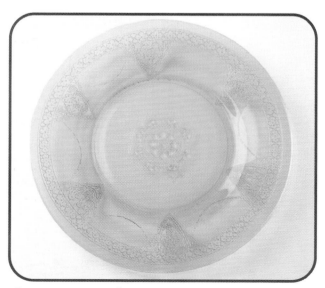

Georgian green plate.

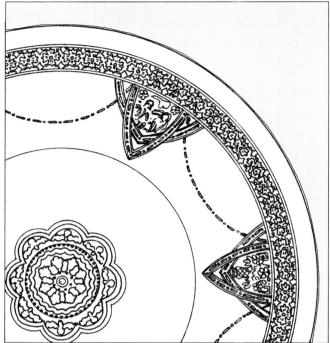

Item	Green
Berry Bowl, 4-1/2" d	7.00
Berry Bowl, 7-1/2" d, large	62.00
Bowl, 6-1/2" d, deep	65.00
Butter Dish, cov	80.00
Cereal Bowl, 5-3/4" d	26.00
Cold Cuts Server, 18-1/2" d, wood, seven openings for 5" d coasters	825.00
Creamer, 3" d, ftd	15.00
Creamer, 4" d, ftd	15.00
Cup	6.50
Cup and Saucer	12.50
Hot Plate, 5" d, center design	48.00
Plate, 6" d, sherbet	6.50
Plate, 8" d, luncheon	10.00
Plate, 9-1/4" d, center design only	25.00
Plate, 9-1/4" d, dinner	30.00
Platter, 11-1/2" l, closed handle	70.00
Saucer	3.50
Sherbet, ftd	16.00
Sugar Cover, 3" d	35.00
Sugar Cover, 4" d	35.00
Sugar, 3" d, ftd	15.00
Sugar, 4" d, ftd	15.00
Tumbler, 9 oz, 4" h, flat	60.00
Tumbler 12 oz, 5-1/4" h, flat	135.00
Vegetable Bowl, 9" l, oval	65.00

Golf Ball #7643

Manufactured by Morgantown Glass, Morgantown, W.V., from 1928 to 1971.

Made in Anna Rose (Pink Champagne), Azure (Gloria Blue), Caramel, Cobalt, Copen Blue, crystal, 14K Topaz (Topaz Mist), India Black, Light Amethyst, Meadow Green (crystal ball and foot), Mission Gold, Old Amethyst, Peach (non-opaque), Ritz Blue, Ruby, Smoke, Spanish Red, Stiegel Green and Venetian Green (Shamrock). There was some production in all-Alabaster (opalescent milk glass) in stemware and vases during the late 1920s and early 1930s.

Decorations include gold and platinum #769 Sparta etching, Berne (platinum #12 border) on Spanish Red; Vernay (platinum #12 border) on Ritz Blue; Avon, Chateau, Eton, Gorton and Toland cuttings; special crest, logo and slogan cuttings, Lotus Decorating Co. silver overlay Hunt Scene. To calculate values for etched pieces, increase crystal by 35% and colors as much as 100% higher. Values for pieces with cuttings, increase value of crystal by 25% and colored wares about 50% higher.

Item	Crystal	India Black	Pastels	Ritz Blue	Spanish Red	Stiegel Green
Bell, 5-1/2" h	-	-	-	225.00	-	-
Bonbon, #2938, Helga, 5-1/4" d	-	375.00	500.00	400.00	400.00	375.00
Bonbon, #7758, Leora, 5" d	-	360.00	-	385.00	385.00	360.00
Bonbon, #9074, Maureen, 4-1/2" d	-	365.00	365.00	385.00	385.00	365.00
Box, cov, #1212, Michael, 7" d	-	-	-	375.00	375.00	-
Brandy Snifter, 21 oz, 6-1/2" h	-	-	-	165.00	185.00	145.00
Cafe Parfait, 5 oz, 6-1/4" h	48.00	-	48.00	70.00	65.00	55.00
Candleholder, 4" h, Jacobi, price for pr	-	255.00	235.00	265.00	265.00	255.00
Candleholder, 4-5/8" h, Dupont, price for pr	-	-	285.00	-	-	-
Candleholder, 6" h, torch, single	-	-	-	225.00	225.00	200.00
Candy Jar, cov, Fairway, 22 oz, 14-1/2"	-	325.00	-	345.00	325.00	325.00
Champagne, 5-1/2 oz, 5" h	35.00	-	40.00	48.00	45.00	40.00
Claret, 4-1/2 oz, 5-1/4" h	45.00	-	52.00	68.00	55.00	55.00
Compote, cov, Celeste, 6" d	-	285.00	285.00	285.00	285.00	260.00
Compote, open, Celeste, 6" d	-	190.00	175.00	21.00	190.00	175.00
Cordial, 1-1/2 oz, 3-1/2" h	40.00	-	48.00	58.00	55.00	48.00
Creamer and Sugar	-	-	255.00	285.00	285.00	285.00
Goblet, 9 oz, 6-3/4" h	38.00	-	45.00	55.00	50.00	45.00
Iced Tea Tumbler, 12 oz, 6-3/4" h, ftd	35.00	-	45.00	50.00	48.00	45.00
Irish Coffee, 6 oz, 5-1/4" h	-	-	-	95.00	-	-
Ivy Ball, #7643, Kennon, 4" d	-	-	-	85.00	85.00	85.00

Item	Crystal	India Black	Pastels	Ritz Blue	Spanish Red	Stiegel Green
Ivy Ball, #7643, Kimball, 4" d . . . . -		-	-	85.00	85.00	85.00
Juice Tumbler, 5 oz, 5" h, ftd 32.00		-	45.00	45.00	45.00	42.00
Lamp, 7643, Amherst . . . . -		-	-	-	-	625.00
Liquor Cocktail, 3-1/2 oz, 4-1/8" h 28.00		-	38.00	38.00	38.00	38.00
Luncheon Tumbler/Goblet, 9 oz, 6-1/8" h, ftd 30.00		-	42.00	55.00	48.00	45.00
Oyster Cocktail, 4 oz, 4-1/4" h, flared . . . 40.00		-	-	55.00	50.00	48.00
Oyster Cocktail, 4-1/2 oz, 4-3/8" h, cupped 40.00		-	-	55.00	50.00	48.00
Pilsner, 11 oz, 9-1/8" h 100.00		-	-	125.00	-	-
Schooner, 32 oz 245.00		-	-	-	-	-
Sherbet/Sundae, 5-1/2 oz, 4-1/8" h 28.00		-	35.00	45.00	38.00	35.00
Sherry, 2-1/2" oz, 4-5/8" h 40.00		-	45.00	60.00	55.00	50.00
Vase, 6-1/2" h, #7643, urn . . . . -		-	-	125.00	125.00	110.00
Vase, 6-1/2" h, #7643-1/2, urn, Stephanie		-	-	165.00	165.00	145.00
Vase, 8" h, #7643, Charlotte . . . . -		-	175.00	165.00	165.00	165.00
Vase, 9-1/2" h, #79, Montague . . . . -		-	-	255.00	255.00	240.00
Vase, 10-1/2" h, #78, Lancaster . . . . -		-	-	245.00	245.00	245.00
Wine Tumbler, 2-1/2 oz, 4-3/8" h, ftd. . . . 32.00		-	45.00	45.00	45.00	42.00
Wine, 3 oz, 4-3/4" h 42.00		-	50.00	65.00	56.00	50.00

Golf Ball Spanish Red goblet.

Harp

Manufactured by Jeannette Glass Company, Jeannette, Pa., from 1954 to 1957.

Made in crystal, crystal with gold trim, limited pieces made in ice blue, iridescent white, pink and shell pink.

Item	Crystal	Other Colors
Ashtray	4.50	-
Cake Stand, 9" d.	25.00	35.00
Coaster	4.50	-
Cup	26.00	-
Parfait	18.50	-
Plate, 7" d.	14.00	12.00
Saucer	10.00	-
Snack Set, cup, saucer, 7" plate	47.00	-
Tray, 2 handles, rectangular	35.00	30.00
Vase, 7-1/2" h	25.00	-

Harp crystal, gold-edge plate and cake stand.

Heritage

Manufactured by Federal Glass Company,
Columbus, Ohio, from 1940 to 1955.
Made in blue, crystal, green and pink.

Item	Blue	Crystal	Green	Pink
Berry Bowl, 5" d	55.00	8.00	50.00	42.00
Berry Bowl, 8-1/2" d	190.00	45.00	190.00	115.00
Creamer, ftd.	-	30.00	-	-
Cup	-	7.00	-	-
Fruit Bowl, 10-1/2" d	-	15.00	-	-
Plate, 8" d, luncheon	-	8.50	-	-
Plate, 9-1/4" d, dinner	-	12.00	-	-
Sandwich Plate, 12" d	-	15.00	-	-
Saucer	-	4.00	-	-
Sugar, open, ftd	-	22.00	-	-

Heritage crystal cup and saucer.

Heritage crystal plate.

Hex Optic *Honeycomb*

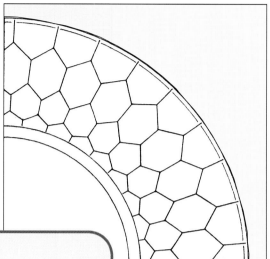

Manufactured by Jeannette Glass Company, Jeannette, Pa., from 1928 to 1932.

Made in green and green. Ultramarine tumblers have been found. Iridescent tumblers and pitchers were made about 1960 and it is assumed that they were made by Jeannette.

Hex Optic green plate and ice tub.

Item	Green	Pink
Berry Bowl, 4-1/4" d, ruffled	5.50	6.00
Berry Bowl, 7-1/2" d	8.00	8.00
Bucket Reamer	60.00	50.00
Butter Dish, cov, rect, 1 lb size .	75.00	72.00
Creamer, two style handles	6.00	7.00
Cup, two style handles	5.00	5.00
Ice Bucket, metal handle	20.00	20.00
Mixing Bowl, 7-1/4" d	14.00	14.00
Mixing Bowl, 8-1/4" d	16.00	16.00
Mixing Bowl, 9" d	18.00	18.00
Mixing Bowl, 10" d	20.00	20.00
Pitcher, 32 oz, 5" h	24.00	24.00
Pitcher, 48 oz, 9" h, ftd	48.00	50.00
Pitcher, 96 oz, 8" h	235.00	245.00
Plate, 6" d, sherbet	3.00	3.00

Item	Green	Pink
Plate, 8" d, luncheon	6.00	6.00
Platter, 11" d, round	14.00	16.00
Refrigerator Dish, 4" x 4"	10.00	10.00
Refrigerator Stack Set, 4 pc	60.00	60.00
Salt and Pepper Shakers, pr. . . .	30.00	30.00
Saucer.	4.00	4.00
Sherbet, 5 oz, ftd.	5.00	5.00
Sugar, two styles of handles	6.00	6.00
Sugar Shaker.	175.00	175.00
Tumbler, 12 oz, 5" h	8.00	8.00
Tumbler, 5-3/4" h, ftd.	10.00	10.00
Tumbler, 7" h, ftd	12.00	12.00
Tumbler, 7 oz, 4-3/4" h, ftd	8.00	8.00
Tumbler, 9 oz, 3-3/4" h	5.00	5.00
Whiskey, 1 oz, 2" h	8.50	8.50

Hobnail

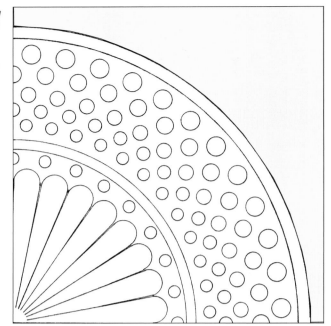

Manufactured by Hocking Glass Company, Lancaster, Ohio, from 1934 to 1936.

Made in crystal, crystal with red trim and pink.

Hobnail pink sherbet.

Item	Crystal	Crystal, red trim	Pink
Cereal Bowl, 5-1/2" d	4.25	4.25	-
Cordial, 5 oz, ftd	6.00	6.00	-
Creamer, ftd	4.00	4.00	-
Cup	4.00	4.00	5.00
Decanter and stopper, 32 oz	27.50	27.50	-
Goblet, 10 oz	7.50	7.50	-
Iced Tea Goblet, 13 oz	8.50	8.50	-
Iced Tea Tumbler, 15 oz	8.50	8.50	-
Juice Tumbler, 5 oz	4.00	4.00	-
Milk Pitcher, 18 oz	22.00	22.00	-
Pitcher, 67 oz	25.00	25.00	-
Plate, 6" d, sherbet	2.00	2.00	3.00
Plate, 8-1/2" d, luncheon	5.50	5.50	4.50
Salad Bowl, 7" d	5.00	5.00	-
Saucer	2.00	2.00	3.00
Sherbet	4.00	4.00	5.00
Sugar, ftd	4.00	4.00	-
Tumbler, 9 oz, 4-3/4" h, flat	5.00	5.00	-
Whiskey, 1-1/2 oz	5.00	5.00	-
Wine, 3 oz, ftd	6.50	6.50	-

Holiday

Button and Bows

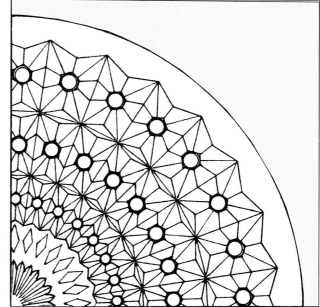

Manufactured by Jeannette Glass Company, Jeannette, Pa., from 1947 to the 1950s.

Made in crystal, iridescent, pink and shell pink. Shell pink production was limited to the console bowl, valued at $45. In crystal look for a pitcher, 16 oz, 4-3/4" h, for $17.50; and a tumbler, 5-1/4 oz, 4-1/4" h, ftd, for $8. In iridescent, there is a pitcher, 16 oz, 4-3/4" h, for $35; a platter, 11-3/8" l, oval, for $12.50; a sandwich tray, 10-1/ 2" l, for $17.50; and a tumbler, 5 oz, 4" h, ftd, for $10.

Holiday pink water pitcher.

Item	Pink
Berry Bowl, 5-1/8" d	14.00
Berry Bowl, 8-1/2" d	25.00
Butter Dish, cov	45.00
Cake Plate, 10-1/2" d, 3 legs	100.00
Candlesticks, pr, 3" h	110.00
Chop Plate, 13-3/4" d	100.00
Console Bowl, 10-1/4" d	120.00
Creamer, ftd	12.50
Cup, plain	3.50
Cup, rayed bottom, 2" d base	7.50
Cup, rayed bottom, 2-3/8" d base	10.00
Juice Tumbler, 5 oz, 4" h, ftd	55.00
Pitcher, 16 oz, 4-3/4" h	60.00
Pitcher, 52 oz, 6-3/4" h	42.00
Plate, 6" d, sherbet	6.00
Plate, 9" d, dinner	17.50
Platter, 11-3/8" l, oval	22.00
Sandwich Tray, 10-1/ 2" l	23.00
Saucer, plain center	4.00
Saucer, rayed center, 2-1/8" d ring	6.00
Saucer, rayed center, 2-1/2" d ring	6.00
Sherbet	8.50
Soup Bowl, 7-3/4" d	50.00
Sugar, cov	25.00
Sugar Lid	16.00
Tumbler, 5 oz, 4" h, ftd	35.00
Tumbler, 5-1/4 oz, 4-1/4" h, ftd	45.00
Tumbler, 6" h, ftd	195.00
Tumbler, 9 oz, 4" h, ftd	25.00
Tumbler, 10 oz, 4" h, flat	24.00
Vegetable Bowl, 9-1/2" l, oval	19.00

Homespun **Fine Rib**

Manufactured by Jeannette Glass Company, Jeannette, Pa., from 1939 to 1949.

Made in crystal and pink.

Item	Crystal	Pink
Ashtray	6.00	6.00
Berry Bowl, 4-1/2" d, closed handles	12.00	13.00
Berry Bowl, 8-1/4" d	20.00	20.00
Butter Dish, cov	50.00	55.00
Cereal Bowl, 5" d, closed handles	25.00	25.00
Coaster	6.00	6.00
Creamer, ftd	12.50	12.50
Cup	12.00	12.00
Iced Tea Tumbler, 13 oz, 5-1/4" h	32.00	32.00
Plate, 6" d, sherbet	7.50	7.50
Plate, 9-1/4" d, dinner	17.00	17.00
Platter, 13" d, closed handles	18.00	18.00
Saucer	5.50	5.50
Sherbet, low, flat	17.50	19.00
Sugar, ftd	12.50	12.50
Tumbler, 5 oz, 4" h, ftd	8.00	8.00
Tumbler, 6 oz, 3-7/8" h, straight	7.00	7.00
Tumbler, 9 oz, 4" h, flared top	17.50	17.50
Tumbler, 9 oz, 4-1/4" h, band at top	17.50	17.50
Tumbler, 15 oz, 6-1/4" h, ftd	38.00	38.00
Tumbler, 15 oz, 6-3/8" h, ftd	36.00	36.00

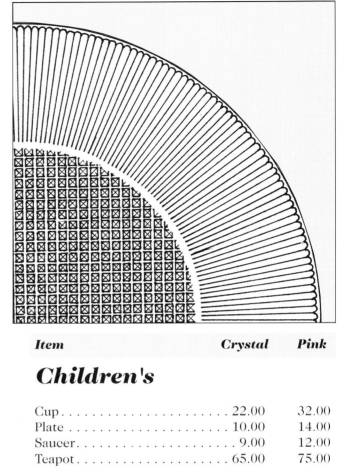

Item	Crystal	Pink
Children's		
Cup	22.00	32.00
Plate	10.00	14.00
Saucer	9.00	12.00
Teapot	65.00	75.00

Homespun pink sugar and tumbler.

Horseshoe *No. 612*

Manufactured by Indiana Glass Company, Dunkirk, Ind., from 1930 to 1933.

Made in crystal, green, pink and yellow. Limited collector interest in crystal and pink at the current time.

Item	Green	Yellow
Berry Bowl, 4-1/2" d	25.00	20.00
Berry Bowl, 9-1/2" d	30.00	35.00
Butter Dish, cov	750.00	-
Candy Dish, metal holder	175.00	-
Cereal Bowl, 6-1/2" d	25.00	25.00
Creamer, ftd	18.00	20.00
Cup and Saucer	16.00	17.50
Pitcher, 64 oz, 8-1/2" h	250.00	300.00
Plate, 6" d, sherbet	9.00	9.00
Plate, 8-3/8" d, salad	10.00	10.00
Plate, 9-3/8" d, luncheon	13.00	15.00
Plate, 10-3/8" d, grill	85.00	85.00
Platter, 10-3/4" l, oval	25.00	25.00
Relish, 3 part ftd	20.00	24.00
Salad Bowl, 7-1/2" d	24.00	24.00
Sandwich Plate, 11-1/2" d	24.00	27.50
Saucer	6.00	6.50
Sherbet	16.00	18.50
Sugar, open	15.00	15.00
Tumbler, 9 oz, ftd	22.00	24.00
Tumbler, 9 oz, 4-1/4" h	150.00	-

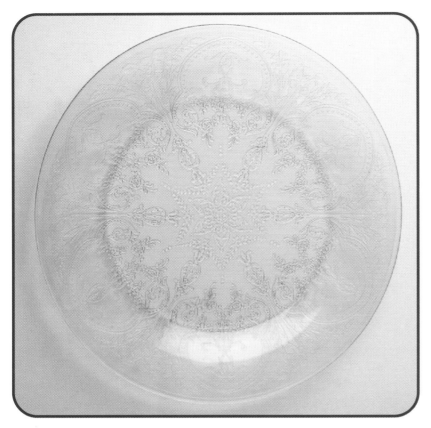

Horseshoe, No. 612 yellow plate.

Horseshoe, No. 612 yellow cup.

Item	Green	Yellow
Tumbler, 12 oz, ftd 140.00		150.00
Tumbler, 12 oz, 4-3/4" h 150.00		-
Vegetable Bowl, 8-1/2" d 30.00		30.00
Vegetable Bowl, 10-1/2" d, oval 25.00		28.50

Indiana Custard

Flower and Leaf Band

Manufactured by Indiana Glass Company, Dunkirk, Ind., in the 1930s and in the 1950s. Made in custard color, known as French Ivory. White was made in the 1950s.

Item	Frech Ivory	White
Berry Bowl, 5-1/2" d	14.00	5.50
Berry Bowl, 9" d, 1-3/4" deep	32.00	-
Butter Dish, cov	68.00	-
Cereal Bowl, 6-1/2" d	4.00	-
Creamer	17.50	-
Cup	38.00	17.00
Plate, 5-3/4" d, bread and butter	7.00	-
Plate, 7-1/2" d, salad	16.00	-
Plate, 8-7/8" d, luncheon	16.00	-
Plate, 9-3/4" d, dinner	28.00	-
Platter, 11-1/2" l, oval	30.00	-
Saucer	12.00	5.00
Sherbet	90.00	-
Soup Bowl, 7-1/2" d, flat	32.00	-
Sugar, cov	30.00	-

Indiana Custard covered sugar.

Iris

Iris and Herringbone

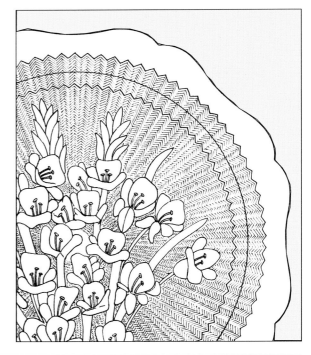

Manufactured by Jeannette Glass Company, Jeannette, Pa., from 1928 to 1932 and in the 1950s and 1970s.

Made in crystal, iridescent, some green and pink. Recent color combinations of yellow and red and blue and green and white have been made. In green, look for a creamer, ftd, for $125; a salad bowl, 9-1/2" d, ruffled, for $120; a sugar, cov, for $120. In pink, look for a creamer, ftd, for $120; a salad bowl, 9-1/2" d, ruffled, for $125; a sugar, cov, for $120; and a vase, 9" h, for $225.

Reproductions: † The candy jar has been reproduced in crystal.

Item	Crystal	Iridescent
Berry Bowl, 4-1/2" d, beaded edge	11.00	12.50
Berry Bowl, 8" d, beaded edge	110.00	30.00
Bowl, 5-1/2" d, scalloped	10.00	23.00
Bowl, 9-1/2" d, scalloped	12.50	10.00
Bread Plate, 11-3/4" d	17.50	38.00
Butter Dish, cov	50.00	45.00
Candlesticks, pr	45.00	48.00
Candy Jar, cov †	150.00	-
Cereal Bowl, 5" d	150.00	-
Coaster	100.00	-
Cocktail, 4 oz, 4-1/4" h	26.00	-
Creamer, ftd	15.00	16.00
Cup	20.00	15.00
Demitasse Cup and Saucer	210.00	350.00
Fruit Bowl, 11" d, straight edge	15.00	-
Fruit Bowl, 11-1/2" d, ruffled	15.00	18.00
Fruit Set	80.00	-
Goblet, 4 oz, 5-3/4" h	30.00	135.00
Goblet, 8 oz, 5-3/4" h	27.50	175.00
Iced Tea Tumbler, 6-1/2" h, ftd	42.00	-
Lamp Shade, 11-1/2"	90.00	-
Nut Set	90.00	-
Pitcher, 9-1/2" h, ftd	45.00	48.00
Plate, 5-1/2" d, sherbet	16.00	15.00
Plate, 7" d	95.00	-
Plate, 8" d, luncheon	125.00	115.00
Plate, 9" d, dinner	55.00	45.00
Salad Bowl, 9-1/2" d, ruffled	15.00	16.00
Sandwich Plate, 11-3/4" d	17.50	38.00
Sauce, 5" d, ruffled	10.00	23.00
Saucer	15.00	11.00
Sherbet, 2-1/2" h, ftd	30.00	15.50
Sherbet, 4" h, ftd	22.00	14.00
Soup Bowl, 7-1/2" d	165.00	80.00
Sugar, cov	32.00	23.00
Tumbler, 4" h, flat	125.00	18.00
Tumbler, 6" h, ftd	25.00	22.00
Tumbler, 6-1/2" h, ftd	32.00	-
Tumbler, flat, water	135.00	-
Vase, 9" h	38.00	35.00
Wine, 4" h	20.00	33.00
Wine, 4-1/4" h, 3 oz	17.50	-
Wine, 5-1/2" h	27.50	-

Iris crystal candlesticks and iridescent plate.

Jubilee

Manufactured by Lancaster Glass Company, Lancaster, Ohio, early 1930s. Made in pink and yellow.

Item	Pink	Yellow
Bowl, 8" d, 5-1/8" h, 3 legs	265.00	215.00
Bowl, 11-1/2" d, 3 legs	250.00	250.00
Bowl, 11-1/2" d, 3 legs, curved in	-	250.00
Bowl, 13" d, 3 legs	250.00	235.00
Cake Tray, 11" d, 2 handles	75.00	85.00
Candlesticks, pr	190.00	190.00
Candy Jar, cov, 3 legs	325.00	325.00
Cheese and Cracker Set	265.00	255.00
Cordial, 1 oz, 4" h	-	245.00
Creamer	45.00	30.00
Cup	40.00	15.00
Fruit Bowl, 9" d, handle	-	125.00
Fruit Bowl, 11-1/2" h, flat	200.00	165.00
Goblet, 3 oz, 4-7/8" h	-	150.00
Goblet, 11 oz, 7-1/2" h	-	75.00
Iced Tea Tumbler, 12-1/2 oz, 6-1/8" h	-	135.00
Juice Tumbler, 6 oz, 5" h, ftd	-	100.00
Mayonnaise, plate, orig ladle	315.00	285.00
Mayonnaise Underplate	125.00	110.00
Plate, 7" d, salad	25.00	14.00
Plate, 8-3/4" d, luncheon	30.00	16.50
Plate, 14" d, 3 legs	-	210.00
Sandwich Plate, 13-1/2" d	95.00	65.00
Sandwich Tray, 11" d, center handle	200.00	250.00
Saucer	15.00	8.00
Sherbet, 8 oz, 3" h	-	75.00
Sherbet/Champagne, 7 oz, 5-1/2" h	-	75.00
Sugar	40.00	24.00
Tumbler, 10 oz, 6" h, ftd	75.00	50.00
Vase, 12" h	-	365.00

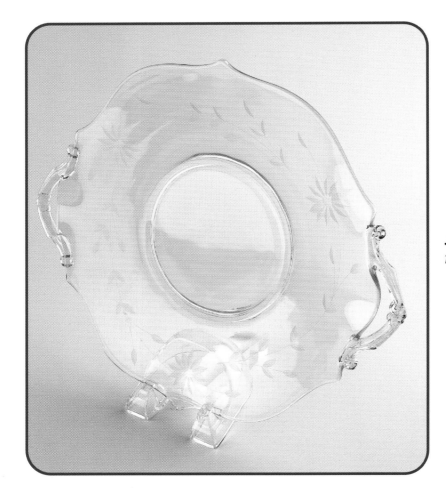

Jubilee yellow serving plate with handles.

Jubilee yellow cup and saucer.

Jubilee yellow goblet.

Laced Edge *Katy Blue*

Manufactured by Imperial Glass Company, Bellaire, Ohio, early 1930s.
Made in blue and green with opalescent edges.

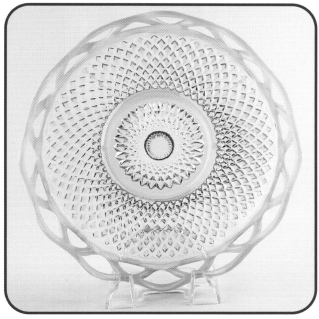

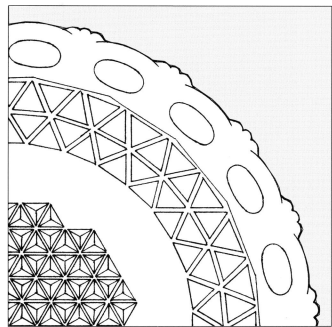

Laced Edge blue-opalescent bowl.

Item	Blue	Green
Bowl, 5" d	40.00	40.00
Bowl, 5-1/2" d	37.50	37.50
Bowl, 5-7/8" d	40.00	40.00
Bowl, 11" l, oval	285.00	285.00
Bowl, 11" l, oval, divided	130.00	130.00
Candlesticks, pr, double light	165.00	180.00
Creamer	45.00	40.00
Cup	35.00	35.00
Fruit Bowl, 4-1/2" d	32.00	30.00
Mayonnaise, 3 piece	100.00	125.00
Plate, 6-1/2" d, bread and butter	20.00	20.00
Plate, 8" d, salad	32.00	32.00
Plate, 10" d, dinner	90.00	85.00
Plate, 12" d, luncheon	85.00	80.00
Platter, 13" l	165.00	150.00
Saucer	18.00	15.00
Soup Bowl, 7" d	85.00	80.00
Sugar	45.00	40.00
Tidbit, 2 tiers, 8" and 10" plates	110.00	100.00
Tumbler, 9 oz	60.00	60.00
Vegetable Bowl, 9" d	95.00	95.00

Lake Como

Manufactured by Hocking Glass Company, Lancaster, Ohio, from 1934 to 1937.

Made in opaque white with a blue scene.

Item	White
Cereal Bowl, 6" d	14.00
Creamer, ftd	31.00
Cup, regular	30.00
Cup, St Denis	30.00
Plate, 7-1/4" d, salad	20.00
Plate, 9-1/4" d, dinner	30.00
Platter, 11" d	65.00
Salt and Pepper Shakers, pr	45.00
Saucer	12.00
Saucer, St Denis	12.00
Soup Bowl, flat	90.00
Sugar, ftd	32.00
Vegetable Bowl, 9-3/4" l	60.00

Lake Como blue and white plate.

Laurel

Manufactured by McKee Glass
Company, Pittsburgh, 1930s.
Made in French Ivory, Jade Green,
Poudre Blue and White Opal.

Item	French Ivory	Jade Green	Poudre Blue	White Opal
Berry Bowl, 4-3/4" d	7.50	6.50	14.00	7.50
Berry Bowl, 9" d	20.00	18.00	45.00	18.00
Bowl, 5-1/2" d	8.00	-	-	-
Bowl, 6" d, three legs	15.00	12.00	-	12.00
Bowl, 10-1/2" d, three legs	35.00	25.00	65.00	25.00
Bowls, 11" d	35.00	35.00	65.00	35.00
Candlesticks, pr, 4" h	50.00	35.00	-	35.00
Cereal Bowl, 6" d	10.00	8.50	20.00	8.50
Cheese Dish, cov	55.00	53.00	-	53.00
Creamer, short	12.00	12.00	-	12.00
Creamer, tall	12.00	12.00	35.00	12.00
Cup	8.50	8.00	20.00	8.00
Plate, 6" d, sherbet	4.00	4.50	10.00	5.00
Plate, 7-1/2" d, salad	9.50	10.00	14.00	10.00
Plate, 9-1/8" d, dinner	12.00	15.00	24.00	15.00
Plate, 9-1/8" d, grill, round	12.50	14.00	-	14.00
Plate, 9-1/8" d, grill, scalloped	12.50	14.00	-	14.00
Platter, 10-3/4" l, oval	27.50	22.00	38.00	24.00
Salt and Pepper Shakers, pr	48.00	60.00	-	60.00
Saucer	2.50	3.00	6.50	3.00
Sherbet	10.00	10.00	-	10.00
Sherbet/champagne, 5"	37.50	40.00	-	40.00
Soup Bowl, 7-7/8" d	30.00	30.00	-	30.00
Sugar, short	12.00	12.00	-	12.00
Sugar, tall	12.00	12.00	35.00	12.00
Tumbler, 12 oz, 5" h, flat	48.00	-	-	-
Tumbler, 9 oz, 4-1/2" h, flat	30.00	40.00	-	40.00
Vegetable Bowl, 9-3/4" l, oval	18.50	20.00	45.00	20.00

Children's

Item	Plain	Green or Decorated	Scotty Dog Green	Scotty Dog Ivory
Creamer	20.00	35.00	115.00	85.00
Cup	18.00	27.50	60.00	40.00
Plate	10.00	17.50	55.00	35.00
Saucer	8.00	10.00	55.00	25.00
Sugar	20.00	40.00	115.00	85.00

Laurel green plate.

Lincoln Inn

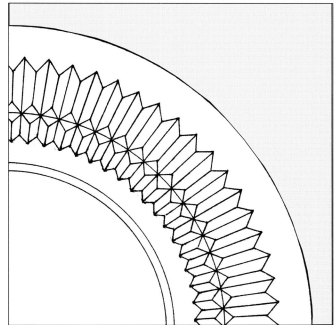

Manufactured by Fenton Art Glass Company, Williamstown, W.V., late 1920s.

Made in amber, amethyst, black, cobalt blue, crystal, green, green opalescent, light blue, opaque jade, pink and red. Production in black was limited to salt and pepper shakers, valued at $315. Some rare pieces have been identified in several other colors.

Item	Cobalt Blue	Crystal	Other Colors	Red
Ashtray	17.50	10.00	10.00	17.50
Bonbon, oval, handle	17.50	10.00	12.00	18.00
Bonbon, sq, handle	15.00	10.00	12.00	15.00
Bowl, 6" d, crimped	14.00	7.50	9.00	14.00
Bowl, 9" d, shallow	-	9.00	-	-
Bowl, 9-1/4" d, ftd	42.00	18.00	20.00	45.00
Bowl, 10-1/2" d, ftd	50.00	28.00	30.00	50.00
Candy Dish, ftd, oval	24.00	14.00	14.00	24.00
Cereal Bowl, 6" d	12.50	7.50	9.50	12.50
Comport	25.00	12.00	15.00	25.00
Creamer	24.00	10.00	15.00	24.00
Cup	17.50	8.50	9.50	18.00
Finger Bowl	20.00	12.00	14.00	20.00
Fruit Bowl, 5" d	12.00	7.00	9.00	12.00
Goblet, 6" h	30.00	14.00	16.00	30.00
Juice Tumbler, 4 oz, flat	27.50	9.00	12.00	27.50
Nut Dish, ftd	20.00	14.00	16.00	20.00
Olive Bowl, handle	15.00	8.50	10.00	15.00
Pitcher, 46 oz, 7-1/4" h	810.00	700.00	715.00	820.00
Plate, 6" d	20.00	10.00	12.50	20.00
Plate, 8" d	27.50	15.00	12.00	27.50
Plate, 9-1/4" d	30.00	15.00	16.50	30.00
Plate, 12" d	35.00	16.00	18.00	35.00
Salt and Pepper Shakers, pr	250.00	150.00	160.00	250.00
Sandwich Server, center handle	100.00	80.00	85.00	100.00
Saucer	5.00	4.00	4.50	5.00
Sherbet, 4-1/2" h, cone shape	18.00	10.00	12.00	18.00
Sherbet, 4-3/4" h	20.00	12.00	14.00	20.00
Sugar	24.00	10.00	15.00	24.00

Item	Cobalt Blue	Crystal	Other Colors	Red
Tumbler, 5 oz, ftd	24.00	12.00	14.00	24.00
Tumbler, 9 oz, flat	-	12.00	15.00	15.00
Tumbler, 9 oz, ftd	28.00	32.00	35.00	30.00
Tumbler, 12 oz, ftd	40.00	20.00	22.00	40.00
Vase, 9-3/4" h	125.00	75.00	85.00	135.00
Vase, 12" h, ftd	150.00	100.00	120.00	160.00
Wine	32.00	15.00	18.00	35.00

Lincoln Inn pink plate.

Lincoln Inn cobalt blue goblet.

Lorain

Manufactured by Indiana Glass Company, Dunkirk, Ind., from 1929 to 1939.

Made in crystal, green and yellow. Sherbert has been reproduced in milk white and dark avocado green.

Lorain yellow plate and tumbler.

Item	Crystal	Green	Yellow
Berry Bowl, 8" d	80.00	85.00	155.00
Cereal Bowl, 6" d	35.00	35.00	59.00
Creamer, ftd	15.00	15.00	27.00
Cup and Saucer	15.00	15.00	20.00
Plate, 5-1/2" d, sherbet	6.50	7.50	12.50
Plate, 7-3/4" d, salad	10.00	10.00	15.00
Plate, 8-3/4" d, luncheon	15.00	15.00	25.00
Plate, 10-1/4" d, dinner	30.00	35.00	60.00
Platter, 11-1/2" l	25.00	25.00	40.00
Relish, 8" d, 4 part	17.50	17.50	35.00
Salad Bowl, 7-3/4" d	36.00	36.00	75.00
Saucer	5.00	5.00	7.00
Sherbet, ftd +	17.50	20.00	35.00
Snack Tray, crystal trim	22.00	25.00	-
Sugar, ftd	15.00	18.00	24.00
Tumbler, 9 oz, 4-3/4" h, ftd	17.50	20.00	36.50
Vegetable Bowl, 9-3/4" l, oval	36.00	40.00	47.00

Madrid

Manufactured by Federal Glass Company, Lancaster, Ohio, from 1932 to 1939.

Made in amber, blue, crystal, green, iridescent and pink. Iridized pieces are limited to a console set, consisting of a low bowl and pair of candlesticks, valued at $35.

Reproductions: † Reproductions include candlesticks, cups, saucers and vegetable bowl. Reproductions are found in amber, blue, crystal and pink. Federal Glass Company reissued this pattern under the name "Recollection." Some of these pieces were dated 1976. When Federal went bankrupt, the molds were sold to Indiana Glass, which removed the date and began production of crystal, then pink. Several pieces were made recently that were not part of the original production and include a footed cake stand, goblet, two-section grill plate, preserves stand, squatty salt and pepper shakers, 11 oz tumbler and vase.

Item	Amber	Blue	Crystal	Green	Pink
Ashtray, 6" sq	265.00	-	250.00	160.00	-
Berry Bowl, small	5.00	-	5.00	-	-
Berry Bowl, 9-3/8" d	22.00	-	22.00	-	20.00
Bowl, 7" d	12.00	-	6.00	15.50	-
Butter Dish, cov	70.00	-	64.00	90.00	-
Cake Plate, 11-1/4" d	24.00	-	20.00	-	28.00
Candlesticks, 2-1/4" h, pr †	18.50	-	15.00	-	28.00
Coaster, 5" d	40.00	-	40.00	35.00	-
Console Bowl, 11" d	20.00	-	18.00	-	36.00
Cookie Jar	48.00	-	40.00	-	34.00
Creamer	12.00	18.00	7.00	10.00	-
Cream Soup, 4-3/4" d	15.00	-	15.00	-	-
Cup †	6.50	18.00	4.50	10.00	7.50
Gelatin Mold, 2-1/2" h	13.50	-	13.50	-	-
Gravy Boat and Platter	500.00	-	500.00	-	-
Iced Tea Tumbler, round	18.00	-	18.00	20.00	-
Jam Dish, 7" d	21.00	33.00	10.00	25.00	-
Juice Pitcher	50.00	-	45.00	-	-
Juice Tumbler, 5 oz, 3-7/8 h, ftd	16.50	40.00	35.00	30.00	-
Pitcher, jug-type	60.00	-	24.00	190.00	-
Pitcher, 60 oz, 8" h, sq	44.00	150.00	150.00	135.00	36.00
Pitcher, 80 oz, 8-1/2" h, ice lip	55.00	-	50.00	200.00	-
Plate, 6" d, sherbet	5.50	12.00	4.00	4.50	4.00
Plate, 7-1/2" d, salad	12.00	17.00	12.00	9.00	9.00
Plate, 8-7/8" d, luncheon	8.50	18.50	5.50	10.00	8.00

Item	Amber	Blue	Crystal	Green	Pink
Plate, 10-1/2" d, dinner	42.50	60.00	21.00	40.00	-
Plate, 10-1/2" d, grill	12.00	-	10.00	18.50	-
Platter, 11-1/2" oval	16.00	24.00	15.00	16.00	15.00
Relish Dish, 10-1/2" d	14.50	-	7.00	16.00	20.00
Salad Bowl, 8" d	17.00	-	9.50	15.50	-
Salad Bowl, 9-1/2" d	32.00	-	30.00	-	-
Salt and Pepper Shakers, 3-1/2" h	125.00	135.00	95.00	68.00	-
Sauce Bowl, 5" d	9.00	-	7.50	8.50	11.00
Saucer †	5.00	8.00	4.00	5.00	5.00
Sherbet, cone	7.00	18.00	6.50	9.50	-
Sherbet, ftd	7.50	15.00	6.00	11.00	-
Soup Bowl, 8" d	15.00	20.00	6.00	15.50	-
Sugar, cov.	46.00	175.00	32.50	48.00	-
Sugar, open	7.00	15.00	6.00	9.00	-
Tumbler, 9 oz, 4-1/2" h	17.50	38.00	15.0	23.50	24.00
Tumbler, 12 oz, 5-1/4" h, ftd	33.50	-	30.00	40.00	-
12 oz, 5-1/4" h	23.00	-	14.00	33.50	-
12 oz, 5-1/2" h, flat	22.50	32.00	20.00	40.00	-
Vegetable Bowl, 10" l, oval †	18.00	33.00	18.00	22.00	27.00

Madrid amber sugar and creamer.

Madrid amber bowl.

Madrid amber grill plate, bowl and cup.

Manhattan *Horizontal Ribbed*

Manufactured by Anchor Hocking Glass Company, from 1938 to 1943.

Made in crystal, green, iridized, pink and ruby. Ruby pieces are limited to relish tray inserts, currently valued at $6 each. Green and iridized production was limited to ftd tumblers, currently valued at $17.50.

Anchor Hocking introduced a similar pattern, Park Avenue, in 1987. Anchor Hocking was very careful to preserve the Manhattan pattern. Collectors should pay careful attention to measurements if they are uncertain of the pattern.

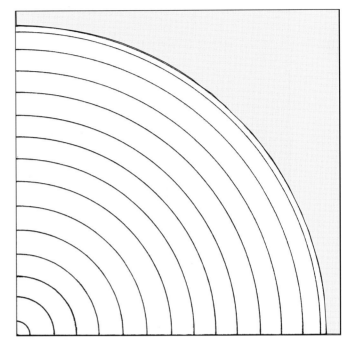

Item	Crystal	Pink
Ashtray, 4" d, round	11.00	8.00
Ashtray, 4-1/2" w, sq	25.00	-
Berry Bowl, 5-3/8" d, handles	18.00	22.00
Berry Bowl, 7-1/2" d	15.00	-
Bowl, 4-1/2" d	9.00	-
Bowl, 8" d, closed handles	28.00	25.00
Bowl, 8" d, metal handle	25.00	-
Bowl, 9-1/2" d, handle	-	45.00
Candlesticks, pr, 4-1/2" h	25.00	-
Candy Dish, 3 legs	-	15.00
Candy Dish, cov	40.00	-
Cereal Bowl, 5-1/4" d, no handles	30.00	-
Coaster, 3-1/2"	20.00	-
Cocktail	15.00	-
Comport, 5-3/4" h	32.00	32.00
Cookie Jar, cov	35.00	30.00
Creamer, oval	9.00	17.50
Cup	20.00	160.00
Fruit Bowl, 9-1/2" d, 2 open handles	40.00	35.00
Juice Pitcher, 24 oz	35.00	-
Pitcher, 80 oz, tilted	55.00	85.00
Plate, 6" d, sherbet	7.00	50.00
Plate, 8-1/2" d, salad	18.00	-
Plate, 10-1/4" d, dinner	24.00	120.00
Relish Tray Insert	2.50	6.00
Relish Tray, 14" d, inserts	22.00	50.00

Item	Crystal	Pink
Relish Tray, 14" d, 4 part	65.00	-
Salad Bowl, 9" d	20.00	-
Salt and Pepper Shakers, pr, 2" h, sq	50.00	48.00
Sandwich Plate, 14" d	22.00	-
Sauce Bowl, 4-1/2" d, handles	10.00	-
Saucer	7.00	50.00
Sherbet	13.50	15.00
Sugar, oval	12.00	17.50
Tumbler, 10 oz, 5-1/4" h, ftd	16.00	25.00
Vase, 8" h	17.50	-
Wine, 3-1/2" h	12.50	-

Manhattan relish tray with ruby inserts and crystal base; and crystal compote, vase and bowl.

Manhattan small crystal bowl (on pedestal); pink sugar and creamer; crystal salt and pepper shakers; crystal iced tea tumbler, pitcher, relish with metal stand; and pink footed bowl.

Mayfair
Federal

Manufactured by Federal Glass Company, Columbus, Ohio, 1934.

Made in amber, crystal and green.

Mayfair Federal amber plate.

Item	Amber	Crystal	Green
Green			
Cereal Bowl, 6" d	16.50	9.50	19.50
Cream Soup, 5" d	18.00	11.00	18.00
Creamer, ftd	13.50	11.00	16.00
Cup	8.50	5.00	8.50
Plate, 6-3/4" d, salad	7.00	4.50	8.50
Plate, 9-1/2" d, dinner	14.00	10.00	14.50
Plate, 9-1/2" d, grill	13.50	8.50	13.50
Platter, 12" l, oval	27.50	20.00	30.00
Sauce Bowl, 5" d	8.50	7.00	12.00
Saucer	4.50	2.50	4.50
Sugar, ftd	14.00	12.00	14.00
Tumbler, 9 oz, 4-1/2" h	27.50	15.00	32.00
Vegetable, 10" l, oval	30.00	30.00	30.00

Mayfair

Open Rose

Manufactured by Hocking Glass Company, Lancaster, OH, from 1931 to 1937.

Made in crystal, green, ice blue, pink and yellow. The lone crystal piece is a juice pitcher, 37oz, 6" h, valued at $18.50.

Reproductions: † This pattern has been plagued with reproductions since 1977. Items reproduced include cookie jars, salt and pepper shakers, juice pitchers and whiskey glasses. Reproductions are found in amethyst, blue, cobalt blue, green, pink and red.

Item	*Green*	*Ice Blue*	*Pink*	*Pink Satin*	*Yellow*
Bowl, 11-3/4" l, flat 33.00		75.00	65.00	70.00	195.00
Butter Dish, cov 1,300.00		295.00	68.00	75.00	1,300.00
Cake Plate, 10" d, ftd 115.00		75.00	35.00	45.00	-
Cake Plate, 12" d, handles 40.00		70.00	48.00	50.00	-
Candy Dish, cov 575.00		285.00	60.00	70.00	475.00
Celery Dish, 9" l, divided 155.00		60.00	-	-	150.00
Celery Dish, 10" l, divided . . . . -		65.00	200.0	-	-
Celery Dish, 10" l, not divided 115.00		80.00	45.00	50.00	115.00
Cereal Bowl, 5-1/2" d 24.00		48.00	30.00	35.00	75.00
Claret, 4-1/2 oz, 5-1/4" h 900.00		-	900.00	-	-
Cocktail, 3 oz, 4" h 375.00		-	75.00	-	-
Console Bowl, 9" d, 3-1/8" h, 3 legs 5,000.00		-	5,000.00	-	-
Cookie Jar, cov † 575.00		295.00	47.00	37.00	860.00
Cordial, 1 oz, 3-3/4" h 925.00		-	1,000.00	-	-
Cream Soup, 5" d . . . . -		-	65.00	68.00	-
Creamer, ftd . . . . -		-	26.00	24.00	-
Cup 150.00		52.00	20.00	25.00	150.00
Decanter, stopper, 32 oz . . . . -		-	225.00	-	-
Fruit Bowl, 12" d, scalloped 45.00		90.00	60.00	65.00	215.00
Goblet, 2-1/2 oz, 4-1/8" 900.00		-	900.00	-	-
Goblet, 9 oz, 5-3/4" h 465.00		-	65.00	-	-
Goblet, 9 oz, 7-1/4" h, thin . . . . -		185.00	220.00	-	-
Iced Tea Tumbler, 13-1/2 oz, 5-1/4" h . . . . -		225.00	60.00	-	-
Iced Tea Tumbler, 15 oz, 6-1/2" h, ftd 225.00		225.00	65.00	65.00	-
Juice Pitcher, 37oz, 6" h † 525.00		150.00	58.00	60.00	500.00
Juice Tumbler, 3 oz, 3-1/4" h, ftd . . . . -		-	80.00	-	-
Juice Tumbler, 5 oz, 3-1/2" . . . . -		120.00	45.00	-	-
Pitcher, 60 oz, 8" h 475.00		175.00	95.00	100.00	425.00
Pitcher, 80 oz, 8-1/2" h 550.00		295.00	125.00	135.00	550.00
Plate, 5-3/4" d 90.00		25.00	13.00	15.00	90.00
Plate, 6-1/2" d, off-center indent 115.00		35.00	30.00	35.00	-
Plate, 6-1/2" d, sherbet . . . . -		24.00	15.00	-	-

Item	Green	Ice Blue	Pink	Pink Satin	Yellow
Plate, 8-1/2" d, luncheon	85.00	55.00	30.00	32.00	80.00
Plate, 9-1/2" d, dinner	150.00	90.00	55.00	60.00	150.00
Plate, 9-1/2" d, grill	75.00	70.00	34.00	30.00	80.00
Plate, 11-1/2" d, grill, handles	-	-	-	-	100.00
Platter, 12" l, oval, open handles	175.00	58.00	38.00	35.00	115.00
Platter, 12-1/2" oval, 8" wide, closed handles	225.00	-	-	-	225.00
Relish, 8-3/8" d, 4 part	160.00	65.00	30.00	22.00	150.00
Relish, 8-3/8" d, non-partitioned	275.00	-	200.00	-	275.00
Salt and Pepper Shakers, pr, flat †	1,000.00	295.00	65.00	70.00	800.00
Salt and Pepper Shakers, pr, ftd	-	-	-	45.00	-
Sandwich Server, center handle	40.00	85.00	50.00	45.00	130.00
Saucer	90.00	27.00	35.00	30.00	140.00
Sherbet, 2-1/4" flat	-	120.00	160.00	-	-
Sherbet, 3" ftd	-	-	18.00	-	-
Sherbet, 4-3/4" ftd	150.00	75.00	75.00	75.00	150.00
Sugar, ftd	195.00	85.00	30.00	35.00	185.00
Sweet Pea Vase	285.00	125.00	140.00	145.00	-
Tumbler, 9 oz, 4-1/4" h	-	100.00	30.00	-	-
Tumbler, 10 oz, 5-1/4" h	-	110.00	77.50	-	185.00
Tumblers, 11 oz, 4-3/4" h	200.00	120.00	185.00	190.00	200.00
Vegetable Bowl, 7" d, 2 handles	33.00	75.00	65.00	70.00	195.00
Vegetable Bowl, 9-1/2" l, oval	110.00	70.00	30.00	30.00	125.00
Vegetable Bowl, 10" d cov	-	120.00	120.00	120.00	900.00
Vegetable Bowl, 10" d open	-	75.00	20.00	19.00	200.00
Whiskey, 1-1/2 oz, 2-1/4" h †	-	-	58.00	-	-
Wine, 3 oz, 4-1/2" h	420.00	-	75.00	-	-

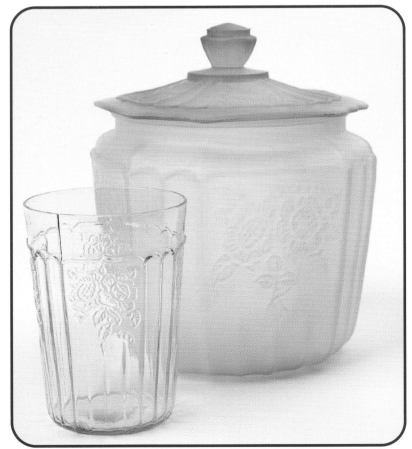

Mayfair Open Rose pink tumbler and pink satin-finish covered cookie jar.

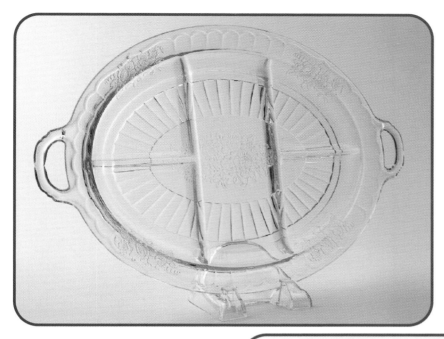

Mayfair Open Rose divided crystal celery dish.

REPRODUCTION! Mayfair Open Rose green and blue cookie jars.

Mayfair Open Rose blue vegetable bowl.

Miss America

Diamond Pattern

Manufactured by Hocking Glass Company, Lancaster, Ohio, from 1935 to 1938.

Made in crystal, green, ice blue, jade-ite, pink, and royal ruby.

Reproductions: † Reproductions include the butter dish, (including a new importer,) creamer, 8" pitcher, salt and pepper shakers, sugar, and tumbler. Reproductions are found in amberina, blue, cobalt blue, crystal, green, pink, red.

Item	Crystal	Green	Ice Blue	Pink	Royal Ruby
Berry Bowl, 4-1/2" d	-	14.00	-	-	-
Bowl, 8" d, curved at top	48.00	-	-	95.00	-
Bowl, 8" d, straight sides	-	-	-	85.00	-
Bowl, 11" d, shallow	-	-	-	-	800.00
Butter Dish, cov †	200.00	-	-	550.00	-
Cake Plate, 12" d, ftd	25.00	-	-	45.00	-
Candy Jar, cov, 11-1/2"	65.00	-	-	175.00	-
Celery Dish, 10-1/2" l, oval	16.50	-	160.00	35.00	-
Cereal Bowl, 6-1/4" d	12.00	18.00	-	25.00	-
Coaster, 5-3/4" d	20.00	-	-	35.00	-
Comport, 5" d	16.00	-	-	28.00	-
Creamer, ftd †	10.00	-	-	20.00	195.00
Cup	11.00	10.00	12.00	22.50	235.00
Fruit Bowl, 8-3/4" d	40.00	-	-	60.00	450.00
Goblet, 10 oz, 5-1/2" h	22.50	-	-	50.00	250.00
Iced Tea Tumbler, 14 oz, 5-3/4" h	25.00	-	-	85.00	-
Juice Goblet, 5 oz, 4-3/4" h	27.50	-	-	95.00	250.00
Juice Tumbler, 5 oz, 4" h	20.00	-	150.00	50.00	200.00
Pitcher, 65 oz, 8" h †	45.00	-	-	175.00	-
Pitcher, 65 oz, 8-1/2" h, ice lip	75.00	-	-	135.00	50.00
Plate, 5-3/4" d, sherbet	7.50	9.00	55.00	12.50	-
Plate, 6-3/4" d	-	12.00	-	-	-
Plate, 8-1/2" d, salad	9.00	14.00	-	32.00	150.00
Plate, 10-1/4" d, dinner	16.50	-	150.00	40.00	-
Plate, 10-1/4" d, grill	11.00	-	-	28.00	-
Platter, 12-1/4" l, oval	15.00	-	-	27.00	-
Relish, 8-3/4" l, 4 part	25.00	-	-	25.00	-
Relish, 11-3/4" d, divided	35.00	-	-	23.00	-
Salt and Pepper Shakers, pr †	33.00	300.00	-	65.00	-
Saucer	4.00	-	-	7.00	60.00

Item	Crystal	Green	Ice Blue	Pink	Royal Ruby
Sherbet	8.00	-	60.00	16.50	135.00
Sugar	10.00	-	-	20.00	175.00
Tumbler, 10 oz, 4-1/2" h, flat †	17.00	45.00	-	38.00	-
Tumbler, 5-3/4" h	28.00	-	-	-	-
Vegetable Bowl, 10" l, oval	18.00	-	-	45.00	-
Whiskey	22.00	-	-	-	-
Wine, 3 oz, 3-3/4" h	24.50	-	-	85.00	250.00

Miss America pink goblet, compote and tumbler with original label.

Close-up view of original label on Miss America pink tumbler.

Miss America green plate and bowl.

Moderntone

Manufactured by Hazel Atlas Glass Company, Clarksburg, W.V., and Zanesville, Ohio, from 1934 to 1942; also, in the late 1940s to early 1950s.

Made in amethyst, cobalt blue, crystal, pink and Platonite fired-on colors. Later period production saw plain white, as well as white with blue or red stripes, a Willow-type design in blue or red on white. Collector interest in crystal is limited and prices remain low, less than 50% of Platonite.

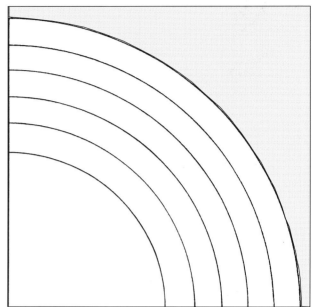

Item	Amethyst	Cobalt Blue	Platonite, Darker Shades	Platonite, Pastel Shades	White or White with Dec	Willow-Type Dec
Ashtray, 7-3/4" d, match holder center. . . -		165.00	-	-	-	-
Berry Bowl, 5" d, rim. 22.00		26.00	-	4.00	4.00	14.00
Berry Bowl, 5" d, without rim . . . . -		-	12.50	25.00	-	-
Berry Bowl, 8-3/4" d 42.00		45.00	-	-	7.50	28.00
Bowl, 8" d, no rim . . . . -		-	36.00	50.00	-	-
Bowl, 8" d, rim. . . . . -		-	-	15.00	6.00	28.00
Butter Dish, metal cov . . . . -		98.00	-	-	-	-
Cereal Bowl, 5" d, deep, no white. . . . . . -		-	16.00	8.00	-	-
Cereal Bowl, 5" d, deep, with white . . . . -		-	-	9.00	4.50	-
Cereal Bowl, 6-1/2" d 70.00		70.00	-	-	-	-
Cheese Dish, 7" d, metal cov . . . . -		460.00	-	-	-	-
Cream Soup, 4-3/4" d 19.00		22.00	-	6.50	5.00	22.00
Cream Soup, 5" d, ruffled 30.00		48.00	-	-	-	-
Creamer 18.00		12.00	12.00	5.50	4.50	20.00
Cup. 9.00		16.00	9.00	4.00	2.50	22.00
Custard Cup 15.00		18.00	-	-	-	-
Mug, 4" h, 8 oz. . . . . -		-	-	-	8.50	-
Mustard, metal lid . . . . -		25.00	-	-	-	-
Plate, 5-7/8" d, sherbet 9.00		6.50	-	-	-	-
Plate, 6-3/4" d, salad 10.00		12.00	9.00	5.00	3.00	8.50
Plate, 7-3/4" d, luncheon 10.00		15.00	-	-	-	-
Plate, 8-7/8" d, dinner 12.00		19.00	15.00	7.00	4.00	20.00
Platter, 11" l, oval 40.00		45.00	-	-	14.00	30.00
Platter, 12" l, oval 48.00		72.00	32.00	15.00	10.00	35.00
Salt and Pepper Shakers, pr 37.50		42.50	-	10.00	12.00	-
Sandwich Plate, 10-1/2" d 18.00		60.00	-	17.50	8.50	-

Item	Amethyst	Cobalt Blue	Platonite, Darker Shades	Platonite, Pastel Shades	White or White with Dec	Willow-Type Dec
Saucer	4.50	5.00	7.50	1.00	1.50	4.50
Sherbet	11.00	13.00	10.00	6.00	2.50	12.00
Soup Bowl, 7-1/2" d.	95.00	135.00	-	-	-	-
Sugar	18.00	12.00	12.00	6.00	4.50	20.00
Tumbler, 5 oz	30.00	50.00	-	-	-	-
Tumbler, 9 oz	27.50	37.50	24.00	9.00	-	-
Tumbler, 12 oz	85.00	95.00	-	-	-	-
Tumbler, cone, ftd	-	-	-	-	4.00	-
Whiskey, 1-1/2 oz	-	42.50	-	10.00	-	-

Children's

Hazel Atlas also manufactured children's sets in the early 1950s, known as Little Hostess Party Dishes. The original box adds to the value. Colorful combinations were found.

Item	Gray/ Rust/ Gold	Green/ Gray/ Chartruse	Lemon/ Beige/ Pink/Aqua	Pastel Pink/ Green/Blue/ Yellow	Pink/ Black/ White
Creamer, 1-3/4".	15.00	14.00	12.00	12.00	12.00
Cup, 3/4"	12.00	9.00	9.00	9.00	9.00
Plate, 5-1/4" d	8.00	9.00	9.00	9.00	9.00
Saucer, 3-7/8" d	8.00	7.00	12.50	7.00	7.00
Sugar, 1-3/4"	12.00	15.00	20.00	15.00	18.00
Teapot, 3-1/2" d	115.00	95.00	75.00	-	75.00

Moderntone cobalt blue cup and saucer, sherbet (on pedestal), salad plate, dinner plate and cream soup.

Moondrops

Manufactured by New Martinsville Glass Company, New Martinsville, W.V., from 1932 to 1940.

Made in amber, amethyst, black, cobalt blue, crystal, dark green, green, ice blue, jadeite, light green, pink, red and smoke.

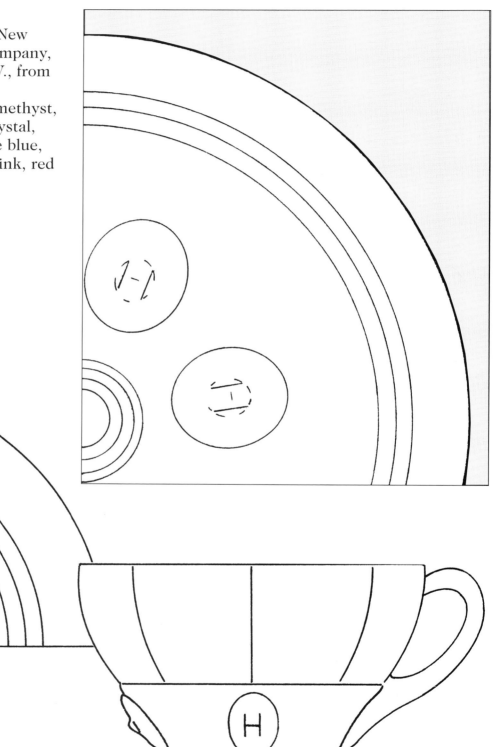

Item	Cobalt Blue	Crystal	Other Colors	Red
Ashtray	30.00	-	18.00	30.00
Berry Bowl, 5-1/4" d	20.00	-	12.00	20.00
Bowl, 8-1/2" d, ftd, concave top	40.00	-	25.00	40.00
Bowl, 9-1/2" d, 3 legs, ruffled	60.00	-	-	60.00
Bowl, 9-3/4" l, oval, handles	50.00	-	30.00	50.00
Butter Dish, cov	250.00	-	250.00	250.00
Candlesticks, pr, 2" h, ruffled	40.00	-	25.00	40.00
Candlesticks, pr, 4" h, sherbet style	30.00	-	18.00	30.00
Candlesticks, pr, 5" h, ruffled	32.00	-	22.00	32.00
Candlesticks, pr, 5" h, wings	90.00	-	60.00	90.00
Candlesticks, pr, 5-1/4" h, triple light	100.00	65.00	65.00	100.00
Candlesticks, pr, 8-1/2" h, metal stem	40.00	-	32.00	40.00
Candy Dish, 8" d, ruffled	40.00	-	20.00	40.00
Casserole, cov, 9-3/4" d	185.00	-	100.00	185.00
Celery Bowl, 11" l, boat-shape	30.00	-	24.00	30.00
Cocktail Shaker, metal top	60.00	-	35.00	60.00
Comport, 4" d	25.00	-	15.00	25.00
Comport, 11-1/2" d	60.00	-	30.00	60.00
Console Bowl, 12" d, round, 3 ftd	-	-	40.00	
Console Bowl, 13" d, wings	-	-	80.00	120.00
Cordial, 3/4 oz, 2-7/8" h	-	-	25.00	48.00
Cream Soup, 4-1/4" d	90.00	-	35.00	90.00
Creamer, 2-3/4" h	15.00	-	10.00	17.00
Creamer, 3-3/4" h	12.00	-	12.00	16.00
Cup	14.00	8.00	10.00	16.00
Decanter, 7-3/4" h	70.00	-	40.00	70.00
Decanter, 8-1/2" h	72.00	-	45.00	72.00
Decanter, 10-1/4" h, rocket-shape	425.00	-	375.00	425.00
Decanter, 11-1/4" h	100.00	-	50.00	110.00
Goblet, 5 oz, 4-3/4" h	25.00	-	15.00	22.00
Goblet, 8 oz, 5-3/4" h	35.00	-	20.00	33.00
Goblet, 9 oz, 6-1/4" h, metal stem	15.00	-	17.50	15.00
Gravy Boat	120.00	-	90.00	125.00
Juice Tumbler, 3 oz, 3-1/4" h, ftd	15.00	-	10.00	15.00
Mayonnaise, 5-1/4" h	32.50	-	30.00	32.50
Mug, 12 oz, 5-1/8" h	40.00	-	24.00	42.00
Perfume Bottle, rocket-shape	200.00	-	150.00	210.00
Pickle, 7-1/2" d	24.00	-	15.00	24.00
Pitcher, 22 oz, 6-7/8" h	175.00	-	90.00	175.00
Pitcher, 32 oz, 8-1/8" h	195.00	-	110.00	195.00
Pitcher, 50 oz, 8" h, lip	200.00	-	115.00	200.00
Pitcher, 53 oz, 8-1/8" h	195.00	-	120.00	195.00
Plate, 5-7/8" d	12.00	-	7.50	12.00
Plate, 6" d, round, off center indent	12.50	-	10.00	12.50
Plate, 6-1/8" d, sherbet	8.00	-	6.00	8.00
Plate, 7-1/8" d, salad	12.00	-	10.00	12.00
Plate, 8-1/2" d, luncheon	15.00	-	12.00	15.00
Plate, 9-1/2" d, dinner	25.00	-	15.00	25.00
Platter, 12" l, oval	35.00	-	20.00	35.00
Powder Jar, 3 ftd	175.00	-	100.00	185.00
Relish, 8-1/2" d, 3 ftd, divided	30.00	-	20.00	30.00
Sandwich Plate, 14" d	40.00	-	20.00	40.00
Sandwich Plate, 14" d, w handles	44.00	-	24.00	45.00
Saucer	6.00	2.00	4.00	6.50
Sherbet, 2-5/8" h	15.00	10.00	11.00	20.00

Item	Cobalt Blue	Crystal	Other Colors	Red
Sherbet, 3-1/2" h.	25.00	-	15.00	25.00
Shot Glass, 2 oz, 2-3/4" h	17.50	-	10.00	17.50
Shot Glass, 2 oz, 2-3/4" h, handle	17.50	-	15.00	17.50
Soup Bowl, 6-3/4" d.	80.00	-	-	80.00
Sugar, 2-3/4" h	10.00	-	10.00	16.00
Tray, 7-1/2" l.	15.00	-	20.00	16.00
Tumbler, 5 oz, 3-5/8" h	15.00	-	10.00	15.00
Tumbler, 7 oz, 4-3/8" h	17.50	-	10.00	17.50
Tumbler, 8 oz, 4-3/8" h	17.50	-	12.00	17.50
Tumbler, 9 oz, 4-7/8" h, handle	30.00	-	15.00	28.00
Tumbler, 9 oz, 4-7/8" h	20.00	-	15.00	19.00
Tumbler, 12 oz, 5-1/8" h	30.00	-	15.00	33.00
Vase, 7-1/4" h, flat, ruffled	60.00	-	60.00	60.00
Vase, 8-1/2" h, bud, rocket-shape	245.00	-	185.00	245.00
Vase, 9-1/4" h, rocket-shape	240.00	-	125.00	240.00
Vegetable Bowl, 9-3/4" l, oval.	48.00	-	24.00	48.00
Wine, 3 oz, 5-1/2" h, metal stem	17.50	-	12.00	16.00
Wine, 4-3/4" h, rocket-shape	27.50	-	30.00	85.00
Wine, 4 oz, 4" h	24.00	-	12.00	24.00
Wine, 4 oz, 5-1/2" h, metal stem	20.00	-	12.00	18.00

Moondrops ruby sugar and creamer.

Moondrops pink cup and saucer.

Moonstone

Manufactured by Anchor Hocking Glass Company, Lancaster, Ohio, from 1941 to 1946.

Made in crystal with opalescent hobnails and Ocean Green with opalescent hobnails.

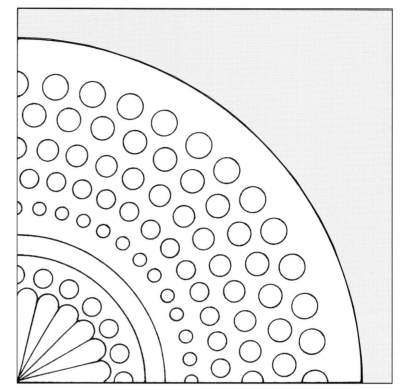

Item	Crystal	Ocean Green
Berry Bowl, 5-1/2" d	18.00	-
Bonbon, heart shape, handle	13.00	-
Bowl, 6-1/2" d, crimped, handle	20.00	-
Bowl, 7-1/4" d, flat	14.00	-
Bowl, 9-1/2" d, crimped	20.00	-
Candleholder, pr.	25.00	-
Candy Jar, cov, 6" h	30.00	-
Cigarette Box, cov	25.00	-
Creamer	9.50	9.50
Cup	8.00	10.00
Dessert Bowl, 5-1/2" d, crimped	9.50	-
Goblet, 10 oz	24.00	24.00
Plate, 6-1/4" d, sherbet	6.00	7.00
Plate, 8-3/8" d, luncheon	15.00	15.00
Puff Box, cov, 4-3/4" d, round	25.00	-
Relish, 7-1/4" d, divided	12.50	-
Relish, cloverleaf	12.50	-
Sandwich Plate, 10-3/4" d	28.00	-
Saucer	6.00	6.00
Sherbet, ftd	7.00	7.00
Sugar, ftd	9.50	9.50
Vase, 5-1/2" h, bud	10.00	-
Vase, 6-1/2" h, ruffled	8.00	-

Moonstone crystal covered candy dish with opalescent hobnails.

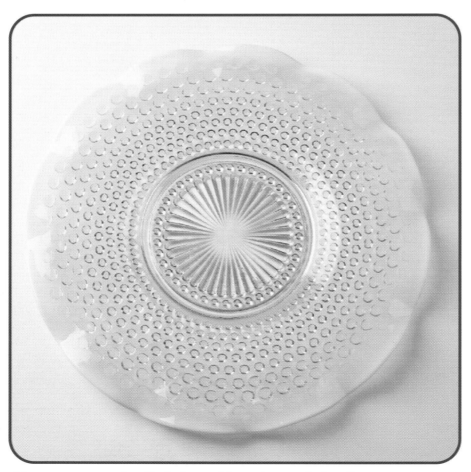

Moonstone crystal ruffled plate with opalescent hobnails.

Moroccan Amethyst

Manufactured by Hazel Ware, division of Continental Can, 1960s.
Made in amethyst.

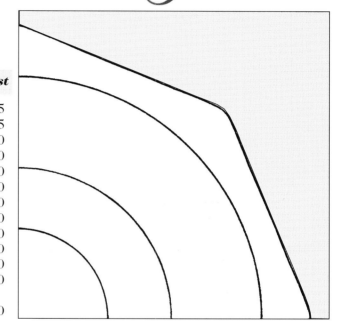

Item	Amethyst
Ashtray, 3-1/4" d, round	5.75
Ashtray, 3-1/4" w, triangular	5.75
Ashtray, 6-7/8" w, triangular	10.00
Ashtray, 8" w, square	14.00
Bowl, 5-3/4" w, deep, square	10.00
Bowl, 6" d, round	8.50
Bowl, 7-3/4" l, oval	17.50
Bowl, 7-3/4" l, rectangular	14.00
Bowl, 7-3/4" l, rectangular, metal handle	17.50
Bowls, 10-3/4" d	30.00
Candy, cov, short	35.00
Candy, cov, tall	32.00
Chip and Dip, 10-3/4" and 5-3/4" bowls in metal frame	40.00
Cocktail Shaker, chrome lid	30.00
Cocktail, stirrer, 16 oz, 6-1/4" h, lip	30.00
Cup	5.00
Fruit Bowl, 4-3/4" d, octagonal	9.00
Goblet, 9 oz, 5-1/2" h	10.00
Ice Bucket, 6" h	35.00
Iced Tea Tumbler, 16 oz, 6-1/2" h	16.00
Juice Goblet, 5-1/2 oz, 4-3/8" h	9.00
Juice Tumbler, 4 oz, 2-1/2" h	10.00
Old Fashioned Tumbler, 8 oz, 3-1/4" h	14.00
Plate, 5-3/4" d, sherbet	4.50
Plate, 7-1/4" d, salad	4.75
Plate, 9-3/4" d, dinner	7.00
Punch Bowl	85.00
Relish, 7-3/4" l	14.00
Salad Fork and Spoon	12.00
Sandwich Plate, 12" d, metal handle	15.00
Saucer	1.00
Sherbet, 7-1/2 oz, 4-1/4" h	8.00
Snack Plate, 10" l, fan shaped, cup rest	8.00
Snack Set, square plate, cup	12.00
Tumbler, 9 oz	10.00
Tumbler, 11 oz, 4-1/4" h, crinkled bottom	12.00
Tumbler, 11 oz, 4-5/8" h	12.00
Vase, 8-1/2" h, ruffled	40.00
Wine, 4-1/2 oz, 4" h	10.00

Moroccan Amethyst cup and saucer.

Mt. Pleasant

Manufactured by L.E. Smith, Mt. Pleasant, Pa., from the 1920s to 1934. Made in amethyst, black, cobalt blue, crystal, green, pink and white.

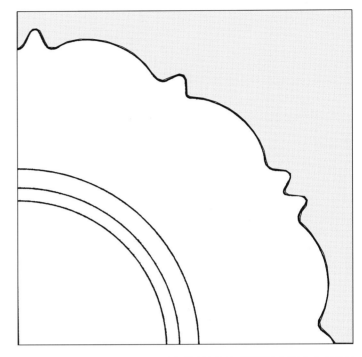

Item	Amethyst	Black	Cobalt Blue	Green	Pink
Bonbon, 7" d, rolled edge	24.00	23.00	24.00	16.00	16.00
Bowl, 6" d, 3 legs	-	25.00	-	-	-
Bowl, 6" w, sq, 2 handles	20.00	15.00	20.00	12.50	12.50
Bowl, 7" d, 3 ftd, rolled out edge	18.50	23.00	18.50	17.50	17.50
Bowl, 8" d, scalloped, 2 handles	37.50	35.00	37.50	20.00	20.00
Bowl, 8" d, sq, 2 handles	38.00	40.00	38.00	20.00	20.00
Bowl, 9" d, scalloped, 1-3/4" deep, ftd	28.00	32.00	30.00	-	-
Bowl, 10" d, 2 handles, turned-up edge	30.00	34.00	32.00	-	-
Cake Plate, 10-1/2" d, 1-1/4" h, ftd	45.00	47.00	40.00	-	-
Cake Plate, 10-1/2" d, 2 handles	26.00	40.00	28.00	17.50	17.50
Candlesticks, pr, 1 light	28.00	42.50	30.00	24.00	28.00
Candlesticks, pr, 2 light	48.00	55.00	50.00	30.00	32.00
Creamer	21.00	19.00	22.50	20.00	24.00
Cup	12.50	15.00	14.00	10.00	10.00
Fruit Bowl, 4-7/8" sq	16.00	20.00	18.00	12.00	10.00
Fruit Bowl, 9-1/4" sq	30.00	50.00	35.00	20.00	20.00
Fruit Bowl, 10" d, scalloped	40.00	40.00	40.00	-	-
Leaf, 8" l	10.00	17.50	16.00	-	-
Leaf, 11-1/4" l	25.00	30.00	28.00	-	-
Mayonnaise, 5-1/2" h, 3 ftd	25.00	28.00	25.00	17.50	17.50
Mint, 6" d, center handle	25.00	26.50	25.00	16.00	16.00
Plate, 7" h, 2 handles, scalloped	15.00	16.00	16.50	10.00	10.00
Plate, 8" d, scalloped	16.00	14.00	16.00	10.00	10.00
Plate, 8" d, scalloped , 3 ftd	17.50	27.00	17.50	10.00	10.00
Plate, 8" w, sq	17.50	25.00	17.50	10.00	10.00

Item	Amethyst	Black	Cobalt Blue	Green	Pink
Plate, 8-1/4" w, sq, indent for cup	17.50	19.00	17.50	-	-
Plate, 9" d, grill	20.00	20.00	20.00	-	-
Plate, 12" d, 2 handles.	35.00	35.00	35.00	20.00	20.00
Rose Bowl, 4" d	25.00	30.00	27.50	20.00	20.00
Salt and Pepper Shakers, pr	45.00	48.00	45.00	25.00	25.00
Sandwich Server, center handle	40.00	37.50	40.00	-	-
Saucer	5.00	5.00	5.00	3.50	3.50
Sherbet.	15.00	16.50	15.00	10.00	10.00
Sugar	9.00	18.00	15.00	20.00	20.00
Tumbler, ftd	25.00	27.50	25.00	-	-
Vase, 7-1/4" h	30.00	35.00	30.00	-	35.00

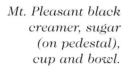

Mt. Pleasant black creamer, sugar (on pedestal), cup and bowl.

Mt. Pleasant black scalloped fruit bowl.

New Century

Manufactured by Hazel Atlas Company, Clarksburg, W.V., and Zanesville, Ohio, from 1930 to 1935.

Made in crystal and green, with limited production in amethyst, cobalt blue and pink.

Item	Amethyst	Cobalt Blue	Crystal	Green	Pink
Ashtray/Coaster, 5-3/8" d	-	-	27.00	28.50	-
Berry Bowl, 4-1/2" d	-	-	18.00	18.00	-
Berry Bowl, 8" d	-	-	20.00	22.00	-
Butter Dish, cov	-	-	55.00	55.00	-
Casserole, cov, 9" d	-	-	60.00	60.00	-
Cocktail, 3-1/4 oz	-	-	20.00	22.00	-
Cream Soup, 4-3/4" d	-	-	20.00	22.00	-
Creamer	-	-	8.50	9.50	-
Cup	20.00	20.00	6.50	8.50	20.00
Decanter, stopper	-	-	55.00	55.00	-
Pitcher, with or without ice lip, 60 oz	35.00	35.00	37.50	37.50	30.00
Pitcher, with or without ice lip, 80 oz	42.00	45.00	40.00	40.00	42.00
Plate, 6" d, sherbet	-	-	3.50	3.50	-
Plate, 7-1/8" d, breakfast	-	-	10.00	10.00	-
Plate, 8-1/2" d, salad	-	-	11.00	11.00	-
Plate, 10" d, dinner	-	-	18.00	18.00	-
Plate, 10" d, grill	-	-	12.00	14.00	-
Platter, 11" l, oval	-	-	18.00	20.00	-
Salt and Pepper Shakers, pr	-	-	35.00	35.00	-
Saucer	7.50	7.50	3.50	3.50	8.00
Sherbet, 3" h	-	-	9.00	9.00	-
Sugar, cov	-	-	24.00	24.00	-
Tumbler, 5 oz, 3-1/2" h	12.00	10.00	12.00	12.00	10.00
Tumbler, 5 oz, 4" h, ftd	-	-	18.00	18.00	-
Tumbler, 8 oz, 3-1/2" h	-	-	20.00	20.00	-
Tumbler, 9 oz, 4-1/4" h	14.00	14.00	17.50	18.00	14.00
Tumbler, 9 oz, 4-7/8" h, ftd	-	-	20.00	20.00	-

Item	Amethyst	Cobalt Blue	Crystal	Green	Pink
Tumbler, 10 oz, 5" h	16.00	16.00	17.50	17.50	16.00
Tumbler, 12 oz, 5-1/4" h	25.00	25.00	25.00	25.00	20.00
Whiskey, 2-1/2" h, 1-1/2 oz	-	-	18.00	20.00	-
Wine, 2-1/2 oz	-	-	25.00	25.00	-

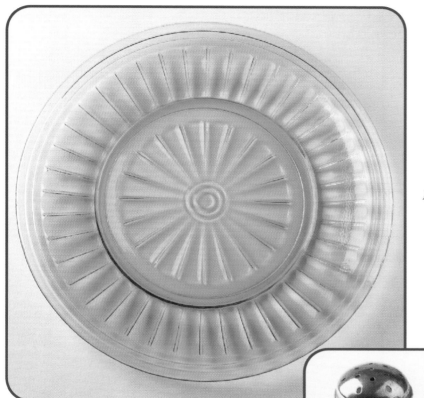

New Century green plate.

New Century green salt and pepper shakers.

Newport *Hairpin*

Manufactured by Hazel Atlas Glass Company, Clarksburg, W.V., and Zanesville, Ohio, from 1936 to the early 1950s.

Made in amethyst, cobalt blue, pink (from 1936 to 1940), Platonite white and fired-on colors (from the 1940s to early 1950s).

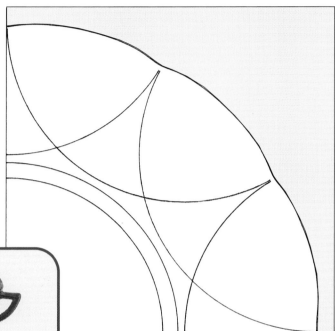

Newport amethyst plate, sugar, creamer and soup bowl.

Item	Amethyst	Cobalt Blue	Fired-On Color	Platonite
Berry Bowl, 4-3/4" d	14.00	19.00	4.00	5.00
Berry Bowl, 8-1/4" d	35.00	22.50	14.00	10.00
Cereal Bowl, 5-1/4" d	30.00	34.00	-	-
Cream Soup, 4-3/4" d	20.00	22.50	6.00	8.50
Creamer	14.00	20.00	8.50	3.00
Cup	12.00	15.00	4.00	2.00
Plate, 6" d, sherbet	7.50	8.00	1.50	1.00
Plate, 8-1/2" d, luncheon	12.00	16.50	5.00	2.50
Plate, 8-13/16" d, dinner	30.00	30.00	15.00	12.00
Platter, 11-3/4" l, oval	35.00	45.00	18.00	12.00
Salt and Pepper Shakers, pr	42.00	45.00	24.00	18.00
Sandwich Plate, 11-1/2" d	48.00	50.00	12.00	10.00
Saucer	5.00	6.00	3.00	2.00
Sherbet	15.00	18.50	7.00	4.00
Sugar	14.00	20.00	9.50	5.00
Tumbler, 9 oz, 4-1/2" h	32.00	38.00	15.00	-

Nora Bird
Line#300

Manufactured by Paden City Glass Company, Paden City, W.V., from 1929 to 1930s.

Made in amber, crystal, green and pink. Amber production is limited; a pair of candlesticks is valued at $115.

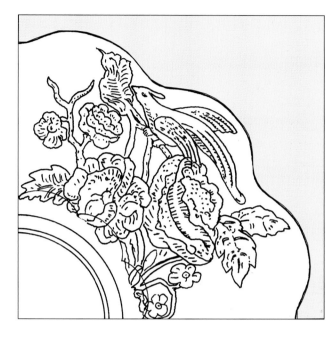

Nora Bird pink mayonnaise liner.

Item	Green	Pink
Candlesticks, pr	85.00	90.00
Candy Dish, cov, 5-1/4" h, ftd	120.00	125.00
Candy Dish, cov, 6-1/2" d, 3 part	120.00	125.00
Creamer, 4-1/2" h, round handle	45.00	48.00
Creamer, 5" h, pointed handle	45.00	48.00
Cup	60.00	60.00
Ice Tub, 6" d	100.00	100.00
Mayonnaise and Liner	90.00	110.00
Plate, 8" d	30.00	35.00
Saucer	15.00	15.00
Sugar, 4-1/2" h, round handle	45.00	48.00
Sugar, 5" h, pointed handle	45.00	48.00
Tumbler, 2-1/4" h, 3 oz	45.00	45.00
Tumbler, 3" h	42.00	42.00
Tumbler, 4" h	50.00	50.00
Tumbler, 4-3/4" h, ftd	60.00	60.00
Tumbler, 5-1/4" h, 10 oz,	60.00	60.00

Normandie

Bouquet and Lattice

Manufactured by Federal Glass Company, Columbus, Ohio, from 1933 to 1940.

Made in amber, crystal, iridescent and pink.

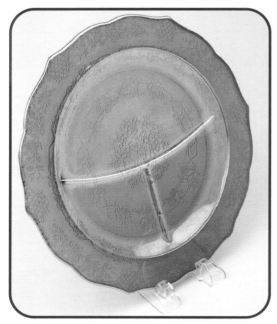

Normandie iridescent grill plate.

Item	Amber	Crystal	Iridescent	Pink
Berry Bowl, 5" d	5.00	4.00	5.00	11.00
Berry Bowl, 8-1/2" d	17.50	12.00	15.00	42.00
Cereal Bowl, 6-1/2" d	25.00	15.00	8.00	30.00
Creamer, ftd	16.00	6.00	4.00	12.00
Cup	7.50	3.50	5.50	8.50
Iced Tea Tumbler, 12 oz, 5" h	50.00	-	-	-
Juice Tumbler, 5 oz, 4" h	38.00	-	-	-
Pitcher, 80 oz, 8" h	89.00	-	-	245.00
Plate, 6" d, sherbet	4.50	2.00	3.00	5.00
Plate, 7-3/4" d, salad	10.00	5.00	55.00	14.00
Plate, 9-1/4" d, luncheon	12.50	6.00	16.50	100.00
Plate, 11" d, dinner	32.00	15.00	10.00	18.00
Plate, 11" d, grill	15.00	8.00	8.00	25.00
Platter, 11-3/4" l	24.00	10.00	12.00	80.00
Salt and Pepper Shakers, pr	50.00	20.00	-	4.00
Saucer	4.00	1.50	3.50	10.00
Sherbet	7.50	5.00	9.00	8.00
Sugar	8.00	6.00	7.00	12.00
Tumbler, 9 oz, 4-1/4" h	25.00	10.00	-	50.00
Vegetable Bowl, 10" l, oval	20.00	10.00	18.50	36.00

Old Café

Manufactured by Hocking Glass Company, Lancaster, Ohio, from 1936 to 1940.
Made in crystal, pink and royal ruby.

Old Café ruby bowl.

Item	Crystal	Pink	Royal Ruby
Berry Bowl, 3-3/4" d	3.50	4.00	6.00
Bowl, 5" d	5.00	5.00	-
Bowl, 9" d, closed handles	10.00	10.00	15.00
Candy Dish, 8" d, low	7.00	11.00	15.00
Candy Jar, 5-1/2" d, crystal with ruby cover	-	-	15.00
Cereal Bowl, 5-1/2" d	8.00	8.00	12.00
Cup	6.00	6.00	10.00
Juice Tumbler, 3" h	10.00	10.00	12.00
Lamp	24.00	24.00	35.00
Olive Dish, 6" l, oblong	6.00	7.50	-
Pitcher, 36 oz, 6" h	72.00	75.00	-
Pitcher, 80 oz	90.00	90.00	-
Plate, 6" d, sherbet	4.00	4.00	-
Plate, 10" d, dinner	35.00	35.00	-
Saucer	4.00	4.00	-
Sherbet, low, ftd	7.00	7.00	12.00
Tumbler, 4" h	12.00	12.00	18.00
Vase, 7-1/4" h	15.00	17.50	22.00

Old Café clear vase and bowl with handles.

Close-up view of original label on Old Café ruby bowl with handles.

Old Café ruby bowl with handles and original label.

Old Colony

Manufactured by Hocking Glass Company, Lancaster, Ohio, from 1935 to 1938.

Made in crystal and pink. Crystal Old Colony pieces are valued at about 50% of pink, as are frosted or satin finish prices. Many other companies made a look-alike to Old Colony, so care must be exercised.

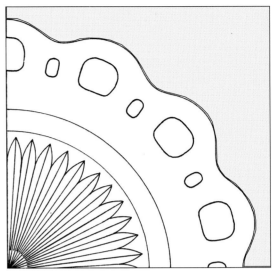

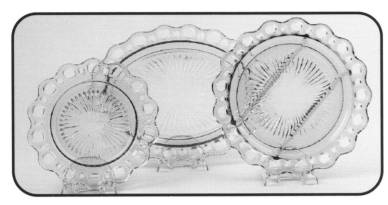

Old Colony, Lace Edge pink plate, platter and divided relish.

Old Colony, Lace Edge pink satin-finish candleholder.

Item	Pink
Bonbon, cov	65.00
Bowl, 9-1/2" d, plain	25.00
Bowl, 9-1/2" d, ribbed	28.00
Butter Dish, cov	65.00
Candlesticks, pr	125.00
Candy Jar, cov, ribbed	45.00
Cereal Bowl, 6-3/8" d	24.00
Comport, 7" d, cov	48.00
Comport, 9" d	750.00
Console Bowl, 10-1/2" d, 3 legs	175.00
Cookie Jar, cov	75.00
Creamer	20.00
Creamer and Sugar	40.00
Cup	24.00
Flower Bowl, crystal frog	25.00
Plate, 7-1/4" d, salad	22.00
Plate, 8-1/4" d, luncheon	24.00
Plate, 10-1/2" d, dinner	30.00
Plate, 10-1/2" d, grill	24.00
Plate, 13" d, 4 part, solid lace	32.00
Plate, 13" d, solid lace	35.00
Platter, 12-3/4" l	35.00
Platter, 12-3/4" l, 5 part	32.00
Relish Dish, 7-1/2" d, 3 part, deep	25.00
Relish Plate, 10-1/2" d, 3 part	25.00
Salad Bowl, 7-3/4" d, ribbed	25.00
Saucer	12.50
Sherbet, ftd	97.50
Sugar	20.00
Tumbler, 5 oz, 3-1/2" h, flat	85.00
Tumbler, 9 oz, 4-1/2" h, flat	18.00
Tumbler, 10-1/2 oz, 5" h, ftd	60.00
Vase, 7" h	365.00

Old English *Threading*

Manufactured by Indiana Glass Company, Dunkirk, Ind., late 1920s.
Made in amber, crystal, green and pink.

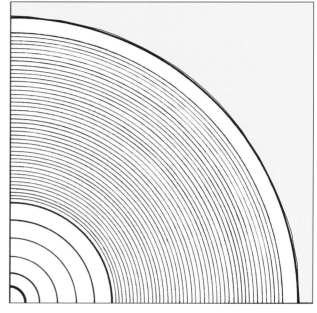

Old English green compote.

Item	Amber	Crystal	Green	Pink
Bowl, 4" d, flat	18.00	15.00	20.00	18.00
Bowl, 9-1/2" d, flat	35.00	25.00	35.00	35.00
Candlesticks, pr, 4" h	35.00	25.00	35.00	35.00
Candy Dish, cov, flat	50.00	40.00	50.00	50.00
Candy Jar, cov	55.00	45.00	55.00	55.00
Cheese Compote, 3-1/2" h	17.50	12.00	17.50	17.50
Cheese Plate, indent	20.00	10.00	20.00	20.00
Compote, 3-1/2" h, 6-3/8" w, 2 handles	24.00	12.00	24.00	24.00
Compote, 3-1/2" h, 7" w	24.00	12.00	24.00	24.00
Creamer	18.00	10.00	18.00	18.00
Egg Cup	-	10.00	-	-
Fruit Bowl, 9" d, ftd	30.00	20.00	30.00	30.00
Fruit Stand, 11" h, ftd	40.00	18.00	40.00	40.00
Goblet, 8 oz, 5-3/4" h	30.00	15.00	30.00	30.00
Pitcher	70.00	35.00	70.00	70.00
Pitcher, cov	125.00	55.00	125.00	125.00
Sandwich Server, center handle	60.00	-	60.00	60.00
Sherbet	20.00	10.00	20.00	20.00
Sugar, cov	38.00	14.00	38.00	38.00
Tumbler, 4-1/2" h, ftd	24.00	12.00	24.00	24.00
Tumbler, 5-1/2" h, ftd	35.00	17.50	35.00	35.00
Vase, 5-3/8" h, 7" w, fan-shape	48.00	24.00	48.00	48.00
Vase, 8" h, 4-1/2" w, ftd	45.00	20.00	45.00	45.00
Vase, 8-1/4" h, 4-1/4" w, ftd	45.00	20.00	45.00	45.00
Vase, 12" h, ftd	60.00	32.00	60.00	60.00

Orchid

Manufactured by Paden City
Glass Company, Paden City, W.V.,
early 1930s.

Made in amber, black, cobalt
blue, green, pink, red and yellow.

Item	Amber	Black	Cobalt Blue	Green	Pink	Red	Yellow
Bowl, 4-1/2" sq	20.00	40.00	37.50	35.00	42.00	40.00	42.00
Bowl, 8-1/2" d, 2 handles	60.00	90.00	85.00	55.00	62.00	90.00	62.00
Bowl, 8-3/4" w, sq.	50.00	75.00	75.00	50.00	50.00	75.00	50.00
Bowl, 10" d, ftd	55.00	115.00	115.00	55.00	55.00	115.00	55.00
Bowl, 11" d, sq	60.00	100.00	100.00	60.00	60.00	100.00	60.00
Candlesticks, pr, 5-3/4" h	80.00	125.00	125.00	80.00	80.00	125.00	80.00
Candy, cov, 6-1/2" w, sq, 3 part . . .	70.00	135.00	135.00	70.00	70.00	135.00	70.00
Comport, 3-1/4" h, 6-1/4" w	24.00	45.00	45.00	24.00	24.00	45.00	24.00
Comport, 6-5/8" h, 7" w	42.00	85.00	85.00	42.00	42.00	85.00	42.00
Creamer.	32.00	60.00	60.00	32.00	32.00	60.00	32.00
Ice Bucket, 6" h	80.00	140.00	140.00	80.00	80.00	140.00	80.00
Mayonnaise, 3 pcs	70.00	115.00	115.00	70.00	70.00	115.00	70.00
Plate, 8-1/2" w, sq	-	50.00	50.00	-	-	50.00	-
Sandwich Server, center handle . . .	45.00	80.00	80.00	45.00	45.00	80.00	45.00
Sugar	32.00	60.00	60.00	32.00	32.00	60.00	32.00
Vase, 8" h.	58.00	125.00	125.00	58.00	58.00	125.00	58.00
Vase, 10" h.	60.00	135.00	135.00	60.00	60.00	135.00	60.00

Orchid yellow compote.

Ovide

Manufactured by Hazel Atlas Glass Company, Clarksburg, W.V., and Zanesville, Ohio, 1930-35 and in the 1950s.

Made in black, green, white Platonite with fired-on colors in the 1950s.

Ovide, informal pink and gray plate.

Item	*Black*	*Green*	*Platonite*
Berry Bowl, 4-3/4" d	-	-	7.50
Berry Bowl, 8" d	-	-	20.00
Candy Dish, cov	45.00	24.00	35.00
Cereal Bowl, 5-1/2" d	10.00	-	12.00
Creamer	7.00	4.50	18.00
Cup	6.50	3.50	14.00
Egg Cup	-	-	22.00
Fruit Cocktail, ftd	5.00	4.50	-
Plate, 6" d, sherbet	-	2.50	6.00
Plate, 8" d, luncheon	-	3.50	15.00
Plate, 9" d, dinner	-	-	25.00
Platter, 11" d	-	-	24.00
Salt and Pepper Shakers, pr	28.00	28.00	25.00
Saucer	3.50	3.50	6.00
Sherbet	6.50	3.50	15.00
Sugar, open	7.00	5.00	18.00
Tumbler	15.00	-	18.00

Oyster & Pearls

Manufactured by Anchor Hocking Glass Corporation, from 1938 to 1940.

Made in crystal, pink, royal ruby and white with fired-on green or pink.

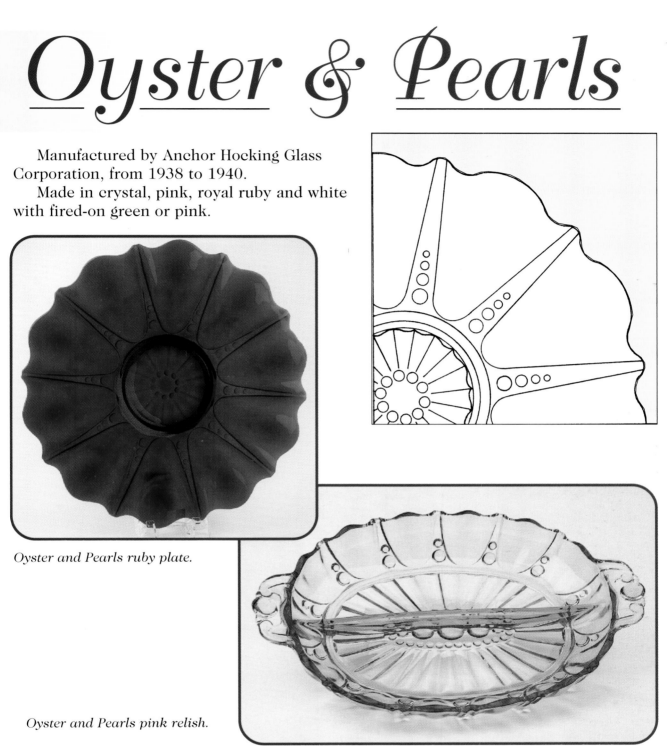

Oyster and Pearls ruby plate.

Oyster and Pearls pink relish.

Item	Crystal	Pink	Royal Ruby	White, Fired-On Green	White, Fired-On Pink
Bowl, 5-1/2" d, handle 8.00	15.00	15.00	-	-
Bowl, 5-1/4" w, handle, heart-shape 8.00	15.00	15.00	8.00	-
Bowl, 6-1/2" d, handle 12.00	11.00	18.00	-	-
Candle Holders, pr, 3-1/2" h 24.00	45.00	48.00	15.00	15.00
Fruit Bowl, 10-1/2" d, deep 20.00	25.00	50.00	15.00	15.00
Relish Dish, 10-1/4" l, divided 8.00	10.00	-	-	-
Sandwich Plate, 13-1/2" d 20.00	34.00	50.00	-	-

Parrot

Sylvan

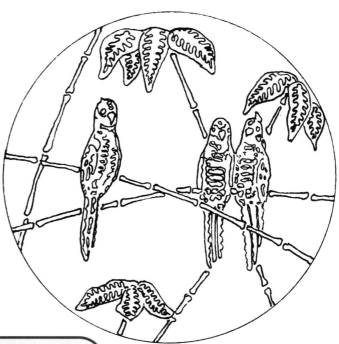

Manufactured by Federal Glass Company, Columbus, Ohio, from 1931 to 1932.

Made in amber and green, with limited production in blue and crystal.

Parrot amber jam bowl and green sherbet plate.

Item	Amber	Green
Berry Bowl, 5" d	22.00	24.00
Berry Bowl, 8" d	75.00	80.00
Butter Dish, cov	1,150.00	375.00
Creamer, ftd	65.00	55.00
Cup	35.00	35.00
Hot Plate, 5" d, pointed	875.00	900.00
Hot Plate, round	-	950.00
Jam Dish, 7" d	35.00	-
Pitcher, 80 oz, 8-1/2" h	-	2,500.00
Plate, 5-3/4" d, sherbet	24.00	35.00
Plate, 7-1/2" d, salad	-	40.00
Plate, 9" d, dinner	49.00	38.00
Plate, 10-1/2" d, grill, round	32.00	-

Item	Amber	Green
Plate, 10-1/2" d, grill, square	-	27.00
Platter, 11-1/4" l, oblong	50.00	55.00
Salt and Pepper Shakers, pr	-	270.00
Saucer	18.00	18.00
Sherbet, ftd, cone	27.00	24.00
Soup Bowl, 7" d	32.00	42.00
Sugar, cov	450.00	175.00
Tumbler, 10 oz, 4-1/4" h	100.00	130.00
Tumbler, 10 oz, 5-1/2" h, ftd, Madrid mold	145.00	-
Tumbler, 12 oz, 5-1/2" h	115.00	160.00
Tumbler, 5-3/4" h, ftd, heavy . . .	100.00	120.00
Vegetable Bowl, 10" l, oval	65.00	57.00

Patrician

Spoke

Manufactured by Federal Glass Company, Columbus, Ohio, from 1933 to 1937.

Made in amber (also called Golden Glo), crystal, green and pink.

Patrician amber bowl, sherbet and cup.

Item	Amber	Crystal	Green	Pink
Berry Bowl, 5" d	12.00	9.50	12.00	17.00
Berry Bowl, 8-1/2" d	47.00	9.00	37.50	35.00
Butter Dish, cov	95.00	100.00	215.00	225.00
Cereal Bowl, 6" d	29.00	27.50	27.50	25.00
Cookie Jar, cov	85.00	80.00	525.00	-
Cream Soup, 4-3/4" d	26.00	24.00	22.50	20.00
Creamer, ftd	12.00	9.00	12.00	12.00
Cup	10.00	8.00	10.00	10.00
Jam Dish	30.00	25.00	35.00	30.00
Pitcher, 75 oz, 8" h, molded handle	120.00	125.00	125.00	115.00
Pitcher, 75 oz, 8-1/4" h, applied handle	150.00	140.00	150.00	145.00
Plate, 6" d, sherbet	10.00	8.50	10.00	10.00
Plate, 7-1/2" d, salad	17.50	15.00	12.50	15.00
Plate, 9" d, luncheon	13.00	12.00	11.00	12.00
Plate, 10-1/2" d, grill	15.00	13.50	20.00	20.00
Plate, 10-1/2 d, dinner	8.00	12.50	32.00	36.00
Platter, 11-1/2" l, oval	32.50	30.00	30.00	28.00
Salt and Pepper Shakers, pr.	55.00	45.00	65.00	85.00
Saucer	10.00	9.25	9.00	9.50
Sherbet	13.00	10.00	14.00	16.00
Sugar	12.00	9.00	12.00	12.00
Tumbler, 5 oz, 4" h	30.00	28.00	30.00	32.00
Tumbler, 8 oz, 5-1/4" h, ftd	47.00	42.00	50.00	-
Tumbler, 9 oz, 4-1/4" h	33.50	28.00	25.00	28.00
Tumbler, 12 oz	42.00	-	-	-
Tumbler, 14 oz, 5-1/2" h	42.00	38.00	40.00	46.00
Vegetable Bowl, 10" l, oval	28.00	30.00	38.50	30.00

Patrick

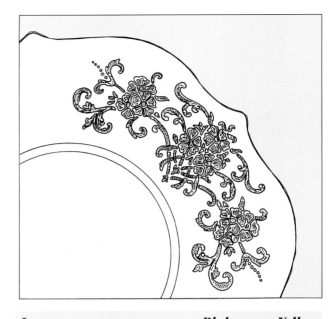

Manufactured by Lancaster Glass
Company, Lancaster, Ohio, early 1930s.
Made in pink and yellow.

Item	Pink	Yellow
Candlesticks, pr	150.00	160.00
Candy Dish, 3 ftd	155.00	165.00
Cheese and Cracker Set	150.00	130.00
Cocktail, 4" h	85.00	85.00
Console Bowl, 11" d	150.00	150.00
Creamer	75.00	40.00
Cup	70.00	40.00
Fruit Bowl, 9" d, handle	172.00	120.00
Goblet, 10 oz, 6" h	100.00	75.00
Juice Goblet, 6 oz, 4-3/4" h . .	95.00	75.00

Item	Pink	Yellow
Mayonnaise, 3 piece	185.00	80.00
Plate, 7" d, sherbet	20.00	15.00
Plate, 7-1/2" d, salad	25.00	20.00
Plate, 8" d, luncheon	45.00	30.00
Saucer	20.00	12.00
Sherbet, 4-3/4" d	65.00	40.00
Sugar	75.00	38.00
Tray, 11" d, center handle . . .	85.00	95.00
Tray, 11" d, two handles	145.00	65.00

Patrick yellow luncheon plate.

Peacock & Wild Rose
Line #1300

Manufactured by Paden City Glass Company, Paden City, W.V., 1930s.

Made in amber, black, cobalt blue, crystal, green, light blue, pink, and red.

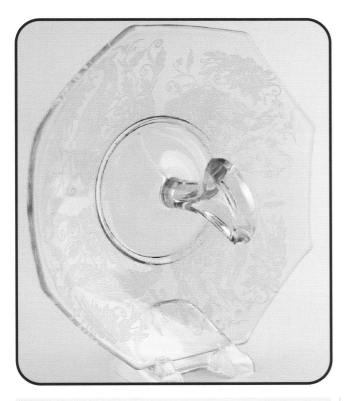

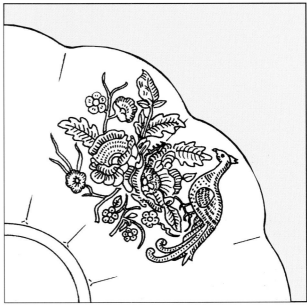

Peacock & Wild Rose pink, server with center handle.

Item	Colors
Bowl, 8-1/2" d, flat	80.00
Bowl, 8-3/4" d, ftd	80.00
Bowl, 9-1/2" d, center handle	175.00
Bowl, 9-1/2" d, ftd	85.00
Bowl, 10-1/2" d, center handle	85.00
Bowl, 10-1/2" d, ftd	95.00
Cake Plate, low foot	195.00
Candlesticks, pr, 5" h	135.00
Candy Dish, cov, 7" d	150.00
Cheese and Cracker Set	120.00
Comport, 3-1/4" h, 6-1/4" w	60.00

Item	Colors
Console Bowl, 11" d	75.00
Console Bowl, 14" d	80.00
Fruit Bowl, 8-1/2" l, oval, ftd	85.00
Fruit Bowl, 10-1/2" d	90.00
Ice Bucket, 6" h	150.00
Ice Tub, 4-3/4" h	140.00
Pitcher, 5" h	150.00
Relish, 3 part	70.00
Vase, 8-1/4" h, elliptical	200.00
Vase, 10" h	115.00
Vase, 12" h	150.00

Peanut Butter

Unknown maker, 1950s.
Made in crystal and milk glass.

Peanut Butter clear tumbler.

Item	Crystal	Milk Glass
Cup	4.00	-
Juice Tumbler, 5-1/4" h	9.00	10.00
Plate, 8" d	5.00	-
Saucer	3.00	-
Sherbet, ftd.	4.00	5.00
Tumbler, 5-3/4" h	6.00	7.00

Petalware

Manufactured by MacBeth-Evans Glass Company, Charleroi, Pa., from 1930 to 1940.

Made in cobalt blue, cremax, crystal, fired-on red, blue, green and yellow, monax and pink. Florette is the name given to a floral dec with a pointed petal. There are other patterns, such as red flower with a red rim, fruit and other floral patterns. Crystal values are about 50% less than those listed for Cremax. Cobalt blue production was limited, the mustard is currently valued at $15, when complete with its metal lid. Monax Regency is priced the same as Monax Florette.

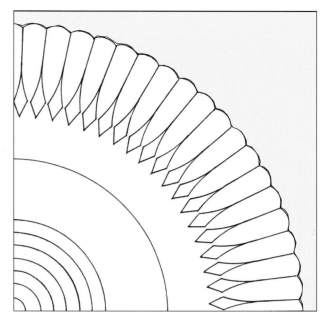

Item	Cremax	Cremax, Gold Trim	Fired-On Colors	Moanax, Florette	Moanax, Plain	Pink
Berry Bowl, 9" d	30.00	32.00	-	35.00	18.00	25.00
Cereal Bowl, 5-1/4" d	15.00	17.50	8.50	12.00	9.00	13.00
Cream Soup Liner	-	-	-	-	19.00	-
Cream Soup, 4-1/2" d	12.50	12.00	12.00	15.00	11.25	17.00
Creamer, ftd	12.50	15.00	8.50	12.00	6.00	10.00
Cup	8.00	10.00	9.50	8.00	4.50	8.00
Lamp Shade, 9" d	17.00	-	-	14.00	18.00	-
Plate, 6" d, sherbet	4.50	50.00	6.00	6.00	2.50	4.50
Plate, 8" d, salad	8.00	8.00	7.50	10.00	4.50	8.50
Plate, 9" d, dinner	15.00	14.00	8.50	16.50	10.00	15.00
Platter, 13" l, oval	25.00	20.00	20.00	25.00	20.00	17.50
Salver, 11" d	14.00	17.00	14.00	16.50	14.00	19.00
Salver, 12" d	-	-	-	-	22.00	19.00
Saucer	3.50	4.00	4.00	4.50	4.00	5.00
Sherbet, 4" h, low ftd	-	-	-	-	32.00	-
Sherbet, 4-1/2" h, low ftd	15.00	12.00	8.00	12.00	10.00	8.50
Soup Bowl, 7" d	65.00	60.00	70.00	65.00	60.00	-
Sugar, ftd	7.50	11.00	12.00	11.00	10.00	10.00
Tumbler, 12 oz, 4-5/8" h	-	-	-	-	-	25.00

Petalware Monax plate.

Petalware Monax sugar and creamer.

Petalware pink sugar, creamer and two plates.

Petalware pink plate, sugar and creamer.

Pineapple & Floral

No. 618

Manufactured by Indiana Glass Company, Dunkirk, Ind., from 1932 to 1937.

Made in amber, avocado (late 1960s), cobalt blue (1980s), crystal, fired-on green, fired-on red and pink (1980s).

Reproductions: † Salad bowl and diamond-shaped comport have been reproduced in several different colors.

Item	Amber	Crystal	Red
Ashtray, 4-1/2" d	20.00	16.50	20.00
Berry Bowl, 4-3/4" d	22.00	20.00	22.00
Cereal Bowl, 6" d	22.00	25.00	22.00
Comport, diamond shape	10.00	3.00	10.00
Creamer, diamond shape	10.00	7.50	10.00
Cream Soup	16.50	18.00	16.50
Cup	10.00	10.00	10.00
Plate, 6" d, sherbet	6.00	5.00	6.00
Plate, 8-3/8" d, salad	8.00	8.00	8.00
Plate, 9-3/8" d, dinner	15.00	17.50	15.00
Plate, 9-3/4" d, indentation	-	25.00	-
Plate, 11" d, closed handles	18.00	17.00	18.00
Plate, 11-1/2" d, indentation	-	25.00	-
Platter, 11" l, closed handles	15.00	18.00	15.00
Relish, 11-1/2" d, divided	20.00	16.50	20.00
Salad Bowl, 7" d †	10.00	3.00	10.00
Sandwich Plate, 11-1/2" d	13.00	20.00	13.00
Saucer	5.00	6.00	5.00
Sherbet, ftd	24.00	20.00	24.00
Sugar, diamond-shape	10.00	6.00	10.00
Tumbler, 8 oz, 4-1/4" h	40.00	40.00	40.00
Tumbler, 12 oz, 5" h	48.00	48.00	48.00
Vase, cone shape	45.00	42.50	45.00
Vegetable Bowl, 10" l, oval	30.00	30.00	30.00

Pineapple & Floral clear sugar and creamer.

Pineapple & Floral amber cream soup.

Pretzel

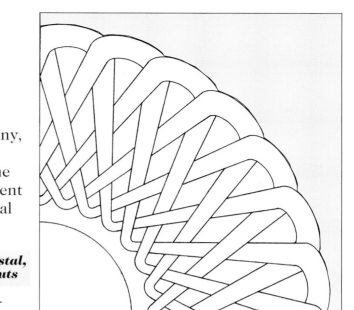

No. 622

Manufactured by Indiana Glass Company, Dunkirk, Ind., from late 1930s to 1960s.

Made in avocado, crystal and teal. Some crystal pieces have a fruit decoration. Recent amber, blue and opaque white issues. A teal cup and saucer is valued at $55.

Item	Crystal, Plain	Crystal, Friuts
Berry Bowl, 9-3/8" d	18.00	-
Bowl, 8" d	7.00	-
Celery Tray, 10-1/4" l	7.50	-
Creamer	6.00	-
Cup	8.00	-
Cup and Saucer	9.50	-
Fruit Cup, 4-1/2" d	8.00	-
Iced Tea Tumbler, 12 oz, 5-1/2" h	77.50	-
Juice Tumbler	35.00	-
Olive, 7" l, leaf-shape	7.00	-
Pickle, 8-1/2" d, two handles	4.00	-
Pitcher, 39 oz	200.00	-
Plate, 6" d	2.50	3.50
Plate, 6" d, tab handle	7.00	-
Plate, 7" sq, wings	9.00	-
Plate, 7-1/4" w, sq, indent	9.00	-
Plate, 7-1/4" w, sq, indent, 3 part	9.00	-
Plate, 8-3/8" d, salad	6.00	6.00
Plate, 9-3/8" d, dinner	10.00	12.00
Plate, 10" d, dinner	10.00	15.00
Relish, 7", 3 part	9.00	-
Sandwich Plate, 11-1/2" d	11.00	12.00
Saucer	1.50	-
Soup Bowl, 7-1/2" d	15.00	10.00
Sugar	6.00	-
Tumbler, 5 oz, 3-1/2" h	50.00	-
Tumbler, 9 oz, 4-1/2" h	55.00	-

Pretzel creamer and clear sugar.

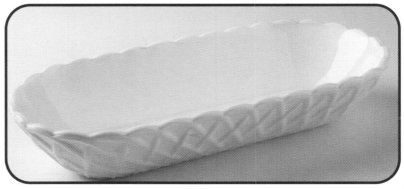

Pretzel milk white celery tray.

Primo

Paneled Aster

Manufactured by U.S. Glass Company, Pittsburgh, early 1930s. Made in green and yellow.

Primo yellow cup.

Item	Green	Yellow
Bowl, 4-1/2"d	15.00	15.00
Bowl, 7-3/4" d	25.00	25.00
Cake Plate, 10" d, 3 ftd	23.50	23.50
Coaster/Ashtray	8.75	8.75
Creamer	12.00	8.50
Cup	14.50	14.50
Plate, 7-1/2" d	10.25	12.00
Plate, 10" d, dinner	22.50	24.00
Plate, 10" d, grill	12.00	11.25
Saucer	3.25	3.25
Sherbet	14.25	14.50
Sugar	12.00	12.00
Tumbler, 9 oz, 5-3/4" h, ftd	23.50	20.00

Princess

Manufactured by Hocking Glass Company, Lancaster, Ohio, from 1931 to 1935.

Made in apricot yellow, blue, green, pink and topaz yellow.

Reproductions: † The candy dish and salt and pepper shakers have been reproduced in blue, green and pink.

Item	Apricot Yellow	Blue	Green	Pink	Topaz Yellow
Ashtray, 4-1/2" d	90.00	-	70.00	80.00	90.00
Berry Bowl, 4-1/2" d	48.00	-	30.00	32.00	48.00
Butter Dish, cov	650.00	-	100.00	95.00	650.00
Cake Plate, 10" d, ftd	-	-	37.50	100.00	-
Candy Dish, cov †	-	-	60.00	85.00	-
Cereal Bowl, 5" d	-	-	36.00	33.00	-
Coaster	90.00	-	35.00	65.00	90.00
Cookie Jar, cov	-	875.00	55.00	75.00	-
Creamer, oval	22.50	-	15.00	17.50	22.50
Cup	5.00	115.00	12.00	12.50	8.00
Hat-Shaped Bowl, 9-1/2" d	125.00	-	45.00	50.00	125.00
Iced Tea Tumbler, 13 oz, 5-1/2" h	28.00	-	125.00	105.00	28.00
Juice Tumbler, 5 oz, 3" h	28.00	-	25.00	28.00	28.00
Pitcher, 24 oz, 7-3/8" h, ftd	-	-	550.00	75.00	-
Pitcher, 37 oz, 6" h	565.00	-	55.00	62.00	565.00
Pitcher, 60 oz, 8" h	95.00	-	65.00	60.00	95.00
Plate, 5-1/2" d, sherbet	2.75	65.00	10.00	10.00	2.75
Plate, 8" d, salad	10.00	-	15.00	15.00	10.00
Plate, 9-1/2" d, dinner	25.00	-	26.00	35.00	25.00
Plate, 9-1/2" d, grill	9.50	115.00	15.00	15.00	9.50
Plate, 10-1/2" d, grill, closed handles	7.50	-	12.00	15.00	7.50
Platter, 12" l, closed handles	60.00	-	23.00	25.00	60.00
Relish, 7-1/2" l, divided, 4 part	100.00	-	30.00	30.00	100.00
Relish, 7-1/2" l, plain	160.00	-	115.00	175.00	160.00
Salad Bowl, 9" d, octagonal	125.00	-	46.00	40.00	125.00
Salt and Pepper Shakers, pr, 4-1/2" h †	75.00	-	60.00	65.00	75.00
Sandwich Plate, 10-1/4" d, 2 closed handles	165.00	-	20.00	35.00	165.00
Saucer, 6" sq	2.75	65.00	10.00	10.00	2.75
Sherbet, ftd	36.00	-	25.00	23.00	36.00
Spice Shakers, pr, 5-1/2" h	-	-	20.00	-	-

Item	Apricot Yellow	Blue	Green	Pink	Topaz Yellow
Sugar, cov	30.00	-	35.00	45.00	30.00
Tumbler, 9 oz, 4" h.	25.00	-	28.00	25.00	25.00
Tumbler, 9 oz, 4-3/4" h, sq, ftd	-	-	65.00	25.00	-
Tumbler, 10 oz, 5-1/4" h, ftd.	28.00	-	35.00	32.00	28.00
Tumbler, 12-1/2 oz, 6-1/2" h, ftd.	20.00	-	85.00	85.00	20.00
Vase, 8" h.	-	-	45.00	50.00	-
Vegetable Bowl, 10" l, oval	60.00	-	28.00	30.00	62.50

Princess green cookie jar.

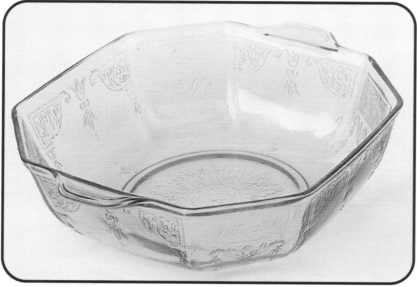

Princess green bowl.

Pyramid

No. 610

Manufactured by Indiana Glass Company, Dunkirk, Ind., from 1926 to 1932.

Made in black (1974-75 by Tiara), blue, crystal, green, pink, white and yellow. Production limited in blue and white. Prices for black not firmly established in secondary market at this time.

Item	Crystal	Green	Pink	Yellow
Berry Bowl, 4-3/4" d.	10.00	25.00	20.00	40.00
Berry Bowl, 8-1/2" d.	17.50	65.00	32.00	60.00
Bowl, 9-1/2" l, oval	25.00	45.00	35.00	55.00
Creamer	15.00	30.00	30.00	40.00
Creamer and Sugar, tray	50.00	175.00	175.00	105.00
Ice Tub	55.00	90.00	80.00	185.00
Pickle Dish, 9-1/2" l, 5-3/4" w	20.00	35.00	35.00	65.00
Pitcher	350.00	210.00	475.00	450.00
Relish, 4 part, handles	25.00	48.00	50.00	65.00
Salt and Pepper Shakers, pr	16.00	-	-	-
Sugar	15.00	30.00	30.00	40.00
Tray for creamer and sugar	20.00	25.00	25.00	35.00
Tumbler, 8 oz, ftd.	50.00	45.00	50.00	75.00
Tumbler, 11 oz, ftd.	60.00	50.00	45.00	70.00

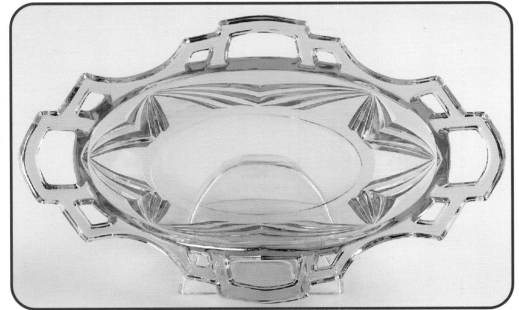

Pyramid green relish.

Queen Mary

Prismatic Line, Vertical Ribbed

Manufactured by Hocking Glass Company, Lancaster, Ohio, from 1936 to 1948.

Made in crystal, pink and royal ruby. The royal ruby pieces include an oval ashtray, 2" x 3-3/4" l, valued at $5, and a pair of 4-1/2" h, two-light candlesticks, valued at $70.

Queen Mary crystal bowl and candlesticks.

Item	Crystal	Pink
Ashtray, 2" x 3-3/4" l, oval	4.00	5.50
Ashtray, 3-1/2" d, round	4.00	-
Berry Bowl, 4-1/2" d	3.00	5.00
Berry Bowl, 5" d	4.00	10.00
Berry Bowl, 8-3/4" d	10.00	17.50
Bowl, 4" d, one handle	4.00	12.50
Bowl, 5-1/2" d, two handles	6.00	13.00
Bowl, 7" d	7.50	35.00
Butter Dish, cov	38.00	125.00
Candlesticks, pr, 2 light, 4-1/2" h	24.00	-
Candy Dish, cov	30.00	38.00
Celery Tray, 5" x 10"	10.00	24.00
Cereal Bowl, 6" d	8.00	24.00
Cigarette Jar, 2" x 3" oval	6.00	7.50
Coaster, 3-1/2" d	4.00	5.00
Coaster/Ashtray, 4-1/4" sq	4.00	6.00
Comport, 5-3/4"	9.00	14.00
Creamer, ftd	6.00	40.00
Creamer, oval	6.00	12.00
Cup, large	5.00	7.00

Item	Crystal	Pink
Cup, small	8.50	10.00
Juice Tumbler, 5 oz, 3-1/2" h	4.50	10.00
Pickle Dish, 5" x 10"	10.00	24.00
Plate, 6" d, sherbet	4.00	5.00
Plate, 6-1/2" d, bread and butter	6.00	-
Plate, 8-1/4" d, salad	6.00	-
Plate, 9-1/2" d, dinner	15.00	60.00
Preserve, cov	30.00	125.00
Relish, clover-shape	15.00	17.50
Relish, 12" d, 3 part	10.00	15.00
Relish, 14" d, 4 part	15.00	17.50
Salt and Pepper Shakers, pr	20.00	-
Sandwich Plate, 12" d	16.00	15.00
Saucer	2.00	5.00
Serving Tray, 14" d	15.00	9.00
Sherbet, ftd	6.50	9.00
Sugar, ftd	-	40.00
Sugar, oval	6.00	12.00
Tumbler, 9 oz, 4" h	6.00	12.00
Tumbler, 10 oz, 5" h, ftd	28.00	66.00

Radiance

Manufactured by New Martinsville Glass Company, New Martinsville, W.V., from 1936 to 1939.

Made in amber, cobalt blue, crystal, emerald green, ice blue, pink and red. Some pieces are found with an etched design. This adds slightly to the value. In emerald green, look for a punch bowl, 9" d, for $135; and a punch bowl liner, 14" d, for $35.

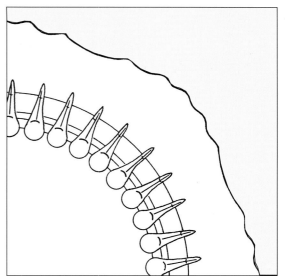

Item	Amber	Cobalt Blue	Crystal	Ice Blue	Pink	Red
Bonbon, 6" d	16.00	-	8.00	32.00	-	32.00
Bonbon, 6" d, cov	48.00	-	24.00	95.00	-	95.00
Bonbon, 6" d, ftd	18.00	-	9.00	35.00	-	35.00
Bowl, 6" d, ruffled	-	-	-	35.00	-	-
Bowl, 6-1/2" d, ftd, metal holder	-	-	-	-	-	32.00
Bowl, 10" d, crimped	28.00	-	14.00	48.00	-	48.00
Bowl, 10" d, flared	22.00	-	11.00	48.00	-	48.00
Bowl, 12" d, crimped	30.00	-	15.00	50.00	-	50.00
Bowl, 12" d, flared	28.00	-	14.00	50.00	-	50.00
Butter Dish, cov	210.00	-	100.00	460.00	-	460.00
Butter Dish, chrome lid	40.00	-	20.00	-	-	-
Cake Salver	-	-	-	175.00	-	175.00
Candlesticks, pr, 2 light	75.00	-	37.50	120.00	-	120.00
Candlesticks, pr, 6" h, ruffled	85.00	-	40.00	175.00	-	175.00
Candlesticks, pr, 8" h	60.00	-	30.00	110.00	-	110.00
Candy Dish, cov, 3 part	-	125.00	-	125.00	-	125.00
Celery Tray, 10" l	18.00	-	9.00	32.00	-	32.00
Cheese and Cracker Set, 11" d plate	32.00	-	15.00	55.00	-	55.00
Comport, 5" h	18.00	-	9.00	30.00	-	30.00
Comport, 6" h	24.00	-	12.00	35.00	-	35.00
Condiment Set., 4 pc, tray	160.00	-	85.00	295.00	-	295.00
Cordial, 1 oz	30.00	-	15.00	45.00	-	45.00
Creamer	14.00	-	7.00	30.00	32.00	32.00
Cruet, individual	40.00	-	20.00	26.00	-	27.50
Cup, ftd	15.00	18.00	8.00	18.00	20.00	20.00
Decanter, stopper, handle	90.00	195.00	45.00	175.00	-	175.00
Lamp, 12" h	60.00	-	30.00	115.00	-	115.00
Mayonnaise, 3 pc set	37.50	-	19.00	85.00	-	85.00
Nut Bowl, 5" d, 2 handles	12.00	-	6.50	20.00	-	24.00
Pickle, 7"d	16.00	-	8.00	25.00	-	27.50
Pitcher, 64 oz	150.00	350.00	75.00	225.00	-	235.00
Pitcher, silver overlay	-	-	-	-	-	125.00
Plate, 8" d, luncheon	10.00	-	5.00	12.00	-	12.00
Punch Bowl, 9" d	110.00	-	65.00	185.00	-	185.00
Punch Bowl Liner, 14" d	48.00	-	24.00	85.00	-	85.00
Punch Cup	8.00	-	5.00	15.00	-	15.00

Item	Amber	Cobalt Blue	Crystal	Ice Blue	Pink	Red
Punch Ladle	100.00	-	45.00	120.00	-	120.00
Relish, 7"d, 2 part	18.00	-	9.00	32.00	-	32.00
Relish, 8" d, 3 part	28.00	-	14.00	35.00	-	35.00
Salt and Pepper Shakers, pr	50.00	-	25.00	90.00	95.00	95.00
Saucer	6.00	7.50	3.50	7.50	8.00	8.00
Sugar	16.00	-	8.00	30.00	32.00	32.00
Tray, oval	25.00	-	15.00	32.00	32.00	32.00
Tumbler, 9" oz	20.00	35.00	10.00	30.00	-	35.00
Vase, 10" h, crimped	48.00	75.00	24.00	60.00	-	70.00
Vase, 10" h, flared	48.00	75.00	24.00	60.00	-	70.00
Vase, 12" h, crimped	60.00	50.00	30.00	55.00	-	85.00
Vase, 12" h, flared	60.00	-	30.00	55.00	-	85.00

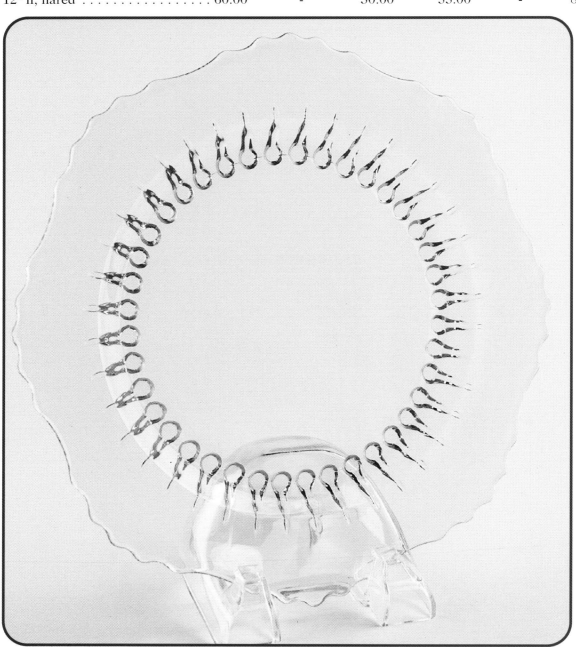

Radiance blue plate.

Raindrops *Optic Design*

Manufactured by Federal Glass Company, Columbus, Ohio, from 1929 to 1933.
Made in crystal and green.

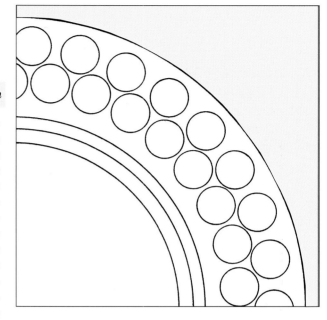

Item	Crystal	Green
Berry Bowl, 7-1/2" d	30.00	45.00
Cereal Bowl, 6" d	10.00	15.00
Creamer	8.00	10.00
Cup	4.00	6.50
Fruit Bowl, 4-1/2" d	5.00	11.00
Plate, 6" d, sherbet	1.50	3.00
Plate, 8" d, luncheon	4.00	7.50
Salt and Pepper Shakers, pr	150.00	315.00
Saucer	1.00	2.50
Sherbet	4.50	7.50
Sugar, cov	7.50	15.00
Tumbler, 2 oz, 2-1/8" h	4.00	7.00
Tumbler, 4 oz, 3" h	4.00	7.00
Tumbler, 5 oz, 3-7/8" h	5.50	9.50
Tumbler, 9-1/2 oz, 4-1/8" h	6.00	12.00
Tumbler, 10 oz, 5" h	6.00	12.00
Tumbler, 14 oz, 5-3/8" h	7.50	15.00
Whiskey, 1 oz, 1-7/8" h	6.50	9.00

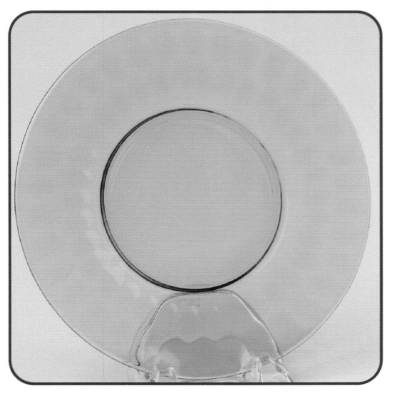

Raindrops green salad plate.

Ribbon

Manufactured by Hazel Atlas Glass Company, Clarksburg, W.V., and Zanesville, Ohio, early 1930s.

Made in black, crystal, green and pink. Production in pink was limited to salt and pepper shakers, valued at $40.

Item	Black	Crystal	Green
Berry Bowl, 4" d	-	20.00	22.00
Berry Bowl, 8" d	-	27.50	30.00
Candy Dish, cov	38.00	30.00	32.00
Cereal Bowl, 5" d	-	20.00	25.00
Creamer, ftd	-	10.00	15.00
Cup	-	3.50	5.50
Plate, 6-1/4" d, sherbet	-	2.50	3.50
Plate, 8" d, luncheon	15.00	4.00	5.50
Salt and Pepper Shakers, pr	45.00	22.00	32.00
Saucer	-	1.00	2.50
Sherbet	-	4.00	6.00
Sugar, ftd	-	10.00	12.00
Tumbler, 10 oz, 6" h	-	27.00	30.00

Ribbon green cup and creamer.

Ring Banded Rings

Manufactured by Hocking Glass Company, Lancaster, Ohio, from 1927 to 1933.

Made in crystal, crystal with rings of black, blue, pink, red, orange, silver, and yellow; green, Mayfair blue, pink and red. Prices for decorated pieces are quite similar to each other.

Item	Crystal	Decorated	Green
Berry Bowl, 5" d.	4.00	9.00	8.00
Berry Bowl, 8" d.	7.50	16.00	16.00
Bowl, 5-1/4" d, divided	12.50	-	-
Butter Tub	24.00	25.00	20.00
Cereal Bowl	-	5.00	8.00
Cocktail Shaker	20.00	30.00	27.50
Cocktail, 3-1/2 oz, 3-3/4" h	12.00	18.00	18.00
Creamer, ftd	5.00	10.00	10.00
Cup	5.00	3.00	5.00
Decanter, stopper	25.00	35.00	32.00
Goblet, 9 oz, 7-1/4" h	7.00	14.00	14.00
Ice Bucket	20.00	33.00	30.00
Ice Tub	24.00	25.00	20.00
Iced Tea Tumbler, 6-1/2" h	8.00	15.00	15.00
Juice Tumbler, 3-1/2" h, ftd	6.50	10.00	15.00
Old Fashioned Tumbler, 8 oz, 4" h	15.00	17.50	17.50
Pitcher, 60 oz, 8" h	22.00	25.00	25.00
Pitcher, 80 oz, 8-1/2" h	17.00	20.00	20.00
Plate, 6-1/2" d, off-center ring	5.00	8.50	8.00
Plate, 6-1/4" d, sherbet	3.00	4.50	4.00
Plate, 8" d, luncheon	3.00	7.00	9.00
Salt and Pepper Shakers, pr, 3" h	20.00	40.00	42.00
Sandwich Plate, 11-3/4" d	8.00	15.00	15.00
Sandwich Server, center handle	15.00	27.50	27.50
Saucer	1.50	2.50	2.50
Sherbet, low	5.00	12.00	12.00
Sherbet, 4-3/4" h	5.00	10.00	12.00
Sherbet, flat, 6-1/2" d underplate	12.00	18.00	21.00
Soup Bowl, 7" d	10.00	9.00	8.00
Sugar, ftd	5.00	10.00	3.00
Tumbler, 4 oz, 3" h	4.00	6.50	6.00

Item	Crystal	Decorated	Green
Tumbler, 5-1/2" h, ftd.	6.00	10.00	10.00
Tumbler, 5 oz, 3-1/2" h	6.50	6.50	12.00
Tumbler, 9 oz, 4-1/4" h	7.50	7.00	9.00
Tumbler, 10 oz, 4-3/4" h	8.50	-	9.00
Tumbler, 12 oz, 5-1/8" h, ftd	5.00	6.00	10.00
Vase, 8" h.	20.00	35.00	37.50
Whiskey, 1-1/2 oz, 2" h	6.50	10.00	12.00
Wine, 3-1/2 oz, 4-1/2" h	14.00	20.00	22.00

Ring green ice tub.

Ring crystal sandwich server.

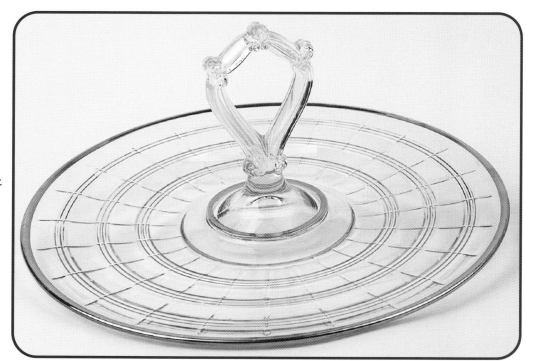

Rock Crystal

Early American Rock Crystal

Manufactured by McKee Glass Company, Pittsburgh, in the 1920s and colors in 1930s.

Made in amber, amberina red, amethyst, aquamarine, blue frosted, cobalt blue, crystal, crystal with goofus dec, crystal with gold dec, dark red, four shades of green, milk glass, pink and frosted pink, red, red slag, vaseline and yellow.

Item	Crystal	Colors	Red
Bonbon, 7-1/2"d, scalloped edge	22.00	35.00	55.00
Bowl, 4" d, scalloped edge	15.00	24.00	35.00
Bowl, 4-1/2" d, scalloped edge	15.00	24.00	35.00
Bowl, 5" d, plain edge	16.00	26.00	45.00
Bowl, 5" d, scalloped edge	16.00	26.00	45.00
Bowl, 8-1/2" d, center handle	-	-	150.00
Bowl, 12-1/2" d, pedestal	80.00	125.00	300.00
Butter Dish, cov	350.00	-	-
Cake Stand, 11" d, 2-3/4" h, ftd	40.00	55.00	135.00
Candelabra, pr, 2-light	50.00	110.00	250.00
Candelabra, pr, 3-light	70.00	135.00	350.00
Candlesticks, pr, 5-1/2" h, low	45.00	70.00	175.00
Candlesticks, pr, 8" h	95.00	70.00	400.00
Candy Dish, cov, ftd, 9-1/2" d	55.00	95.00	225.00
Candy Dish, cov, round	50.00	75.00	175.00
Celery Tray, 12" l, oblong	30.00	40.00	85.00
Center Bowl, 12-1/2" d, ftd	80.00	125.00	300.00
Champagne, 6 oz, ftd	16.00	25.00	35.00
Claret, 3 oz	-	65.00	-
Cocktail, 3-1/2 oz, ftd	15.00	22.00	23.00
Comport, 7" d	35.00	50.00	90.00
Cordial, 1 oz, ftd	25.00	45.00	65.00
Creamer, 9 oz, ftd	20.00	35.00	70.00
Creamer, flat, scalloped edge	40.00	-	-
Cruet, stopper, 6 oz,	95.00	-	-

Item	Crystal	Colors	Red
Cup, 7 oz	17.00	25.00	70.00
Deviled Egg Plate	50.00	-	-
Egg Cup, 3-1/2 oz, ftd	8.50	20.00	25.00
Finger Bowl, 5" d bowl, 7" d plate, pie-crust edge	27.50	48.00	60.00
Goblet, 8 oz, ftd	16.00	27.50	60.00
Goblet, 8 oz, 7-1/2" h, low, ftd	18.00	30.00	60.00
Ice Dish	35.00	-	-
Iced Tea Goblet, 11 oz	25.00	35.00	70.00
Jelly, 5" d, ftd, scalloped edge	18.00	30.00	50.00
Juice Tumbler, 5 oz	17.50	25.00	50.00
Lamp, electric	185.00	300.00	650.00
Old Fashioned Tumbler, 5 oz	18.00	30.00	60.00
Parfait, 3-1/2 oz, low, ftd	18.00	40.00	75.00
Pickle, 7" l	20.00	40.00	65.00
Pitcher, covered, 9" h	175.00	300.00	675.00
Pitcher, half gallon, 7-1/2" h	100.00	165.00	-
Pitcher, quart, scalloped edge	150.00	220.00	-
Pitcher, tankard	190.00	495.00	900.00
Plate, 6" d, bread & butter, scalloped edge	6.50	9.50	20.00
Plate, 7-1/2" d, pie-crust edge	8.00	12.00	22.00
Plate, 7-1/2" d, scalloped edge	8.00	12.00	22.00
Plate, 8-1/2" d, pie-crust edge	9.00	12.00	30.00
Plate, 8-1/2" d, scalloped edge	9.00	12.00	30.00
Plate, 9" d, scalloped edge	18.50	24.00	55.00
Plate, 10-1/2" d, center design, scalloped edge	47.50	75.00	175.00
Plate, 10-1/2" d, scalloped edge	27.50	35.00	65.00
Plate, 11-1/2" d, scalloped edge	20.00	30.00	60.00
Punch Bowl and Stand, 14"	550.00	-	-
Relish, 11-1/2" d, 2 part	35.00	50.00	75.00
Relish, 12-1/2" d, 5 part	45.00	-	-
Relish, 14" d, 6 part	40.00	65.00	-
Roll Tray, 13" d	35.00	60.00	125.00
Salad Bowl, 7" d, scalloped edge	25.00	40.00	65.00
Salad Bowl, 8" d, scalloped edge	32.00	42.00	67.50
Salad Bowl, 9" d, scalloped edge	35.00	50.00	85.00
Salad Bowl, 10-1/2" d, scalloped edge	25.00	50.00	90.00
Salt and Pepper Shakers, pr	80.00	135.00	-
Salt Dip	35.00	-	-
Sandwich Server, center handle	32.00	40.00	140.00
Saucer	5.00	6.50	20.00
Sherbet, 3-1/2 oz, ftd	15.00	20.00	25.00
Spoon Tray, 7" l	20.00	40.00	65.00
Spooner	42.00	-	-
Stemware, 7 oz	18.00	25.00	50.00
Sugar, cov	50.00	65.00	155.00
Sugar, 10 oz, open	18.00	20.00	40.00
Sundae, 6 oz, low, ftd	10.00	15.00	35.00
Syrup, lid	165.00	-	-
Tray, 5-3/8" x 7-3/8", 7/8" h	70.00	-	-

Item	Crystal	Colors	Red
Tumbler, 9 oz, concave	15.00	26.00	30.00
Tumbler, 9 oz, straight	15.00	26.00	30.00
Tumbler, 12 oz, concave	35.00	40.00	70.00
Tumbler, 12 oz, straight	35.00	40.00	70.00
Vase, 11" h, ftd.	75.00	95.00	170.00
Vase, cornucopia	70.00	95.00	-
Whiskey, 2-1/2 oz	25.00	35.00	66.50
Wine, 2 oz	16.00	27.50	50.00

Rock Crystal amber plate.

Rose Cameo

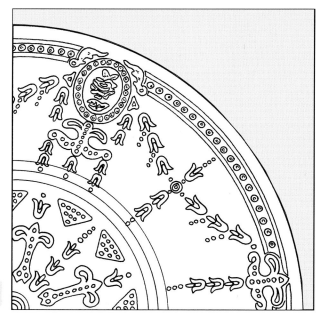

Manufactured by Belmont Tumbler
Company, Bellaire, Ohio, in 1931.
Made in green.

Item	Green
Berry Bowl, 4-1/2" d	12.00
Cereal Bowl, 5" d	26.50
Bowl, 6" d, straight sides	24.00
Plate, 7" d, salad	16.00
Sherbet	16.00
Tumbler, 5" h, ftd	22.50
Tumbler, 5" h, ftd, sterling silver trim	25.00

Rose Cameo green tumbler.

Rosemary

Dutch Rose

Manufactured by Federal Glass Company,
Columbus, Ohio, from 1935 to 1937.
Made in amber, green and pink.

Item	Amber	Green	Pink
Berry Bowl, 5" d	6.00	15.00	15.00
Cereal Bowl, 6" d	33.50	32.00	35.00
Cream Soup, 5" d	17.50	24.00	29.00
Creamer, ftd	10.00	16.00	20.00
Cup.	8.50	12.50	15.00
Plate, 6-3/4" d, salad	6.00	11.00	12.50
Plate, 9-1/2" d, dinner	10.00	15.00	21.00
Plate, 9-1/2" d, grill	8.50	15.00	21.00
Platter, 12" l, oval	17.50	24.00	33.00
Saucer	4.00	6.50	6.50
Sugar, ftd	10.00	16.00	20.00
Tumbler, 9 oz, 4-1/4" h	33.00	30.00	50.00
Vegetable Bowl, 10" l, oval. .	16.50	37.00	40.00

Rosemary amber vegetable bowl and berry bowl.

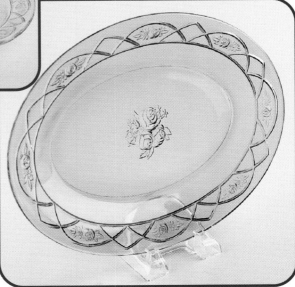

Rosemary green platter.

Roulette

Many Windows

Manufactured by Hocking Glass Company, Lancaster, Ohio, from 1935 to 1939.

Made in crystal, green and pink.

Item	Crystal	Green	Pink
Cup	35.00	6.00	6.50
Fruit Bowl, 9" d	10.00	15.00	15.00
Iced Tea Tumbler, 12 oz, 5-1/8" h	16.00	25.00	27.50
Juice Tumbler, 5 oz, 3-1/4" h	7.50	20.00	22.00
Old Fashioned Tumbler, 7-1/2 oz, 3-1/4" h	22.00	40.00	40.00
Pitcher, 65 oz, 8" h	30.00	35.00	35.00
Plate, 6" d, sherbet	3.50	4.50	5.00
Plate, 8-1/2" d, luncheon	7.00	6.00	6.00
Sandwich Plate, 12" d	12.00	14.00	15.00
Saucer	1.50	3.00	3.00
Sherbet	7.00	6.00	6.00
Tumbler, 9 oz, 4-1/8" h	13.00	20.00	22.00
Tumbler, 10 oz, 5-1/2" h, ftd	15.00	25.00	27.50
Whiskey, 1-1/2 oz, 2-1/2" h	8.00	15.00	15.00

Roulette green plate and sherbet.

Round Robin

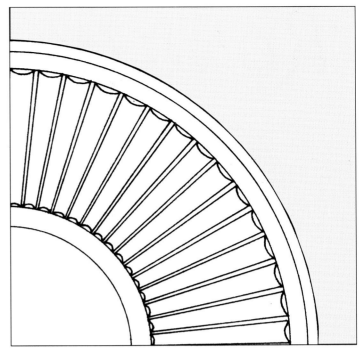

Unknown maker, early 1930s. Made in crystal, iridescent and green. Crystal, produced as the base for iridescent pieces, is found occasionally.

Item	Iridescent	Green
Berry Bowl, 4" d.	5.00	6.00
Creamer, ftd.	7.50	8.50
Cup	7.50	7.00
Domino Tray	-	40.00
Plate, 6" d, sherbet.	3.00	3.00
Plate, 8" d, luncheon	7.00	7.00
Sandwich Plate, 12" d	9.00	12.50
Saucer	2.00	2.00
Sherbet	8.50	10.00
Sugar	7.50	8.50

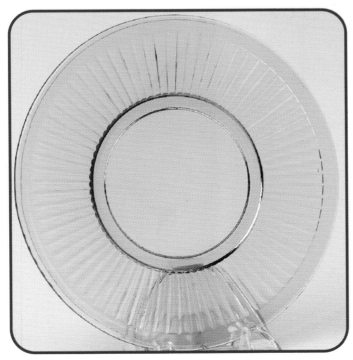

Round Robin green plate.

Roxana

Manufactured by Hazel Atlas Glass Company, Clarksburg, W.V., and Zanesville, Ohio, in 1932.

Made in crystal, golden topaz and white. Production in white was limited to a 4-1/2" bowl, valued at $15.

Item	Crystal	Gold Topaz
Berry Bowl, 5" d	6.00	12.00
Bowl, 4-1/2" x 2-3/8"	6.00	12.00
Cereal Bowl, 6" d	7.50	15.00
Plate, 5-1/2" d	4.50	9.00
Plate, 6" d, sherbet	4.00	8.00
Sherbet, ftd	6.00	12.00
Tumbler, 9 oz, 4-1/4" h	8.50	17.00

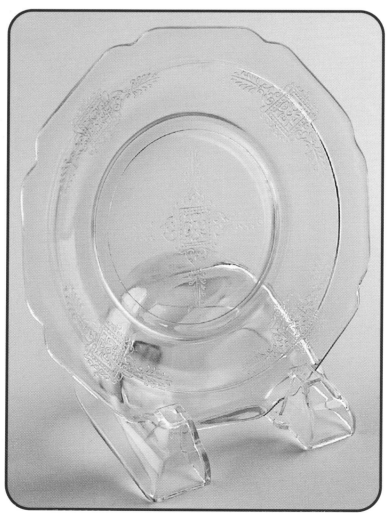

Roxana yellow saucer.

Royal Lace

Manufactured by Hazel Atlas Glass Company, Clarksburg, W.V., and Zanesville, Ohio, from 1934 to 1941.

Made in cobalt blue, crystal, green, pink and some amethyst.

Reproductions: † Reproductions include an 5 oz, 3-1/2" h tumbler, found in a darker cobalt blue.

Item	Cobalt Blue	Crystal	Green	Pink
Berry Bowl, 5" d	30.00	15.00	30.00	27.00
Berry Bowl, 10" d	60.00	20.00	32.00	28.00
Bowl, 10" d, 3 legs, rolled edge	-	190.00	75.00	50.00
Bowl, 10" d, 3 legs, ruffled edge	-	42.00	65.00	100.00
Bowl, 10" d, 3 legs, straight edge	-	24.00	45.00	40.00
Butter Dish, cov	-	65.00	250.00	150.00
Candlesticks, pr, rolled edge	-	45.00	85.00	60.00
Candlesticks, pr, ruffled edge	-	28.00	70.00	60.00
Candlesticks, pr, straight edge	-	30.00	75.00	55.00
Cookie Jar, cov	495.00	45.00	75.00	55.00
Cream Soup, 4-3/4" d	35.00	14.00	35.00	24.00
Creamer, ftd	60.00	15.00	25.00	20.00
Cup and Saucer	45.00	16.00	25.00	18.00
Nut Bowl	990.00	190.00	375.00	375.00
Pitcher, 48 oz, straight sides	150.00	40.00	110.00	85.00
Pitcher, 64 oz, 8" h	225.00	45.00	110.00	120.00
Pitcher, 68 oz, 8" h ice lip	240.00	50.00	-	95.00
Pitcher, 86 oz, 8" h	-	50.00	135.00	95.00
Pitcher, 96 oz, 9-1/2" h, ice lip	265.00	70.00	140.00	100.00
Plate, 6" d, sherbet	14.00	5.00	10.00	15.00
Plate, 8-1/2" d, luncheon	30.00	7.50	15.00	20.00
Plate, 9-7/8" d, dinner	40.00	18.00	25.00	20.00
Plate, 9-7/8" d, grill	35.00	15.00	23.00	20.00
Platter, 13" l, oval	50.00	27.00	40.00	39.00
Salt and Pepper Shakers, pr	250.00	45.00	128.00	65.00
Sherbet, ftd	40.00	17.00	25.00	18.00
Sherbet, metal holder	28.00	4.00	-	-

Item	Cobalt Blue	Crystal	Green	Pink
Sugar, cov. 42.00	32.00	30.00	50.00
Toddy or Cider Set 225.00	-	-	-
Tumbler, 5 oz, 3-1/2" h † 65.00	15.00	30.00	35.00
Tumbler, 9 oz, 4-1/8" h 45.00	16.00	30.00	20.00
Tumbler, 10 oz, 4-7/8" h 100.00	25.00	60.00	60.00
Tumbler, 12 oz, 5-3/8" h 125.00	25.00	50.00	55.00
Vegetable Bowl, 11" l, oval. 60.00	25.00	35.00	35.00

Royal Lace clear plate.

Royal Ruby

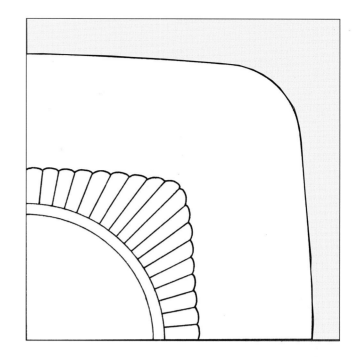

Manufactured by Anchor Hocking Glass Corporation, Lancaster, Pa., from 1938 to 1967.

Made only in Royal Ruby.

Item	Royal Ruby
Ashtray, 4-1/2", leaf	5.00
Beer Bottle, 7 oz	30.00
Beer Bottle, 12 oz	32.00
Beer Bottle, 16 oz	35.00
Beer Bottle, 32 oz	40.00
Berry, 4-5/8" d, small, square	7.50
Berry, 8-1/2" d, round	17.50
Bonbon, 6-1/2" d	18.00
Bowl, 7-3/8" w, sq	17.50
Bowl, 11" d, Rachael	50.00
Bowl, 12" l, oval, Rachael	50.00
Cereal Bowl, 5-1/4" d	12.00
Cigarette Box, card holder, 6-1/8" x 4"	90.00
Cocktail, 3-1/2 oz, Boopie	8.50
Cocktail, 3-1/2 oz, tumbler	10.00
Creamer, flat	8.00
Creamer, ftd	8.00
Cup, round	5.00
Cup, square	6.00
Cup and Saucer, round	12.00
Cup and Saucer, square	8.50
Dessert Bowl, 4-3/4" w, sq	5.25
Fruit Bowl, 4-1/4" d	6.00
Goblet, 9 oz	9.00
Goblet, 9-1/2 oz	14.00
Goblet, ball stem	12.00
Ice Bucket	55.00
Iced Tea Goblet, 14 oz, Boopie	20.00
Iced Tea Tumbler, 13 oz, 6" h, ftd	10.00
Ivy Ball, 4" h, Wilson	4.00
Juice Tumbler, 4 oz	5.00
Juice Tumbler, 5-1/2 oz	7.00
Juice Tumbler, 5 oz, flat or ftd	9.00
Juice Pitcher	40.00
Lamp	35.00
Pitcher, 3 qt, tilted	45.00
Pitcher, 3 qt, upright	35.00
Pitcher, 42 oz, tilted	32.00
Pitcher, 42 oz, upright	35.00
Plate, 6-1/4" d, sherbet	4.00
Plate, 7" d, salad	3.00
Plate, 7-3/4" w, sq, salad	2.00
Plate, 8-3/8" w, sq, luncheon	11.00
Plate, 9-1/8" d, dinner	14.00
Plate, 13-3/4" d	35.00
Popcorn Bowl, 5-1/4" d	12.50
Popcorn Bowl, 10" d, deep	40.00
Punch Bowl and Stand	75.00
Punch Set, 14 pieces	110.00
Punch Cup	3.00
Salad Bowl, 8-1/2" d	19.00
Salad Bowl, 11-1/2" d	40.00
Saucer, 5-3/8" w, sq	4.00
Saucer, round	4.00
Set, 50 pcs, orig labels, orig box	325.00
Sherbet, 6-1/2 oz, stemmed	7.50
Sherbet, 6 oz, Boopie	8.00
Soup Bowl, 7-1/2" d	14.00
Sugar, flat	8.00
Sugar, footed	8.00
Sugar Lid, notched	11.00
Tray, center handle, ruffled	16.50

Item	Royal Ruby	Item	Royal Ruby
Tumbler, 5 oz, 3-1/2" h	5.00	Vase, 6-5/8" h, Coolidge	12.00
Tumbler, 9 oz	5.00	Vase, 9" h, Hoover	16.00
Tumbler, 10 oz, 5" h, ftd	5.00	Vase, 10" h, fluted, star base	35.00
Tumbler, 14 oz, 5" h	9.00	Vase, 10" h, ftd, Rachael,	50.00
Tumbler, 15 oz, long boy	15.00	Vegetable Bowl, 8" l, oval	45.00
Vase, 3-3/4" h, Roosevelt	7.50	Wine, 2-1/2 oz, ftd	12.50
Vase, 6-3/8" h, Harding	10.00		

Royal Ruby punch set, punch bowl and six cups.

Royal Ruby sugar, creamer, (on pedestal), cup and saucer.

S-Pattern

Stippled Rose Band

Manufactured by MacBeth-Evans Glass Company, Charleroi, Pa., from 1930 to 1933.

Made in amber, crystal, crystal with amber, blue, green, pink or silver trims, fired-on red, green, light yellow and monax.

Item	Amber	Crystal	Crystal with Trims	Fired-On Colors	Yellow
Berry Bowl, 8-1/2" d	7.50	12.00	-	-	7.50
Cake Plate, 11-3/4" d	48.00	45.00	50.00	-	48.00
Cake Plate, 13" d	80.00	65.00	75.00	-	75.00
Cereal Bowl, 5-1/2" d	6.00	4.00	6.00	12.00	6.00
Creamer, thick	7.50	6.50	8.00	15.00	7.50
Creamer, thin	7.50	6.50	8.00	15.00	7.50
Cup, thick	5.00	4.00	5.50	10.00	5.00
Cup, thin	5.00	4.00	5.50	10.00	5.00
Pitcher, 80 oz	-	65.00	-	-	-
Plate, 6" d, sherbet	3.50	3.00	4.00	-	3.50
Plate, 8-1/4" d, luncheon	3.50	4.50	3.50	-	3.50
Plate, 9-1/4" d, dinner	6.50	-	7.50	-	6.50
Plate, grill	8.50	6.50	9.00	-	8.50
Saucer	4.00	3.00	4.00	-	4.00
Sherbet, low, ftd	8.00	5.50	8.50	-	8.00
Sugar, thick	7.50	6.50	8.00	15.00	7.50
Sugar, thin	7.50	6.50	8.00	15.00	7.50
Tumbler, 5 oz, 3-1/2" h	6.50	5.00	6.50	-	6.50
Tumbler, 10 oz, 4-3/4" h	8.50	7.00	7.50	-	8.50
Tumbler, 12 oz, 5" h	15.00	10.00	16.50	-	15.00

S-Pattern yellow tumbler.

S-Pattern crystal yellow-satin plate.

Sandwich *Hocking*

Manufactured by Hocking Glass Company, and later Anchor Hocking Corporation, from 1939 to 1964.

Made in crystal, Desert Gold, 1961-64; Forest Green, 1956-1960s; pink, 1939-1940; Royal Ruby, 1938-1939; and white/ivory (opaque) 1957-1960s.

Reproductions: † The cookie jar has been reproduced in crystal.

* No cover is known for cookie jar in Forest Green.

Item	Crystal	Desert Gold	Forest Green	Pink	Royal Ruby	White
Bowl, 4-5/16" d, smooth	3.00	-	2.00	-	-	-
Bowl, 4-7/8" d, smooth	3.00	3.50	-	4.50	17.50	-
Bowl, 4-7/8" d, crimped	12.00	-	-	-	-	-
Bowl, 5-1/4" d, scalloped	5.00	6.00	-	-	20.00	-
Bowl, 5-1/4" d, smooth	-	-	-	7.00	20.00	-
Bowl, 6-1/2" d, scalloped	5.00	8.00	40.00	-	27.50	-
Bowl, 6-1/2" d, smooth	7.50	8.00	-	-	-	-
Bowl, 7-1/4" d, scalloped	6.00	-	-	-	-	-
Bowl, 8-1/4" d, oval	5.00	-	-	-	-	-
Bowl, 8-1/4" d, scalloped	6.00	-	70.00	18.00	55.00	-
Butter Dish, cov	40.00	-	-	-	-	-
Cereal Bowl, 6-3/4" d	32.00	12.00	-	-	-	-
Cookie Jar, cov † *	35.00	40.00	20.00	-	-	-
Creamer	5.50	-	25.00	-	-	-
Cup, coffee	2.00	11.00	24.00	-	-	-
Cup, tea	3.00	11.00	24.00	-	-	-
Custard Cup	7.00	-	1.00	-	-	-
Custard Cup Liner	5.50	-	1.50	-	-	-
Custard Cup, crimped	12.50	-	-	-	-	-
Dessert Bowl, 5" d, crimped	10.50	-	-	-	-	-
Juice Pitcher, 6" h	75.00	-	135.00	-	-	-
Juice Tumbler, 3 oz, 3-3/8" h	12.00	-	6.00	-	-	-
Juice Tumbler, 5 oz, 3-9/16" h	7.50	-	2.50	-	-	-
Pitcher, 1/2 gallon, ice lip	80.00	-	350.00	-	-	-
Plate, 6" d	3.00	-	-	-	-	-
Plate, 7" d, dessert	10.00	-	-	-	-	-
Plate, 8" d, luncheon	4.00	-	-	-	-	-

Item	Crystal	Desert Gold	Forest Green	Pink	Royal Ruby	White
Plate, 9" d, dinner 18.00		9.00	85.00	6.00	-	-
Plate, 9" d, indent for punch cup 6.00		-	-	-	-	-
Punch Bowl, 9-3/4" d 18.00		-	-	-	-	15.00
Punch Bowl and Stand 32.00		-	-	-	-	30.00
Punch Bowl Set, bowl, base, 12 cups . . 60.00		-	-	-	-	-
Punch Cup. 3.00		-	-	-	-	2.00
Salad Bowl, 7" d 8.00		25.00	-	-	-	-
Salad Bowl, 7-5/8" d . . . . -		-	60.00	-	-	-
Salad Bowl, 9" d 24.00		-	-	-	-	-
Sandwich Plate, 12" d. 14.00		17.50	-	-	-	-
Saucer 2.00		4.00	15.00	-	-	-
Sherbet, ftd 8.00		8.00	-	-	-	-
Snack Set, plate and cup 9.00		-	-	-	-	-
Sugar, cov 30.00		-	-	-	-	-
Sugar, no cover 5.50		-	25.00	-	-	-
Tumbler, 9 oz, ftd. 27.50		125.00	-	-	-	-
Tumbler, 9 oz, water 9.00		-	5.00	-	-	-
Vase . . . . -		-	24.00	-	-	-
Vegetable, 8-1/2" l, oval 6.00		-	-	-	-	-

*Sandwich, Hocking
crystal oval bowl.*

*Sandwich, Hocking
amber round bowl.*

Sandwich *Indiana*

Manufactured by Indiana Glass Company, Dunkirk, Ind., 1920s to 1980s.

Made in crystal, late 1920s to 1990s; amber, late 1920s to 1980s; milk white, mid 1950s; teal blue, 1950s to 1960s; red, 1933 and early 1970s; and smoky blue, 1976-1977.

Item	Amber	Crystal	Teal Blue	Red
Ashtray, club	2.00	3.00	-	-
Ashtray, diamond	2.00	3.00	-	-
Ashtray, heart	2.00	3.00	1.00	-
Ashtray, set	8.00	12.00	-	-
Ashtray, spade	2.00	3.00	-	-
Basket, 10" h	35.00	35.00	-	-
Berry Bowl, 4-1/4" d	3.00	4.00	-	-
Bowl, 6" w, hexagonal	4.50	4.00	15.00	-
Bowl, 8-1/2" d	10.00	11.00	-	-
Butter Dish, cov	25.00	25.00	150.00	-
Candlesticks, pr, 3-1/2" h	18.00	18.00	-	-
Candlesticks, pr, 7" h	25.00	25.00	-	-
Celery Tray, 10-1/2" l	17.50	14.00	-	-
Cereal Bowl, 6" d	12.00	6.50	-	-
Cocktail, 3 oz, ftd	7.50	7.50	-	-
Console Bowl, 9" d	17.50	17.50	-	-
Console Bowl, 11-1/2" d	20.00	20.00	-	-
Creamer	6.00	6.00	-	48.00
Creamer and Sugar, tray	18.00	18.00	35.00	-
Cruet, 6-1/2 oz, stopper	-	-	145.00	-
Cup	4.00	4.00	8.50	30.00
Decanter, stopper	25.00	25.00	-	90.00
Fairy Lamp	15.00	-	-	-
Goblet, 9 oz	10.00	13.00	-	45.00
Iced Tea Tumbler, 12 oz, ftd	10.00	10.00	-	-
Mayonnaise, ftd	14.00	14.00	-	-
Pitcher, 68 oz	24.00	24.00	-	175.00

Item	Amber	Crystal	Teal Blue	Red
Plate, 6" d, sherbet	3.50	3.50	7.50	-
Plate, 7" d, bread and butter	4.00	4.00	-	-
Plate, 8" d, oval, indent	-	4.00	6.50	15.00
Plate, 8-3/8" d, luncheon	7.50	8.00	-	20.00
Plate, 10-1/2" d, dinner	9.00	8.50	-	-
Puff Box	18.00	18.00	-	-
Salt and Pepper Shakers, pr.	18.00	18.00	-	-
Sandwich Plate, 13" d	14.50	14.50	25.00	35.00
Sandwich Server, center handle	20.00	20.00	-	50.00
Saucer	2.50	1.50	7.00	7.50
Sherbet, 3-1/4" h	6.00	5.00	12.00	-
Sugar, cov, large	20.00	20.00	-	48.00
Tumbler, 8 oz, ftd, water	10.00	10.00	-	-
Wine, 3" h, 4 oz	10.00	11.00	-	15.00

Sandwich, Indiana crystal creamer, sugar and tray.

Sharon

Cabbage Rose

Manufactured by Federal Glass Company, Columbus, Ohio, from 1935 to 1939.

Made in amber, crystal, green and pink.

Reproductions: † Reproductions include the butter dish, cov candy dish, creamer, cov sugar and salt and pepper shakers. Reproduction colors include dark amber, blue, green and pink.

Item	Amber	Crystal	Green	Pink
Berry Bowl, 5" d	8.50	4.00	15.00	14.00
Berry Bowl, 8-1/2" d	9.50	12.00	40.00	45.00
Butter Dish, cov †	48.00	20.00	85.00	63.00
Cake Plate, 11-1/2" d, ftd	30.00	10.00	65.00	48.00
Candy Dish, cov †	45.00	15.00	100.00	50.00
Cereal, 6" d	20.00	10.00	28.00	25.00
Champagne, 5" d bowl	-	-	-	10.00
Cheese Dish, cov	225.00	1,500.00	-	950.00
Cream Soup, 5" d	28.00	14.00	50.00	48.00
Creamer, ftd †	25.00	14.00	20.00	30.00
Cup	15.00	6.00	18.00	18.00
Fruit Bowl, 10-1/2" d	22.00	15.00	36.00	42.00
Iced Tea Tumbler, ftd	125.00	15.00	-	62.50
Jam Dish, 7-1/2" d	40.00	-	48.00	215.00
Pitcher, 80 oz, ice lip	145.00	-	150.00	165.00
Pitcher, 80 oz, without ice lip	140.00	-	150.00	150.00
Plate, 6" d, bread and butter	16.00	5.00	8.50	16.50
Plate, 7-1/2" d, salad	16.50	6.50	8.00	30.00
Plate, 9-1/2" d, dinner	12.00	7.50	24.00	22.00
Platter, 12-1/2" l, oval	16.00	-	30.00	30.00
Salt and Pepper Shakers, pr †	40.00	-	60.00	55.00
Saucer	5.00	2.00	36.00	15.00
Sherbet, ftd	12.00	6.00	35.00	16.50
Soup, flat, 7-3/4" d, 1-7/8" deep	50.00	-	-	52.00
Sugar, cov †	25.00	8.00	50.00	45.00

Item	Amber	Crystal	Green	Pink
Tumbler, 9 oz, 4-1/8" h, thick 27.00		-	65.00	45.00
Tumbler, 9 oz, 4-1/8" h, thin 27.00		-	65.00	42.00
Tumbler, 12 oz, 5-1/4" h, thick 55.00		-	95.00	50.00
Tumbler, 12 oz, 5-1/4" h, thin 55.00		-	95.00	52.50
Tumbler, 15 oz, 6-1/2" h, thick 125.00		15.00	-	60.00
Vegetable Bowl, 9-1/2" l, oval 22.00		-	30.00	32.00

Sharon pink sherbet, two bowls and creamer.

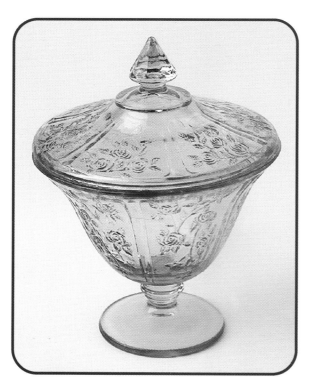

REPRODUCTION!
Sharon pink covered
candy dish.

Ships

Sailboat, Sportsman Series

Manufactured by Hazel Atlas Glass Company, Clarksburg, W.V., and Zanesville, Ohio, late 1930s.

Made in cobalt blue with white, yellow, and red decoration. Pieces with yellow or red decoration are valued slightly higher than the traditional white decoration.

Item	Cobalt Blue with White Decoration
Cocktail Mixer, stirrer	25.00
Cocktail Shaker	35.00
Cup	12.00
Ice Bowl	45.00
Iced Tea Tumbler, 10-1/2 oz, 4-7/8" h	18.00
Iced Tea Tumbler, 12 oz	24.00
Juice Tumbler, 5 oz, 3-3/4" h	12.50
Old Fashioned Tumbler, 8 oz, 3-3/8" h	18.00
Pitcher, 82 oz, no ice lip	50.00
Pitcher, 86 oz, ice lip	50.00
Plate, 5-7/8" d, bread and butter	24.00
Plate, 8" d, salad	27.50
Plate, 9" d, dinner	32.00
Roly Poly, 6 oz	10.00
Saucer	18.00
Shot Glass, 2 oz, 2-1/4" h	165.00
Tumbler, 4 oz, 3-1/4" h, heavy bottom	27.50
Tumbler, 4 oz, heavy bottom	11.00
Tumbler, 9 oz, 3-3/4" h	11.00
Tumbler, 9 oz, 4-5/8" h	14.00
Whiskey, 3-1/2" h	30.00

Ships cobalt blue cocktail shaker.

Ships cobalt blue luncheon plate.

Ships cobalt blue dinner plate.

Sierra Pinwheel

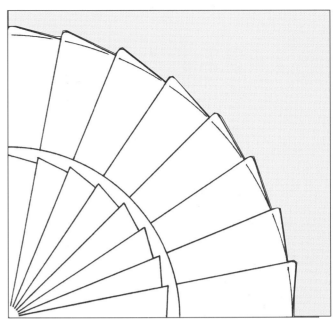

Manufactured by Jeannette Glass Company, Jeannette, Pa., from 1931 to 1933.

Made in green and pink. A few forms are known in Ultramarine.

Item	Green	Pink
Berry, small	13.50	16.00
Berry Bowl, 8-1/2" d	14.00	20.00
Butter Dish, cov	75.00	70.00
Cereal Bowl, 5-1/2" d	18.00	14.00
Creamer	20.00	17.50
Cup	17.50	15.00
Pitcher, 32 oz, 6-1/2" h	160.00	110.00
Plate, 9" d, dinner	18.00	22.50
Platter, 11" l, oval	48.00	40.00
Salt and Pepper Shakers, pr	36.00	36.00
Saucer	6.00	5.00
Serving Tray, 10-1/4" l, 2 handles	20.00	25.00
Sugar, cov	25.00	20.00
Tumbler, 9 oz, 4-1/2" h, ftd	100.00	80.00
Vegetable Bowl, 9-1/4" l, oval	115.00	50.00

Sierra Pinwheel green butter dish and pink cup and saucer.

Sierra Pinwheel pink plate.

197

Spiral

Manufactured by Hocking Glass Company, Lancaster, Ohio, from 1928 to 1930.

Made in crystal, green, and pink. Collector interest is strongest in green.

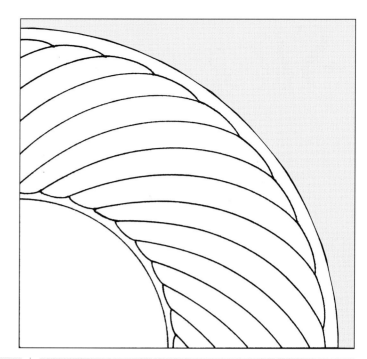

Item	Green
Berry Bowl, 4-3/4" d	6.00
Berry Bowl, 8" d	14.00
Butter Tub	25.00
Creamer, flat	8.00
Creamer, footed	8.00
Cup	5.00
Ice Tub	25.00
Juice Tumbler, 5 oz, 3" h	5.00
Mixing Bowl, 7" d	9.00
Pitcher, 58 oz, 7-5/8" h	35.00
Plate, 6" d, sherbet	3.00

Item	Green
Plate, 8" d, luncheon	4.00
Platter, 12" l	30.00
Preserve, cov	30.00
Salt and Pepper Shakers, pr	37.50
Sandwich Server, center handle	30.00
Saucer	2.00
Sherbet	5.00
Sugar, flat	8.00
Sugar, footed	8.00
Tumbler, 5-7/8" h, ftd	24.00
Tumbler, 9 oz, 5" h	10.00

Spiral green plate and sherbet.

Star

Manufactured by Federal Glass Company, Columbus, Ohio, 1950s.

Made in amber, crystal and crystal with gold trim. Crystal pieces with gold trim would be valued the same as plain crystal.

Item	Amber	Crystal
Dessert Bowl, 4-5/8" d 4.00		5.00
Iced Tea Tumbler, 12 oz, 5-1/8" h . . 8.00		9.00
Juice Pitcher, 36 oz, 5-3/4" h . . . 10.00		12.00
Juice Tumbler, 4-1/2 oz, 3-3/8" h . . 4.00		5.00
Pitcher, 60 oz, 7" h 12.00		14.00
Pitcher, 85 oz, 9-1/4" h, ice lip. . 15.00		15.00

Item	Amber	Crystal
Plate, 6-3/16" d, salad 2.00		3.00
Plate, 9-3/8" d, dinner 6.00		7.50
Sugar, cov 12.00		15.00
Tumbler, 9 oz, 3-7/8" h, water . . . 6.00		7.50
Vegetable Bowl, 8-3/8" d. 10.00		15.00
Whiskey, 1-1/2 oz, 2-1/4" h 4.00		5.00

Star crystal bowl and two pitchers.

Starlight

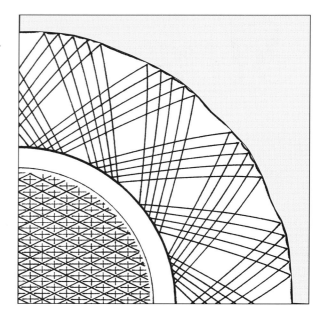

Manufactured by Hazel Atlas Glass Company, Clarksburg, W.V., and Zanesville, Ohio, from 1938 to 1940.

Made in cobalt blue, crystal, pink and white. Production in cobalt blue was limited to 8-1/2" d bowl, valued at $30. In pink, look for a bowl, 8-1/2" d, two handles, for $20; a cereal bowl, 5-1/2" d, two handles, for $10; and a sandwich plate, 13" d, for $20.

Item	Crystal	White
Bowl, 8-1/2" d, 2 handles 17.00		17.00
Bowl, 11-1/2" d, deep 25.00		25.00
Bowl, 12" d, 2-3/4" deep 25.00		25.00
Cereal Bowl, 5-1/2" d, 2 handles . . 7.00		7.00
Creamer, oval 5.00		5.00
Cup 6.00		4.00
Plate, 6" d, sherbet 4.50		4.00
Plate, 7-1/2" d, salad 5.00		4.50
Plate, 8-1/2" d, luncheon 5.00		5.00

Item	Crystal	White
Plate, 9" d, dinner 8.50		8.50
Relish Dish 15.00		15.00
Salad Bowl, 11-1/2" d, deep 25.00		25.00
Salt and Pepper Shakers, pr 23.00		23.00
Sandwich Plate, 13" d 23.00		-
Saucer 4.00		2.00
Sherbet 14.00		12.00
Sugar, oval 5.00		5.00

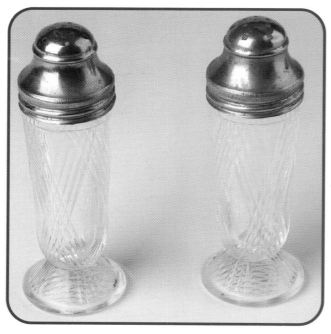

Starlight crystal salt and pepper shakers.

Starlight crystal plate.

Strawberry

Manufactured by U.S. Glass Company, Pittsburgh, early 1930s.

Made in crystal, green, pink and iridescent.

Strawberry pink plate.

Item	Crystal	Green	Iridescent	Pink
Berry Bowl, 4" d.	6.50	9.00	6.50	10.00
Berry Bowl, 7-1/2" d.	16.00	20.00	16.00	20.00
Bowl, 6-1/4" d, 2" deep	40.00	60.00	40.00	60.00
Butter Dish, cov.	125.00	150.00	125.00	150.00
Comport, 5-3/4" d	55.00	60.00	55.00	60.00
Creamer, large, 4-5/8" h	24.00	35.00	24.00	35.00
Creamer, small.	12.00	17.50	12.00	17.50
Olive Dish, 5" l, one handle	8.50	14.00	8.50	14.00
Pickle Dish, 8-1/4" l, oval	8.00	14.00	8.00	14.00
Pitcher, 7-3/4" h	150.00	150.00	150.00	150.00
Plate, 6" d, sherbet.	5.00	7.00	5.00	8.00
Plate, 7-1/2" d, salad.	10.00	14.00	10.00	15.00
Salad Bowl, 6-1/2" d.	15.00	20.00	15.00	20.00
Sherbet	6.00	7.00	6.00	7.00
Sugar, large, cov.	60.00	85.00	60.00	85.00
Sugar, small, open	12.00	32.00	12.00	32.00
Tumbler, 8 oz, 3-5/8" h.	20.00	30.00	20.00	30.00

Sunburst

Herringbone

Manufactured by Jeannette Glass Company, Jeannette, Pa., late 1930s.
Made in crystal.

Item	Crystal
Berry Bowl, 4-3/4" d	6.50
Berry Bowl, 8-1/2" d	15.00
Bowl, 10-1/2" d	20.00
Candlesticks, pr, double	35.00
Creamer, ftd	16.00
Cup	7.50
Cup and Saucer	8.00
Plate, 5-1/2" d	11.00

Item	Crystal
Plate, 9-1/4" d, dinner	15.00
Relish, 2 part	14.00
Sandwich Plate, 11-3/4" d	15.00
Saucer	3.00
Sherbet	12.00
Sugar	16.00
Tumbler, 4" h, 9 oz, flat	18.00

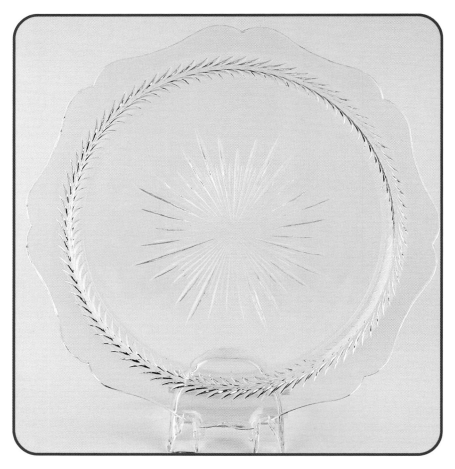

Sunburst clear serving plate.

Sunflower

Manufactured by Jeannette Glass Company, Jeannette, Pa., 1930s.

Made in Delphite, green, pink and some opaque colors. Look for a creamer in Delphite, valued at $85.

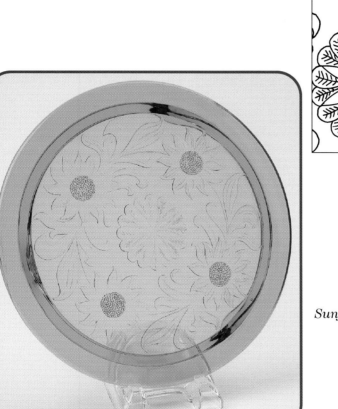

Sunflower green cake plate.

Item	Green	Pink	Opaque
Ashtray, 5" d	14.00	10.00	-
Cake Plate, 10" d, 3 legs	16.00	16.00	-
Creamer	20.00	20.00	85.00
Cup	15.00	12.50	75.00
Plate, 9" d, dinner	20.00	16.00	-
Saucer	13.50	10.00	85.00
Sugar	23.00	20.00	-
Trivet, 7" d, 3 legs, turned up edge	315.00	300.00	
Tumbler, 8 oz, 4-3/8" h, ftd	35.00	30.00	-

Swankyswigs

Swankyswigs are small tumblers that originally contained a Kraft cheese-spread product. Made from the 1930s until the 1950s, these colorful tumblers are popular with collectors. Lids are valued at $5 each when found in good condition. Certain advertisements can bring a higher price. Glasses with original labels will command approximately 50% more.

Item	Value

Antelope and Star
Black and Red, 3-1/2" h 4.00

Antique Pattern (3-3/4" h)
Churn and Cradle, Orange. 5.00
Coal and Coal Bucket, Brown. 5.00
Coffee Grinder and Plate, Green 5.00
Coffee Pot and Trivet, Black. 5.00
Spinning Wheel and Bellows, Red 5.00
Teapot and Lamp, Blue 5.00

Band #2
Red and Black, 3-3/8" h 2.50

Band #3
Blue and White, 3-3/8" h 3.00

Bustlin' Betsy
All colors, 3-3/4" h, each 3.00

Carnival (3-1/2" h)
Blue. 4.25
Green 4.50
Red 3.00
Yellow 4.00

Cars and Wagon
Black and White, 3-3/4" h 4.00

Item	Value

Checkerboard
Red and White, 3-1/2" h 16.00

Circle and Dot (3-1/2" h)
Black 4.25
Blue. 4.25
Red 4.25

Cornflower
#1, Light Blue, 3-1/2" h 9.00
#1, Light Blue, 3-3/4" h 15.00
#1, Light Blue, 4-1/2" h 18.00
#2, Dark Blue, 3-1/4" h 12.75
#2, Light Blue, 3-1/4" h 12.50
#2, Yellow, 3-1/4" h 12.00
#2, Dark Blue, 3-1/2" h 2.75
#2, Light Blue, 3-1/2" h 2.50
#2, Red, 3-1/2" h 2.50
#2, Yellow, 3-1/2" h 2.00

Daisy
Red and White, 3-1/4" h 35.00
Red, White and Green, 3-1/4" h 15.00
Red and White, 3-1/2" h 25.00
Red, White and Green, 3-3/4" h 2.00
Red, White and Green, 4-1/2" h 17.50

Davy Crockett
3-1/2" h 8.50

Item	Value

Dots
Red, 3-1/2" h 3.00

Flying Geese
Red, Yellow and Blue, 3-1/2" h 4.00

Forget-Me-Not
Dark Blue, 3-1/4" h. 15.00
Light Blue, 3-1/4" h 12.75
Red, 3-1/4" h 14.00
Yellow, 3-1/4" h 13.00
Dark Blue, 3-1/2" h 2.75
Light Blue, 3-1/2" h 2.75
Red, 3-1/2" h 4.00
Yellow, 3-1/2" h 3.00

Horizontal Lines
Black and Red, 3-1/4" h 3.00

Kiddie Cups
Bear and Pig, Blue, 3-1/4" h 12.75
Bird and Elephant, Red, 3-1/4" h 12.75
Dog and Rooster, Orange, 3-1/4" h 12.75
Duck and Horse, Black, 3-1/4" h. 13.50
Squirrel and Deer, Brown, 3-1/4" h 12.75
Rabbit and Cat, Green, 3-1/4" h 12.75
Bear and Pig, Blue, 3-3/4" h 4.00
Bird and Elephant, Red, 3-3/4" h 4.00
Dog and Rooster, Orange, 3-3/4" h 4.00
Duck and Horse, Black, 3-3/4" h 4.00
Rabbit and Cat, Green, 3-3/4" h 4.00
Squirrel and Deer, Brown, 3-3/4" h 4.00
Bear and Pig, Blue, 4-1/2" h 18.00
Bird and Elephant, Red, 4-1/2" h 18.00
Dog and Rooster, Orange, 4-1/2" h 18.00
Duck and Horse, Black, 4-1/2" h. 20.00
Rabbit and Cat, Green, 4-1/2" h 18.00
Squirrel and Deer, Brown, 4-1/2" h. 18.00

Posy
Jonquil, Yellow, 3-1/4" h 18.00
Jonquil, Yellow, 3-1/2" h 6.00
Jonquil, Yellow, 4-1/2" h 20.00
Tulip, Red, 3-1/4" h 15.00
Tulip, Red, 3-1/2" h 4.00
Tulip, Red, 4-1/2" h 12.00
Violet, Purple, 3-1/4" h 18.00
Violet, Purple, 3-1/2" h 5.00
Violet, Purple, 4-1/2" h 20.00

Scotty
Red Dog, Blue Fence, 3-1/2" h 6.00

Spaceships
Blue, 3-1/2" d 6.00

Stars (3-1/2" h)
Black 2.00
Green 3.00
Red 4.00

Tulip
#1, Green, 3-1/4" h 14.00
#1, Black, 3-1/2" h 3.00
#1, Dark Blue, 3-1/2" h 2.75
#1, Green, 3-1/2" h 2.75
#1, Red, 3-1/2" h 3.50
#1, Blue, 4-1/2" h 15.00
#1, Green, 4-1/2" h 14.00
#1, Red, 4-1/2" h 15.00
#2, Dark Blue, 3-1/4" h 15.00
#2, Dark Blue, 3-3/4" h 4.00
#2, Dark Blue, 4-1/2" h 18.00
#3, Light Blue, 3-1/4" h 14.00
#3, Yellow, 3-1/4" h 14.00
#3, Dark Blue, 3-3/4" h 2.75
#3, Light Blue, 3-3/4" h 2.75
#3, Red, 3-3/4" h 2.75
#3, Yellow, 3-3/4" h 3.00
#3, Red, 4-1/2" h 15.00

Swankyswigs Posy Tulip.

Swankyswigs Posy Violet.

Swankyswigs: six styles of Kiddie Cups.

Swankyswigs (from left): red Tulip No. 3 and yellow Tulip No. 3.

Swankyswigs (from left): blue Forget-Me-Not, blue Cornflower No. 2 and black Tulip No. 1.

Swankyswigs (from left): orange Antique, brown Antique and green Bustlin' Betsy.

Swirl

Petal Swirl

Manufactured by Jeannette Glass Company, Jeannette, Pa., from 1937 to 1938.

Made in amber, Delphite, ice blue, pink and Ultramarine. Production was limited in amber and ice blue.

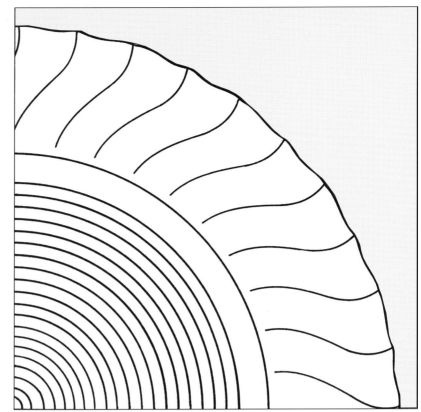

Item	Delphite	Pink	Ultramarine
Bowl, 10" d, ftd, closed handles	-	24.00	28.00
Butter Dish, cov	-	175.00	245.00
Candleholders, pr, double branch	-	40.00	45.00
Candleholders, pr, single branch	115.00	-	-
Candy Dish, cov	-	130.00	150.00
Candy Dish, open, 3 legs	-	16.00	24.00
Cereal Bowl, 5-1/4" d	14.00	10.00	15.00
Coaster, 1" x 3-1/4"	-	15.00	14.00
Console Bowl, 10-1/2" d, ftd	-	18.00	30.00
Creamer	12.00	7.50	15.00
Cup and Saucer	14.00	12.00	20.00
Plate, 6-1/2" d, sherbet	6.50	4.50	7.50
Plate, 7-1/4" d, luncheon	-	6.50	11.00
Plate, 8" d, salad	9.00	8.50	12.00
Plate, 9-1/4" d, dinner	12.00	13.00	19.00
Plate, 10-1/2" d, dinner	18.00	-	30.00
Platter, 12" l, oval	35.00	-	-
Salad Bowl, 9" d	30.00	18.00	26.00
Salad Bowl, 9" d, rimmed	-	20.00	28.00
Salt and Pepper Shakers, pr	-	-	45.00
Sandwich Plate, 12-1/2" d	-	20.00	27.50
Sherbet, low, ftd	-	13.00	23.00
Soup, tab handles, lug	-	25.00	35.00
Sugar, ftd	-	12.00	17.50
Tray, 10-1/2" l, two handles	25.00	-	-

Item	Delphite	Pink	Ultramarine
Tumbler, 9 oz, 4" h	-	18.00	42.00
Tumbler, 9 oz, 4-5/8" h	-	18.00	-
Tumbler, 13 oz, 5-1/8" h	-	45.00	90.00
Vase, 6-1/2" h, ftd, ruffled	-	22.00	-
Vase, 8-1/2" h, ftd	-	-	30.00

Swirl Ultramarine sugar and creamer.

Swirl Ultramarine plate and bowl.

Tea Room

Manufactured by Indiana Glass Company, Dunkirk, Ind., from 1926 to 1931.

Made in amber, crystal, green and pink.

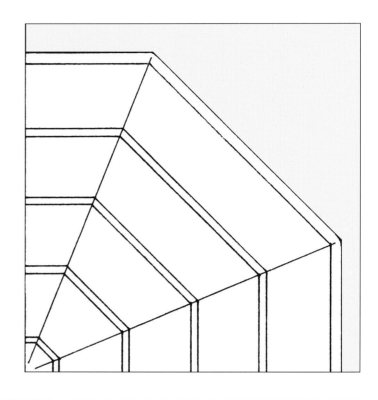

Item	Amber	Crystal	Green	Pink
Banana Split Bowl, 7-1/2" l	-	75.00	100.00	145.00
Candlesticks, pr, low	-	-	48.00	85.00
Celery Bowl, 8-1/2"d	-	-	35.00	27.50
Creamer, 3-1/4" h	-	-	30.00	28.00
Creamer, 4-1/2" h, ftd	80.00	-	20.00	18.00
Creamer and Sugar on Tray	-	-	180.00	75.00
Cup	-	-	65.00	60.00
Finger Bowl	-	79.00	50.00	40.00
Goblet, 9 oz	-	-	75.00	65.00
Ice Bucket	-	-	85.00	80.00
Lamp, electric	-	140.00	175.00	145.00
Mustard, cov	-	-	160.00	140.00
Parfait	-	-	72.00	65.00
Pitcher, 64 oz	425.00	400.00	150.00	135.00
Plate, 6-1/2" d, sherbet	-	-	35.00	32.00
Plate, 8-1/4" d, luncheon	-	-	37.50	35.00
Plates, 10-1/2" d, two handles	-	-	50.00	45.00
Relish, divided	-	-	30.00	25.00
Salad Bowl, 8-3/4" d, deep	-	-	150.00	135.00
Salt and Pepper Shakers, pr, ftd	-	-	60.00	55.00
Saucer	-	-	30.00	25.00
Sherbet	-	-	35.00	30.00

Item	Amber	Crystal	Green	Pink
Sugar, 3" h, cov . . . . -	-	-	115.00	100.00
Sugar, 4-1/2" h, ftd 80.00		-	20.00	18.00
Sugar, cov, flat . . . . -	-	-	200.00	170.00
Sundae, ftd, ruffled . . . . -	-	-	85.00	70.00
Tumbler, 6 oz, ftd . . . . -	-	-	35.00	32.00
Tumbler, 8 oz, 5-1/4" h, ftd 75.00		-	35.00	32.00
Tumbler, 11 oz, ftd . . . . -	-	-	45.00	40.00
Tumbler, 12 oz, ftd . . . . -	-	-	60.00	55.00
Vase, 6-1/2" h, ruffled edge . . . . -	-	-	145.00	125.00
Vase, 9-1/2" h, ruffled . . . . -	-	50.00	110.00	100.00
Vase, 9-1/2"h, straight . . . . -	-	175.00	95.00	225.00
Vase, 11" h, ruffled edge . . . . -	-	-	350.00	400.00
Vase, 11" h, straight . . . . -	-	-	200.00	400.00
Vegetable Bowl, 9-1/2" l, oval . . . . -	-	-	75.00	65.00

Tea Room pink sugar and creamer.

Thistle

Manufactured by MacBeth-Evans, Charleroi, Pa., about 1929-1930.

Made in crystal, green, pink and yellow. Production was limited in crystal and yellow.

Item	Green	Pink
Cake Plate, 13" d, heavy	150.00	125.00
Cereal Bowl, 5-1/2" d	27.50	80.00
Cup, thin	32.00	24.00
Fruit Bowl, 10-1/4" d	300.00	200.00
Plate, 8" d, luncheon	22.00	18.00
Plate, 10-1/4" d, grill	32.00	28.00
Saucer	12.00	12.00

Thistle green plate.

Thumbprint

Manufactured by Federal Glass Company, Columbus, Ohio, from 1927 to 1930.
Made in green.

Item	Green
Berry Bowl, 4-3/4" d	7.00
Berry Bowl, 8" d	10.00
Cereal Bowl, 5" d	9.00
Creamer, ftd	8.00
Cup	6.00
Juice Tumbler, 4" h	6.00
Plate, 6" d, sherbet	3.00
Plate, 8" d, luncheon	5.00
Plate, 9-1/4" d, dinner	7.00
Salt and Pepper Shakers, pr.	25.00
Saucer	2.00
Sherbet	7.00
Sugar, ftd	8.00
Tumbler, 5" h	8.00
Tumbler, 5-1/2" h	10.00
Whiskey, 2-1/4" h	6.50

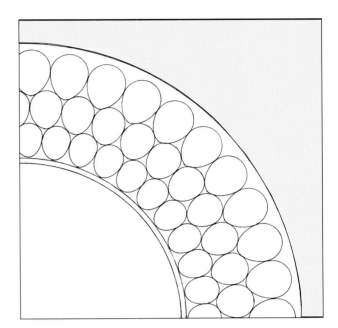

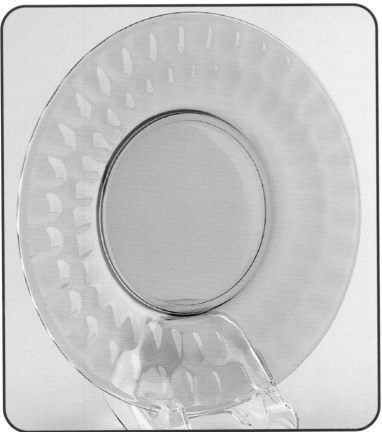

Thumbprint green plate.

Tulip

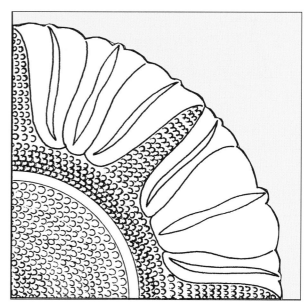

Manufactured by Dell Glass Company, early 1930s.

Made in amber, amethyst, blue, crystal and green.

Item	Amber	Amethyst	Blue	Crystal	Green
Bowl, 6" d.	10.00	14.00	14.00	10.00	10.00
Bowl, 13-1/4" l, oblong oval	40.00	50.00	50.00	40.00	40.00
Candleholders, pr, 3-3/4" h	22.00	25.00	25.00	22.00	22.00
Candy, cov	32.00	45.00	45.00	32.00	32.00
Creamer	15.00	20.00	20.00	15.00	15.00
Cup	12.00	18.00	18.00	12.00	16.00
Decanter, orig stopper	42.00	50.00	50.00	42.00	42.00
Ice Tub, 4-7/8" wide, 3" deep	24.00	35.00	35.00	24.00	24.00
Juice Tumbler	15.00	17.50	17.50	15.00	15.00
Plate, 6" d.	8.00	9.00	10.00	7.50	8.50
Plate, 7-1/4" d.	9.00	10.00	12.00	9.50	10.00
Plate, 10-1/4" d	-	-	-	-	34.00
Saucer	4.00	6.00	6.00	3.00	5.00
Sherbet, 3-3/4" h, flat	8.50	12.00	12.00	8.00	10.00
Sugar	15.00	20.00	20.00	15.00	15.00
Whiskey	17.50	20.00	22.00	17.00	20.00

Tulip green creamer.

Twisted Optic

Manufactured by Imperial Glass Company, Bellaire, Ohio, from 1927 to 1930.
Made in amber, blue, canary, green and pink.

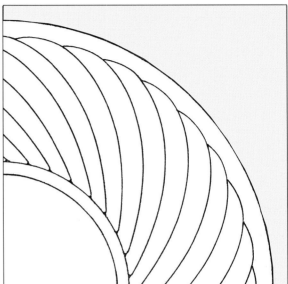

Item	Amber	Blue	Canary	Green	Pink
Basket, 10" h	42.00	75.00	75.00	45.00	45.00
Bowl, 7" d, ruffled	-	-	-	-	8.00
Bowl, 9" d	18.50	28.50	28.50	18.50	18.50
Bowl, 11-1/2" d, 4-1/4" h	24.00	48.00	48.00	24.00	24.00
Candlesticks, pr, 3" h	22.00	40.00	40.00	22.00	22.00
Candlesticks, pr, 8" h	30.00	50.00	50.00	30.00	30.00
Candy Jar, cov, flat	25.00	50.00	50.00	25.00	25.00
Candy Jar, cov, flat, flange edge	35.00	60.00	60.00	33.00	33.00
Candy Jar, cov, ftd, flange edge	35.00	60.00	60.00	33.00	33.00
Candy Jar, cov, ftd, short	40.00	70.00	70.00	40.00	40.00
Candy Jar, cov, ftd, tall	40.00	65.00	65.00	40.00	40.00
Cereal Bowl, 5"d	6.50	10.00	10.00	6.50	6.50
Cologne Bottle, stopper	45.00	65.00	65.00	45.00	45.00
Console Bowl, 10-1/2" d	25.00	35.00	35.00	25.00	25.00
Cream Soup, 4-3/4" d	12.00	18.00	18.00	12.00	12.00
Creamer	8.00	14.00	14.00	8.00	8.00
Cup	7.50	10.00	12.50	5.00	6.00
Mayonnaise	20.00	35.00	35.00	20.00	20.00
Pitcher, 64 oz.	32.00	-	-	30.00	32.00
Plate, 6" d, sherbet	2.50	4.50	5.00	2.50	2.00
Plate, 7" d, salad	3.50	6.50	7.00	3.50	3.50
Plate, 7-1/2 x 9" l, oval	6.00	10.00	10.00	6.00	6.00
Plate, 8" d, luncheon	4.00	9.00	10.00	4.00	4.00
Powder Jar, cov	38.00	65.00	65.00	38.00	38.00
Preserve Jar	30.00	-	-	30.00	30.00
Salad Bowl, 7"d	12.00	15.00	15.00	12.00	12.00
Sandwich Plate, 10" d	10.00	17.50	17.50	10.00	10.00
Sandwich Server, center handle	22.00	35.00	35.00	22.00	22.00

Item	Amber	Blue	Canary	Green	Pink
Sandwich Server, two-handles, flat	15.00	20.00	20.00	15.00	15.00
Saucer	2.50	4.50	4.50	2.50	2.50
Sherbet	7.50	12.00	12.50	7.00	7.50
Sugar	8.00	14.00	14.00	8.00	8.00
Tumbler, 4-1/2" h, 9 oz	6.50	-	-	6.50	7.00
Tumbler, .5-1/4" h, 12 oz	9.50	-	-	9.50	10.00
Vase, 7-1/4" h, 2 handles, rolled edge	20.00	50.00	-	-	-
Vase, 8" h, 2 handles, fan	32.00	65.00	65.00	30.00	30.00
Vase, 8" h, 2 handles, straight edge	30.00	65.00	65.00	30.00	27.50

Twisted Optic pink candle holders.

U.S. Swirl

Manufactured by U.S. Glass Company, late 1920s.

Made in crystal, green, iridescent and pink. Production in crystal and iridescent was limited.

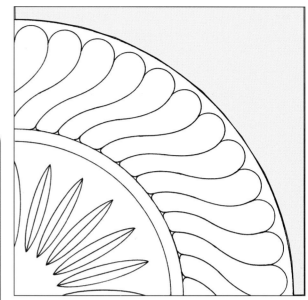

U.S. Swirl green pitcher.

Item	Green	Pink
Berry Bowl, 4-3/8" d	6.00	7.00
Berry Bowl, 7-7/8" d	15.00	17.00
Bowl, 5-1/2" d, handle	10.00	12.00
Bowl, 8-1/4" l, 2-3/4" h, oval	40.00	40.00
Bowl, 8-3/8" l, 1-3/4" h, oval	50.00	50.00
Butter Dish, cov	115.00	115.00
Candy, cov, 2 handles	30.00	32.00
Creamer	15.00	17.50
Pitcher, 48 oz, 8" h	55.00	50.00
Plate, 6-1/8" d, sherbet	3.00	2.50
Plate, 7-7/8" d, salad	6.00	6.50
Salt and Pepper Shakers, pr	48.00	45.00
Sherbet, 3-1/4" h	5.00	6.00
Sugar, cov	35.00	32.00
Tumbler, 8 oz, 3-5/8" h	12.00	10.00
Tumbler, 12 oz, 4-3/4" h	15.00	15.00
Vase, 6-1/2" h	20.00	20.00

Vernon

No. 616

Manufactured by Indiana Glass Company, Dunkirk, Ind., from 1930 to 1932.

Made in crystal, green and yellow.

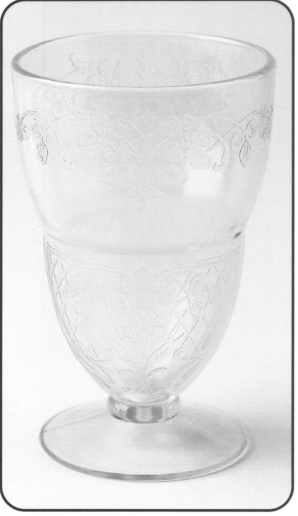

Item	Crystal	Green	Yellow
Creamer, ftd	12.00	25.00	25.00
Cup	10.00	15.00	15.00
Plate, 8" d, luncheon	7.00	10.00	10.00
Sandwich Plate, 11-1/2" d	14.00	25.00	25.00
Saucer	4.00	6.00	6.00
Sugar, ftd	12.00	25.00	25.00
Tumbler, 5" h, ftd	15.00	35.00	35.00

Vernon yellow tumbler.

Victory

Manufactured by Diamond Glass-Ware Company, Indiana, Pa., from 1929 to 1932. Made in amber, black, cobalt blue green and pink.

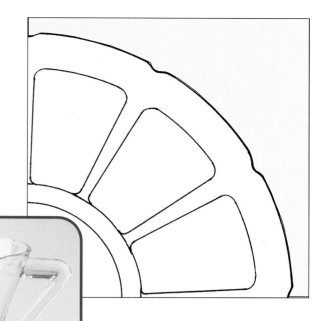

Victory pink creamer and sugar.

Item	Amber	Black	Cobalt Blue	Green	Pink
Bonbon, 7" d	12.00	20.00	20.00	12.00	12.00
Bowl, 11" d, rolled edge	30.00	50.00	50.00	30.00	30.00
Bowl, 12-1/2" d, flat edge	30.00	60.00	60.00	30.00	30.00
Candlesticks, pr, 3" h	35.00	100.00	100.00	35.00	35.00
Cereal Bowl, 6-1/2" d	12.00	30.00	30.00	12.00	12.00
Cheese and Cracker Set, 12" d indented plate and comport	45.00	-	-	45.00	45.00
Comport, 6" h, 6-1/4" d	18.00	-	-	18.00	18.00
Console Bowl, 12" d	35.00	65.00	65.00	35.00	35.00
Creamer	17.50	45.00	45.00	15.00	15.00
Cup	10.00	35.00	35.00	10.00	10.00
Goblet, 7 oz, 5" h	20.00	-	-	20.00	20.00
Gravy Boat, underplate	185.00	325.00	325.00	185.00	185.00
Mayonnaise Set, 3-1/2" h, 5-1/2" d bowl, 8-1/2" d indented plate, ladle	45.00	100.00	100.00	45.00	45.00
Plate, 6" d, bread and butter	6.50	17.50	17.50	6.50	6.50
Plate, 7" d, salad	7.50	20.00	20.00	8.00	7.00
Plate, 8" d, luncheon	8.00	27.00	27.00	7.00	7.00
Plate, 9" d, dinner	20.00	40.00	40.00	22.00	20.00
Platter, 12" l, oval	30.00	70.00	70.00	32.00	32.00
Sandwich Server, center handle	30.00	65.00	65.00	32.00	30.00
Saucer	5.00	12.50	12.50	5.00	5.00
Sherbet, ftd	15.00	27.50	27.50	15.00	15.00
Soup Bowl, 8-1/2" d, flat	20.00	45.00	45.00	20.00	20.00
Sugar	15.00	45.00	45.00	15.00	15.00
Vegetable Bowl, 9" l, oval	35.00	85.00	85.00	35.00	35.00

Vitrock

Flower Rim

Manufactured by Hocking Glass Company, Lancaster, Ohio, from 1934 to 1937.

Made in white and white with fire-on colors.

Item	White
Berry Bowl, 4" d	5.00
Cereal Bowl, 7-1/2" d	6.50
Cream Soup, 5-1/2" d	12.50
Creamer, oval	5.00
Cup	4.00
Fruit Bowl, 6" d	6.00
Plate, 7-1/4" d, salad	2.50
Plate, 8-3/4" d. luncheon	4.50

Item	White
Plate, 10" d, dinner	7.50
Platter, 11-1/2" l	25.00
Saucer	2.50
Soup Bowl, flat	50.00
Soup Plate, 9" d	15.00
Sugar	5.00
Vegetable Bowl, 9-1/2" d	14.50

Vitrock opaque white bowl and plate.

Waterford *Waffle*

Manufactured by Hocking Glass Company, Lancaster, Ohio, from 1938 to 1944.

Made in crystal, forest green (1950s), pink, white and yellow. Forest Green production was limited; currently an ashtray is valued at $4. Yellow was also limited, and a small berry bowl is valued at $3.50. Collector interest is low in white.

Item	Crystal	Pink
Ashtray, 4" d	5.00	5.00
Berry Bowl, 4-3/4" d	7.50	16.00
Berry Bowl, 8-1/4" d	10.00	27.00
Butter Dish, cov	28.00	225.00
Cake Plate, 10-1/4" d, handles	11.50	16.00
Cereal Bowl, 5-1/2" d	17.50	30.00
Coaster, 4" d	2.50	-
Creamer, Miss America style	37.50	-
Creamer, oval	5.00	12.00
Cup	6.50	15.00
Cup, Miss America style	-	42.00
Goblet, 5-1/2" h, Miss America style	35.00	85.00
Goblet, 5-1/4" h	12.00	-
Goblet, 5-5/8" h	17.50	-
Juice Pitcher, 42 oz, tilted	28.00	-
Juice Tumbler, 5 oz, 3-1/2" h, Miss America style	-	62.00
Lamp, 4" spherical base	28.00	-
Pitcher, 80 oz, tilted, ice lip	32.00	150.00
Plate, 6" d, sherbet	3.50	6.50
Plate, 7-1/8" d, salad	7.00	8.00
Plate, 9-5/8" d, dinner	12.50	24.00
Platter, 14" l	8.00	-
Relish, 13-3/4" d, 5 part	16.00	-
Salt and Pepper Shakers, pr	6.50	-
Sandwich Plate, 13-3/4" d	12.00	30.00
Saucer	3.00	5.00
Sherbet, ftd	3.50	15.00
Sherbet, ftd, scalloped base	8.00	-
Sugar	5.00	12.00
Sugar, Miss America style	35.00	-
Sugar Lid, oval	5.00	25.00
Tray	6.00	-
Tumbler, 10 oz, 4-7/8" h, ftd	16.00	23.00

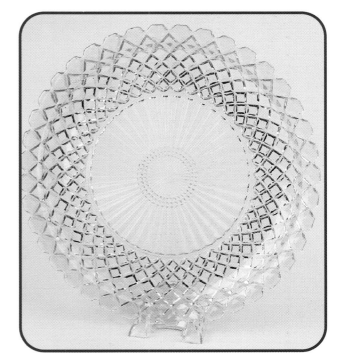

Waterford crystal plate.

Windsor

Windsor Diamond

Manufactured by Jeannette Glass Company, Jeannette, Pa., from 1936 to 1946.

Made in crystal, green and pink with limited production in amberina red, Delphite and ice blue.

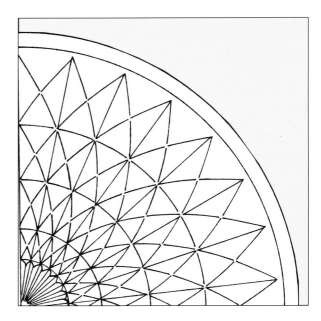

Item	Crystal	Green	Pink
Ashtray, 5-3/4" d	13.50	45.00	35.00
Berry Bowl, 4-3/4" d	4.00	11.00	9.00
Berry Bowl, 8-1/2" d	6.50	17.50	18.50
Bowl, 5" l, pointed edge	5.00	-	17.50
Bowl, 7" x 11-3/4", boat shape	18.00	35.00	32.00
Bowl, 7-1/2" d, 3 legs	8.00	-	24.00
Bowl, 8" d, 2 handles	9.00	24.00	20.00
Bowl, 8" l, pointed edge	10.00	-	48.00
Bowl, 10-1/2" l, pointed edge	25.00	-	32.00
Butter Dish, cov	27.50	95.00	60.00
Cake Plate, 10-3/4" d, ftd	9.00	22.00	20.00
Candlesticks, pr, 3" h	20.00	-	85.00
Candy Jar, cov	18.00	-	-
Cereal Bowl, 5-3/8" d	9.00	22.00	25.00
Chop Plate, 13-5/8" d	19.00	40.00	42.00
Coaster, 3-1/4" d	8.50	18.00	25.00
Comport	9.00	-	-
Cream Soup, 5" d	6.00	30.00	25.00
Creamer	5.00	15.00	20.00
Creamer, Holiday shape	7.50	-	-
Cup and Saucer	9.00	24.00	15.00
Fruit Console, 12-1/2" d	25.00	-	95.00
Pitcher, 16 oz, 4-1/2" h	24.00	-	115.00
Pitcher, 52 oz, 6-3/4" h	15.00	55.00	33.00
Plate, 6" d, sherbet	3.75	8.00	5.00
Plate, 7" d, salad	4.50	20.00	18.00
Plate, 9" d, dinner	9.00	25.00	25.00
Platter, 11-1/2" l, oval	7.00	25.00	22.00
Powder Jar	15.00	-	55.00
Relish Platter, 11-1/2" l, divided	10.00	-	200.00
Salad Bowl, 10-1/2" d	12.00	-	-
Salt and Pepper Shakers, pr	16.00	48.00	39.00
Sandwich Plate, 10" d, closed handles	-	-	24.00
Sandwich Plate, 10" d, open handles	7.50	17.00	17.00

Item	Crystal	Green	Pink
Sherbet, ftd	3.50	15.00	13.00
Sugar, cov	9.00	40.00	19.00
Sugar, cov, Holiday shape	12.00	-	100.00
Tray, 4" sq	5.00	12.00	10.00
Tray, 4" sq, handles	6.00	-	40.00
Tray, 4-1/8" x 9"	5.00	16.00	10.00
Tray, 4-1/8" x 9", handles	9.00	-	50.00
Tray, 8-1/2" x 9-3/4"	7.00	35.00	25.00
Tray, 8-1/2" x 9-3/4", handles	14.00	45.00	85.00
Tumbler, 4" h, ftd	7.00	-	-
Tumbler, 5 oz, 3-1/4" h	9.00	42.00	25.00
Tumbler, 7-1/4" h, ftd	19.00	-	-
Tumbler, 9 oz, 4" h	7.50	38.00	22.00
Tumbler, 11 oz, 4-5/8" h	8.00	-	-
Tumbler, 12 oz, 5" h	11.00	55.00	30.00
Tumbler, 11 oz, 5" h, ftd	12.00	-	-
Vegetable Bowl, 9-1/2" l, oval	7.50	30.00	25.00

Windsor crystal plate and pink pitcher.

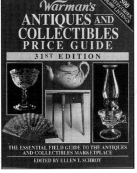